PROFESSIONALISM

REACHING THE HEIGHTS OF
SUCCESS IN YOUR CAREER

KAPLAN PUBLISHING

New York

© 2010 by Kaplan, Inc.
Published by Kaplan Publishing, a division of Kaplan, Inc.
1 Liberty Plaza, 24th Floor
New York, NY 10006

Permissions

All excerpts and adaptations in this book are done so with permission of Kaplan Publishing, which acknowledges the following works:

Dempsey, David, *Legally Speaking,* revised and updated edition, 2009
Greene, Brenda, *Get the Interview Every Time,* revised and expanded edition, 2008
Johnson, Cynthia and Drew, *Caffeine Will Not Help You Pass That Test,* 2005
Kaplan, *Sharp Vocab: Build Better Vocabulary Skills,* 2008
Kaplan, *Sharp Writing: Build Better Writing Skills,* 2008
Lawrence, Judy, *The Budget Kit,* 5th ed., 2008
Lewis, Allyson, *The 7-Minute Difference,* 2008
Martinez, Diane; Peterson, Tanya; Wells, Carrie; Hannigan, Carrie; Stevenson, Carolyn, *Technical Writing,* 2008
Pinkett, Randal, *Campus CEO,* 2007
Schawbel, Dan, *Me 2.0,* 2009
Thiederman, Sondra, *Making Diversity Work,* revised and updated edition, 2008

Reproduced with permission of publisher:

MindTools.com, "The Inverted-U relationship between pressure and performance." © Mind Tools Ltd., 1995–2010, www.mindtools.com/stress/UnderstandStress/StressPerformance.htm.

Robert Throop and Marion Castellucci, "Six Rules for Stating Goals," *Reaching Your Potential: Personal and Professional Development,* 1E. © Wadsworth, a part of Cengage Learning, Inc. www.cengage.com/permissions.

Printed in the United States of America

ISBN-13: 978-1-60714-175-4

Contents

Introduction

You have taken the first step to designing your new career.

This book will teach you everything you need to know.

Keep in mind that your career requires more from you than simply memorizing facts that you will learn in this book. Reading the material presented in this book is an essential component to getting what you want in your life, but it's up to you to make it work. You have to see the big picture.

Simply put, you need to understand that you are now in sales. Everyone looking for a job is a salesperson. And the product that you are selling is you! In order to sell yourself effectively you must be aware of how other people perceive you. You have to understand how you come off in a meeting, on the street, and over the phone. You need to take responsibility for your image and actively manage it.

In order to be a good salesperson you need to figure out how to produce the results you are looking for. Here are some steps that will help you get those results.

First, commit to school and growing your talent in a powerful way. Here's how to do it. You cannot look at any of your courses as "just a class." You have to look at your Kaplan program as the first step toward your new career. This is your future! Everything you are about to learn will help you meet your career goals. You are on your way.

Second, when you walk into the Kaplan classroom—it's a whole new you. You can either act like a professional powerhouse or a part-time pushover. Consider this your dress rehearsal. You have to conduct yourself professionally while you are a student. This new attitude will help you take advantage of the talents you already have.

Third, give your all to this program and make every second of it count. You are here because you want something larger for yourself. Stay focused and put in the time. Your courses will help you realize your full potential. If you put in the time, these Kaplan classes will have an amazing impact on your professional career. Kaplan is going to support you the entire way. Now is the time to put your head down and get everything you can out of it.

Here's how to get the most out of the professionalism segment of your program:

1 Set Goals

To be successful at anything, you need to set a goal. Your career is like a road trip. To plan a road trip, you need to know two things—where you are going and how long you have to get there. The same is true with your career. Where do you want to end up and by when? Knowing the answers to these questions will help get you closer to having a career. Let's set your goals now.

These statements will help you set your goals:

My future career is _____.

This class will help me achieve it because _____.

I want to get the following grade: _____.

I want to improve in the following ways: _____.

2 Design Your Schedule for Success

School is not just going to "fit in" to your existing schedule. To prepare for a rewarding career, you have to make the time. You must plan your success, and it starts with your calendar. Sit down now, and plan out a couple blocks of time every week that you can dedicate to your future. You will use the time to study, develop a professional network, and complete tasks that will get you closer to your goal. If you live with someone, or if you have a spouse or kids, it is very important to discuss your schedule with them as well. Ask for their support. Thinking you can do this alone or in spite of them isn't going to work. They can help you stick to the schedule you are creating for yourself. It's a powerful tool. Design your schedule for success and make yourself accountable to it. It works.

3 Visualize Your Future

This sounds cheesy and maybe it is. The funny thing is, it works. Think about it: Before you go to the grocery store you make a list of the ingredients for specific meals you envision creating in the days ahead. You then go get those items. That saves time (and money). You are planning your future. You are crystal clear about what you want. Only now can you go and get it. When you "see" or plan for something, you actually have something to strive for. The same works for your future YOU. Start planning for it, and start planning by visualizing the future YOU.

Find a picture in a magazine that represents your future. It could be a picture of someone in your newly chosen field, or a photo you take of the building you hope to work in, or something you plan to buy yourself as a reward when you finish the course and land a job. This is your shopping list for your career. This is what you want. This is what you are working toward. As corny as you feel, find the picture and stick it on the wall where you study. Whenever you want, look up and let it remind you of what you are working toward. Ask yourself the following questions: Where do you picture yourself in the next one, two, five, ten years? How will a new career help you reach those goals? You are visualizing the future you are actively creating for yourself. Nice.

4 Create a Weekly Routine

The more your week falls into a routine, the easier it will be to stick to your schedule and be successful. You go to class on certain days. You study on certain days. You have family time on certain days. Keep your busy life simple by keeping your routine consistent. This is the key to success. Make time to pursue your dream by making that time easier to find. Make finding a routine a priority.

5 Create a Relationship with Your Instructors

Your instructors are there because they want to help you succeed. Your instructors are there to help you grow your talent. Your instructors have information to teach you that will help you in your new career. They can help you get a job by writing a recommendation for you or helping you network. Your instructors are people you should get to know. How do you do that? Simple: show up for class and be interested. Ask questions after class. Email questions during the week. Ask your instructor for advice about finding a mentor. Trust me, the more enthusiasm you show for the coursework and your future, the faster you'll create that relationship! Believe it or not, this is a very important skill. You want to learn how to create relationships.

6 Build Your Personal and Professional Network

Ninety percent of all jobs come from networking, not through online job searches. The majority of new jobs are never posted online. How are you supposed to get a job? By networking.

Your courses at Kaplan are a tremendous opportunity to build up your network of relationships. Get to know the other students. Form study groups. Find out your classmates' career goals. You never know who other people know. Someone you are about to go to school with could introduce you to your next boss. But you'll never know that if you don't take the time to build the relationship. Your network is one of the most important things you'll need in your career, so start building it now. If you feel like starting your career is a solitary endeavor, just like studying, you are wrong. It's not. Contacts get jobs. You have to build a network of contacts so you can request information, assistance, and so on, if you need to. Check your ego at the door.

7 Do Your Homework and Classroom Activities Like They Matter

You're here. Let's do it right. Your homework and your classroom activities matter a great deal. So why not put your best foot forward—at all times. During the professionalism segment of your program, keep a journal where you can record your responses to some of the exercises presented in the book. The journal doesn't have to be anything fancy—a simple spiral notebook will do. What's important is that you keep track of all the thought and effort that you put into planning your career. These reflections will help you when you are looking for a job. Your new career may be many months off, but the effort you put in now will pay off later. There are two reasons why you should do this. First, if you do well in class, you will have more job opportunities. And second, the study habits you create now are directly transferable to your career. So take the opportunity to create good ones now! The little stuff matters. How you act matters.

Now that you know what to do to make the most of your courses, you need to focus on taking control of your professional reputation. This book will help you do that.

It's time to take control of how people see you: your professional reputation. Large companies like McDonald's and Coca-Cola spend millions of dollars to figure out how to control how we think and feel about their products. What if you were to put some time and effort into a similar process? What if you come up with a way to control how a potential employer thinks of you? You will have the biggest advantage if you start doing that right now. You have a "brand" to build and protect. You may not have thought about it, but you are turning yourself into a valuable product that a future employer will buy. You are in sales. Let's ready the product for market.

So how do you know what your brand should be? It's simple. What do people say about you when you leave a room? Think about that for a minute. *What do people say about me when I leave a room?* Don't know? Ask someone. Promise the person full immunity and ask him or her to give you the good, the bad, and the ugly. If you don't like what you hear, you have work to do.

A person with a great professional reputation is courteous, trustworthy, reliable, thorough, knowledgeable, and a team player.

It is easy to make a great impression if you conduct yourself the following way: dress the part, act the part, respect other people, and be interested.

First, dress the part. Donald Trump talks about how he got started in real estate. He dressed the part. As soon as he graduated from business school, he went out and bought the best suit he could afford. He wanted to make sure he "looked" like someone who was successful in real estate, even though he was only just starting out. He said it was a little weird because you feel like a phony, but dressing the part is one way to make a great impression. Do you need to wear a suit to class? No. But you shouldn't be casual either. Wear professional clothes and become someone who has their act together. It will make a great impression on people.

Act the part. By signing up to take this program, it is evident you take your future seriously. So act like you mean it, too. Show up on time for your classes. Stay for the entire class period. Come to class prepared. Complete your assignments on time. Put your phone away. Lose the gum. Take those earbuds out. Pay attention. Turn in work that you'd want your future employer or boss to see. You might not feel like doing it, but you must push yourself to act the part.

Respect others. Always. If you want a terrific reputation, then treat everyone with the utmost respect. Don't text while someone is talking to you. Listen, without interrupting. Gossiping will get you nowhere good. Being polite to people doesn't mean you are weak; on the contrary, it can take you farther than you think.

Be interested. Most people think they need to be interesting. Wrong. You want a job? You want to leave a lasting impression? Be interested. Ask questions about the job, the company, the course work. Show you are interested and you are prepared.

These days, the impression you make on people goes way beyond just how you look and act. You also have a reputation online, and it is essential that you know what it is and how to manage it.

Manage your digital footprint. What you find about yourself online and whatever you post online is what's referred to as your "digital footprint." And as technology advances and you do more and more online with Facebook, Twitter, blogs, and so forth, your footprint will get bigger and bigger. Since potential employers may look at the material you post online, it's important that you tailor your online image in the same way you would your personal image. Your profile on social networking sites should be PG-rated. The photos of scantily dressed people drunk at a party may be fun for friends, but if a future employer ever sees them, guess who's NOT getting a job? You! Set the privacy controls so only people with permission can see your stuff. Clean up the photos. Untag yourself from any "compromising" photos that other people have posted of you. Clean up the language. Think twice about posting strong political or religious views on your profile page. It's fine to have strong views—but keep them private if there is any chance of alienating a future employer. Conduct yourself online as if your future bosses are watching. They are.

Get a new email account. Everyone communicates by email these days. For professional reasons your email address needs to be your name. So lose the shopaholic$@ gmail.com or monstertruckfan@yahoo.com or momof3kids@yahoo.com addresses, and create a new account with just your name. If your name is taken, add digits to the end to make it unique.

Voicemail messages and ringtones. It's great that you have a favorite song or that your little 3-year-old cousin has learned to talk, but a potential employer may not want to know that. Be sure that your outgoing voicemail message is very professional and that a standard ring tone is set for business calls.

Google yourself. Speaking of your future boss, the first thing he or she will do to determine whether or not to interview you for your dream job is "Google" you. So, go ahead. Google yourself and see what you find. And if there is anything bad there, be prepared to explain it or counteract it. If you have a Twitter account, your employer will likely be following you. So watch what you say.

Pretend everyone is watching. The easiest way to do the right thing online is just pretend everyone in the world can see everything you are doing (because they probably can). If you don't want your mother, your spiritual advisor, your spouse, or your employer seeing what you are about to write or post, then don't do it. You may have had a colorful past, but if you want a professional future, don't post the evidence of it online.

Master the essential skills for employment. There are skills that every employer wants, and you can master them while you are doing this class. These skills will be examined throughout the book, but it's not enough to just learn about them. You have to make them your own. You have to demonstrate these qualities in real life, right now and throughout your life.

There are essential skills you are being graded on every time you show up to a job interview: dependability, punctuality, attitude, and politeness.

Your Kaplan program will teach you the skills you will need for your specific career. But there are skills just as important—maybe more important—than the ones you learn in order to perform a particular job. In addition to specialized skills you need to succeed in your field, every employer is expecting you to have mastered these essential basic skills:

Dependability. First and foremost, employers hire people they can depend on. Are you the kind of person who will get the task done? Are you someone who works hard?

Punctuality. Another quality that employers look for is someone who is one time. Arriving to work on time, showing up at meetings on time, and completing work assignments on time is absolutely crucial. You can practice all these as a student.

Attitude. Attitude is everything. It is a little known secret for landing a great job. When a future employer invites you to an interview, they've already decided that you are competent to do the job. What they want to know is whether or not they'll "like" working with you. Many employers do the airport test. If they got stuck at an airport on a delayed flight and had to spend four hours with you, what would it be like? Do you have the right attitude or not? Are you negative or positive? Are you someone you want to be around? Attitude is everything in life. You should start cultivating a positive attitude about class, about homework, and about your future now. You'll need it for that interview you're working toward.

Politeness. In the busy, rushed world of our personal lives, we've all gotten used to texting, multitasking, and racing around. Old-fashioned politeness has been dropped for the sake of efficiency. In the professional world, politeness is not only appreciated, it is required. If you want to make it in your career, start conducting yourself with politeness. It's a requirement. Pleases. Thank yous. Listening. Following through on what you commit to doing. The things your parents taught you. Cultivate them now, and your career success will be your reward.

Be on the ball. Paying attention and taking good notes is hard to do when you're tired from a long day. However, you'll need to do these everyday things as part of your job, so start doing them now. Techniques to help you pay attention include arriving prepared with everything you need (notebook, pen, highlighter), sitting in the front of the class so you are forced to pay attention, and taking notes and participating in the class. If you are busy doing something, you are less likely to start day-dreaming or dozing.

Relationship building. A skill that will help you in your career and in your life is the ability to connect with people and build relationships. If you are interested in people, then they will find you interesting. Being interested means asking questions, giving them your full attention, and maintaining eye contact. Here are some other simple techniques to master to help you become more effective at building relationships.

Connecting with people is all about listening, not talking. When you are listening, you are learning what the other person needs, wants, and is interested in. You can and should use this information to help you forge a relationship with the person and help you get what you want.

Remember some small detail about the person or something from the conversation. Next time you see him or her, bring it up. *Is your daughter feeling better? How'd that interview go? Hey, I remembered the name of that book we were talking about. Did you land the business?* Anything at all, no matter how small. By doing so you will make the other person feel important (because you remembered something) and you will be creating continuity from the first conversation. This makes your connection that much more meaningful.

High personal standards. If you want to change your life, just raise your standards. Think about the standards you have for yourself. Are they high or low? Do you expect a lot of yourself, or not much at all? If you start raising your standards for yourself now, your entire life will change. Do you eat healthy? Do you take care of yourself? Are you on time? Do you tell the truth? Do you take on too much? Do you think highly of yourself?

Another thing about standards: look at who you hang out with. There's a body of scientific research that has proven that your peers have more influence over you than anyone else. If your friends have low standards, then you probably do too. As you start to make new connections, look to connect with people who have high standards. It will help you stay on track as you launch your new future.

There's a lot to manage when you go to school to learn a new career. But don't make the mistake of leaving your past behind completely. Your life experience has tremendous value, and you should use it to propel yourself forward in the classroom. Anytime you see an opportunity to share an insight or experience relevant to the discussion—do it. Particularly if you don't want to.

Bring your life to the classroom. The more you find ways to tie your life experience and prior work experience into the discussion, the classroom exercises, and your homework, the more you will learn, the more you will get out of it, and the more you will stand out as a student. It will also help you build confidence to use what you already know to establish your voice in class and add to what you are learning.

Bring your classroom to your life. Another thing you can do to raise your confidence and empower yourself is to share what you are learning with your family and friends. They can support you much better in your goals if they know what you are doing when you are in class. It's easier for everyone to be quiet and give you the time you need to study if they feel connected to what you are working toward. Also, you never know who has an uncle or a cousin in a relevant field. They'd never know to introduce you if they don't know what you are up to.

Immerse yourself now. The more you immerse yourself in the world of your new career, the faster and easier it will come to you. One way to do that is on the Web. There are online forums, social networking sites, and professional association sites for just about every profession out there—including yours. If you start participating in those online communities now, you'll be surprised how "fluent" you will become in your new profession by the time you are done with your training. You'll be up on the trends in the industry, know the major employers, and have a healthy contact list of people who can give you the advice you need to land a job.

Ninety percent of jobs come from networking, so start building a network NOW. Networking is nothing more than developing positive relationships with people in your related field. Why do you want a network? What can these "contacts" do for you? A lot. People who are already working in your new profession are the first to hear about job openings. You can use contacts in your network to distinguish you from the other people applying for the same job by using their names when you apply.

Develop an elevator pitch about yourself. Take the time to come up with a 15-second explanation of what kind of job you'll be looking for when you finish school or the industry you hope to work in. This isn't a long speech; rather, it's something fast and simple that gives anyone you are talking to an idea of who you are and what you are looking to do:

Hi, I'm (your name). I am currently studying to become (insert profession). I finish my courses in (month, year) and hope to start working as a (insert job). I wanted to meet you because I would love your help with . . .

Tap your existing contacts. You already have a network! Your family, friends, high school classmates, former coworkers, and neighbors are all part of your network. Spread the word (using your elevator speech) that you are looking to speak with people who may be able offer you advice. Set up meetings. Always ask every contact for two or three more people they can recommend you speak with. "Do you know anyone else who could give me advice about the healthcare industry?" "May I use your name when I contact them?"

Seek advice. Don't ask your contacts for a job. Always lead with the request for advice. The job opportunities will arise in those conversations as you are seeking advice.

Join professional associations. There are professional associations that you can join now—as a student—to start meeting people in your field. The time to start building your network is NOT when you are looking for a job. Rather, the time to start building it is NOW when you can just show up and be interested. That way, when you are looking for a job several months from now in the related field, you will feel more comfortable and you will already have the relationships established that will help you get a job. To meet people, volunteer for committees or help with events and special projects.

People will find you interesting only if you are interested in them. It's the easiest trick in the book for connecting with people and making a good impression. It's been said of many successful people that their secret is in making the person they are speaking to feel as if that person is the only one in the room. That's how focused they are on them! So when you are interacting with people, be interested. Ask questions.

Follow through. Always take the time to meet new contacts face-to-face. Follow up with a handwritten thank you note or a formal email. Make sure you stay in touch every month or two to keep them updated on your search and your meetings with the contacts they referred you to.

Form study groups. Classmates are wonderful additions to your network of contacts. A great way to deepen the relationships with your classmates is to form study groups. Particularly if you are a shy person—it's a great way to break the ice and get to know other people.

By now you realize that your future begins now. That means now is the time to start setting yourself up for success in the job market. Think sales. You have to know what impression you are making. Now is the time to start honing that skill.

It is important to define your career goals now, so you know what you are building toward. Forget about what you think you are capable of . . . what do you dream you'll be able to do in this field? What are you really going for? What's the first job you hope to get? Is there a particular company you would love to work for when you are done? It's kind of embarrassing to admit what you'd really love to have happen, but you can't get your dream job if you don't plan for it!

You can't be ashamed or afraid to ask for help. People do like to help other people. That's why being polite helps. Finding someone who has gone before you and who can give you contacts and information about your chosen field is invaluable.

The first thing you need to do to begin building your network is find a mentor.

Find a mentor. A mentor is someone who will help you grow in any area of your career. Anyone can be your mentor. So keep an open mind as to who this person might be. Look for someone who has the skills, experience, or traits that you want to cultivate in yourself. Look for someone who is doing the job you would love or works in the industry you hope to break into. Ask people if they know anyone who does what you want to do. You want to talk to that person.

You can find a suitable mentor outside of work. Look to industry associations, clergy or congregation, online communities, local business owners, your instructors, retirees, or simply people you know socially. You may find a mentoring relationship naturally, but being proactive and simply asking your friends, instructors, and family for referrals for a mentor to help you with specific goals will help you find someone faster.

Be honest with yourself. Unless you know what help you need and what areas you need to grow in your professional development, no one can help you. Think also about people who have mentored you or made an impact on you in the past. Use that relationship as an example of what you are looking for in a new mentor.

Once you have your career goals in place and a network of contacts helping you out, it's time to start thinking about your job search. You're probably asking, *But how am I going to get a job in my new field when I have no experience in that field?* Right? It might seem impossible. But remember: you are a salesperson now. And your product is you. You have the power to sell yourself to potential employers, and you have some valuable tools to help you.

Resume. You may not have experience working in your new field, but you already have many skills. *But how are those skills relevant,* you ask? That's easy. Many of the skills that you've developed over your lifetime—in your current job, in previous jobs, in your outside activities, even in the things you do for fun—are called transferable skills. These are skills that you learned in one situation that can be applied to other situations as well. Your resume is where you will highlight these skills. A well-crafted resume will outline your strengths so employers can see exactly how you will be right for a new position. With a host of resume dos and don'ts and the Optimal Resume program to guide you through the process, you will be able to put together a resume that highlights your unique skills and the qualifications you've gained from this program.

Portfolio. Your resume tells an employer what you can do; your portfolio *shows* people what you can do. This course will provide you with the tools you need to develop a portfolio that showcases the skills you've developed throughout the program. By providing potential employers with samples of your work, they can see exactly how well you can put your skills to work—and how well you could put your skills to work for them.

Interview. Uh-oh, the interview. Just the thought of the interview may send your pulse racing. But like many things that seem intimidating and complicated, the key to success is something small and simple: be prepared. Not so hard, right? This book will provide you with the resources you need to sharpen your interviewing skills and get that job offer. By knowing exactly what you can expect from a typical job interview and by rehearsing answers to key questions, you will go into every interview fully prepared and ready for a new career.

Kaplan has your back. Your instructors and all the Kaplan staff are here to provide you with the real-world knowledge and skills you need to succeed beyond the classroom. Whether it's help with basic skills such as personal finances or providing advice that is specific to your field, your instructors are dedicated to your success and to your future—while you're here in the classroom and when you are out in the real world.

Your future is now. Make the most of it!

As you make your way through *Professionalism*, you will find answers to the following and many other important career-related questions. Read them now so you can look out for solutions in the book, during classroom activities, and from your instructors. Remember, your professional future starts here.

- How can writing down your goals help you achieve more?
- Why is it important to develop an effective time management plan?
- How can you present a positive image as you prepare for your new career?
- In addition to the words you choose, what other elements of communication influence meaning in a conversation?
- How can you improve your business writing without learning a million grammar rules?
- How can you engage an audience when you give a presentation?
- What can you do to get along with difficult co-workers and customers?
- How can you create a professional resume if you don't have a lot of work experience?
- How can you demonstrate your skills during an interview?
- How can strategies designed to sell products be used to help you find a job?
- Why is it important to have a personal statement summing up who you are and what you want?
- How can you develop a network of connections in your field while you are still a student?
- What questions are illegal to ask during an interview?
- What should you know about your employer beyond what they sell?
- How can you keep your personal biases out of the workplace?
- What qualities make someone a good team player?
- How are ethics important in the workplace?
- How can employee benefits increase your bank account?
- What should you take away from an employee appraisal at work?

—Mel Robbins

About the Editor

Mel Robbins has run a successful coaching and keynote-speaking business for almost a decade. She serves Fortune 500 corporations, conferences and media events, as well as high-level executives and individual clients, helping them reach their professional and personal goals. Mel is a graduate of Dartmouth College and Boston College Law School. She was a trial attorney and dot-com executive for several years, before launching her coaching career. Mel and her company Advice for Living, Inc. write a monthly column for *Success Magazine* and are co-developing and distributing personal improvement products with Success Media.

Mel is a no-nonsense life and business coach who has turned her expertise and love for helping people into an impressive media career. She hosts and produces a syndicated radio show, *The Mel Robbins Show*, which broadcasts in more than twenty markets across the country. Mel also hosts a Saturday morning show on Boston's Talk Evolution, 96.9 WTKK, and will debut on WABC Radio in New York City in January 2010. *The Mel Robbins Show* airs live every day from a custom built radio booth in Borders' flagship downtown Boston store. Her fast-moving show aims to change your life through honest and entertaining coaching, storytelling, and problem solving. Mel focuses each show on current events, real life problems, career and business issues, and conflict resolution.

Acknowledgments

Thank you to the following editors for their contributions.

Michelle Cox
Director of Career Services
Kaplan College Dallas/Ft. Worth
Dallas, Texas

Monica Hill-Sumlin
Director of Career Services
Kaplan College Dayton
Dayton, Ohio

Anna Howell
Director of Career Services
Florida Education Center
Lauderhill, Florida

Jennifer M. Kelly, MSHR, PHR
Director
Kaplan Career Institute, ICM Campus
Pittsburgh, Pennsylvania

Charlotte D. Lofton, MBA
Chair, Medical Program Management Dept.
Kaplan Career Institute
Brooklyn, Ohio

Nova S. Pena
Director of Career Services
Career Centers of Texas, El Paso
El Paso, Texas

Greg Witkowski
Instructor
Kaplan Career Insitute, ICM Campus
Pittsburgh, Pennsylvania

1 | Goal Setting

KEYS TO SUCCESS

- Understanding what a goal is and why it is important
- Recognizing the difference between long-term, intermediate, and short-term goals
- Assessing your values and setting goals that are appropriate
- Developing a plan to reach your goals
- Knowing when to reevaluate your goals
- Developing strategies for staying motivated

What Is a Goal?

Setting and keeping realistic goals are two of the most important things you can do to achieve success. Having well-defined goals gives you direction and purpose, which in turn can help you stay focused and motivated.

1

Before you start thinking about setting goals, let's look at what a goal is. A goal is a specific, measurable objective that can be achieved through your own actions. A goal is always linked to a plan, which makes it different from a wish or a dream. Wishes and dreams are things that you hope for; a goal is something that you take steps to achieve. Think of a goal as being a dream defined, accompanied by an action plan.

The Value of Goals

One of the most valuable things about having goals is the goal-setting process itself. Setting goals forces you to look at your life and think about important things like these:

- What you want
- What you don't want
- What you want but could live without

Once you set some personal goals, you have a destination. Compare your career path to taking a road trip to a city in another state. When you set off on a long trip, you generally have a map to rely on. You can pull out the map when you get turned around or when you think you might be heading in the wrong direction. Goals can serve the same purpose: when you have clearly defined goals, you can rely on them as a map to guide you. You can refer back to them any time you need motivation or focus.

Long-Term, Intermediate, and Short-Term Goals

The process of setting goals can be intimidating. One thing that can make it easier is to break big goals down into smaller ones. Goals can come in three sizes:

- Long-term goals
- Intermediate goals
- Short-term goals

Long-term goals are big and lofty and take many years to achieve. A long-term goal is something that may take up to five years or even longer to accomplish. A long-term goal will typically have a big impact on your life when you have achieved it. It's a "big deal" goal. For example, your long-term goal might be to get a job with one of the leading companies in your field.

On the way to your long-term goals, you'll have to meet smaller objectives that will help you get there. These are called intermediate goals and short-term goals. An intermediate goal is a step toward a long-term goal. Meeting it is a big achievement in itself, but it takes less time than a long-term goal to achieve, often one to three years. Earning a degree or a certificate is an example of an intermediate goal.

A short-term goal may take a few weeks, several months, or even a year to achieve. It's an accomplishment in itself, and it's also a step that leads you closer to your larger goals. Passing a particular course on the way to getting a degree is an example of a short-term goal.

You can think of short-term goals and intermediate goals as markers, or milestones, on the way to your greater destination. On your road trip, they're the cities and towns you pass through on the way.

Short-Term, Intermediate, and Long-Term Goals Work Together

It's important to have all three kinds of goals: short-term, intermediate, and long-term. For one thing, short-term and intermediate goals help make your long-term goals seem more attainable by reminding you that you need to take a series of small steps to get what you want. And when you realize these small steps will help you reach your bigger goal, you stay motivated to do the daily tasks that you sometimes might not want to do. What if it's raining out, you're tired, and you don't want to go to your pharmacology class? Thinking about how your bigger goal—becoming a certified pharmacy technician—is related to succeeding in class makes it easier to get up and head out the door. When you begin to see how your daily activities can add up to something bigger, it's easier to get those little things done.

Goals for Different Areas of Your Life

The goal-setting techniques described in this chapter can be applied to many different areas of your life, for example:

- Personal
- Financial
- Educational
- Career
- Spiritual
- Health

When you set goals for yourself, make sure you choose goals that cover a range of these categories. It's important to have a balanced life. For example, if you focus only on financial goals, other areas of your life may suffer. It's great—and necessary—to have money, but other aspects of your life are important as well. Focusing instead on finding a career that is rewarding—both financially and personally—can have a positive impact on many areas of your life. Your financial needs will be satisfied with the increased income that comes from a professional position. Selecting a career that gives you a sense of purpose will provide personal satisfaction and increased self-confidence. Job satisfaction may even carry over into other areas of your life, such as health or spiritual well-being.

Internal and External Rewards

Consider the ways in which activities can be rewarding. There are things that you do just because you like them, things that may not have a tangible reward but that you like to do because they are challenging or satisfying. Your pleasure comes from the task itself, not from an outside source. For example, you may enjoy taking pictures of your family in different settings. You don't sell the photos, or exhibit them in an art museum, but you still enjoy doing this because of the internal reward: it makes you feel good.

There are other things that you do because there is an external reward associated with the task. The reward comes not from the activity itself but from what you get after you complete the activity. Money is an example of an external reward. You may want to spend time with friends or family rather than going to work, but the paycheck motivates you to go anyway.

Many activities combine both internal and external rewards. When you are setting your goals, include goals that cover both internal and external rewards so you have personal satisfaction as well as material gain.

Self-Assessment

Before you can start setting goals, you need to first assess yourself. Take a moment to consider the things you value, the things to which you are most willing to devote your time, energy, and attention. You can consciously identify the things you value and plan your actions based on them, or you can let unconscious actions and unexamined habits create priorities for you. Some of those "accidental" priorities might be positive and worthwhile; many others will not be. By identifying the things that are truly meaningful to you, you begin to tailor your actions in a way that will support the things you value.

Grab a blank sheet of paper and make a short, simple list of what's important in your life. Arrange the items in order, beginning with the most important. Ask yourself, "What things are most important to me?" Here is an example of a list someone might come up with:

1. Family
2. Friends
3. Personal growth
4. Career

5. Finances
6. Travel
7. Health
8. Hobbies

> ### *Practice Critical Thinking*
>
> The Case of Two Friends and Their Goals
>
> At lunch one day, Danisha and Vicki were talking about what they wanted out of life. Danisha wanted to get married and have three children. She didn't care much about school or jobs because she thought she'd be too busy raising her kids.
>
> Vicki, on the other hand, wanted to get an associate's degree, work with children for a couple of years and save money, and then go back to school to become a social worker. Vicki also wanted to get married and have children someday, but she wanted to have a professional career as well.
>
> 1. Whose goals are more balanced? Why?
> 2. What does Danisha risk by focusing exclusively on one goal?

As you can see, you don't need to take the time to dig deeply into specific actions associated with these priorities. Simply take a few minutes to consider and list the things that are most important to you.

Six Rules for Stating Goals*

Once you've taken a look at yourself and listed some things that are important to you, start thinking about how to set your goals. In *Reaching Your Potential*, Robert K. Throop and Marion B. Castellucci offer some guidelines:

1. **Express your goals in positive language.** For example, "I will change my eating habits to maintain a weight of 120 pounds," rather than "I will not eat candy or cookies." Or "I will get at least a B in English," rather than "I won't fail English." When writing goals, you will find that positive language has beneficial effects.

2. **Make your goals as specific as possible.** Avoid vague, general language such as "I would like to travel." Instead, be specific and say something like "I will vacation in Aruba." Making goals specific makes them more vivid and helps you focus your efforts on achieving them.

3. **Make your goals measurable.** For example, suppose you want to save some money. How will you know whether you've reached your goal? When you've saved $100? $1,000? You have to have some way to measure whether you've achieved your goal. If you say you want to save $1,000 of your part-time earnings, you have a measurable goal. When you state a goal, ask yourself, "What do I want to accomplish? How will I know that I have accomplished it?" Your goal will be measurable if you can respond to these questions.

4. **Set yourself a deadline.** When do you want to achieve this goal? In two months? In two years? Whatever the answer, commit yourself to a time frame. Decide when you will start and when you will be done.

5. **Have a variety of goals.** It's important not to channel your efforts toward only one goal or one type of goal. If all your goals are professional, for example, you will find yourself neglecting other aspects of your life. Try to achieve a balance of personal, educational, professional, and community service goals, as well as short-term, intermediate, and long-term goals.

6. **Make your goals your own.** Having others set goals for you, even well-meaning people like parents, spouses, and friends, means that the goals are not truly your own. Your goals must be just that—yours. That way, you'll be committed to achieving them. Accomplishing your goals ought to give *you* pleasure and satisfaction.

Setting Your Goals

Now that you know some rules for stating goals, it's time to set some goals that will support the things that are meaningful for you. Think about the things that are most important to you. Consider the different kinds of rewards and the need to have a well-balanced life, and make sure your goals don't focus too much on only one aspect of your life. Also consider which activities will give you the best return on investment of your time and effort. If you decide to devote several years to achieving a goal, make sure it's something you're certain you want. Consider other options that may give you the same satisfaction in a shorter time frame.

Write It Down

Always put your goals in writing. Keep a separate notebook or a file on your computer that you can use for documenting your goals. Start by listing a couple of long-term goals. Think about where you are now, and for each long-term goal think about what you need to do to reach it. Set some intermediate and short-term goals that will help you reach your larger goal. Identify possible obstacles to your progress and think about things you can do to overcome them. Create a list with your long-term goal at the top followed by your intermediate and short-term goals, as shown in the goal-setting tips box below. Make sure your goals are specific and make sure you include a time frame for completing them.

Goal-Setting Tips

If your long-term goal is to get a job as a certified medical assistant, your list of goals might look something like this:

TIMELINE	
March 2012	Long-term goal: To get a job as a certified medical assistant
February 2012	Intermediate goal: Pass certification exam
January 2012	Intermediate goal: Complete medical assistant program and earn degree
January 2011	Intermediate goal: Complete first year of medical assistant program
Ongoing	Short-term goals: Pass all classes with at least a B
	Engage with instructors and other students
	Keep up on all coursework and reading
	Attend all classes

Review and Revise

Once you have your goals down in writing, go back to the rules for setting goals. Do your goals follow the rules? Think about your skills and your strengths. Are your goals realistic? Focus on goals that can be achieved through your own efforts, not those that depend on things that are out of your control.

Is there a logical progression from your short-term and intermediate goals to your desired outcome? Is there anything on your list that isn't necessary? Take it off. Continue to make adjustments.

Creating and Sticking to a Plan

Once you have your goals down in writing, it's time to come up with a specific action plan for achieving them. Start by looking over your list of long-term, intermediate, and short-term goals. What do you need to do each week to bring you closer to achieving your goals? You can think of these as "mini-goals." Then make a list of what you'd like to accomplish in the week that is related to your goals. Break it down further into a daily task list.

Of course, you'll still need to balance your goals with all your other daily commitments. That's where having a good time management plan can help. Creating a schedule to keep track of your daily and weekly obligations will help you stay organized. There are many tools available to help you do this, from computer calendars to plain old pencil and paper. Chapter 2, Time Management Strategies, discusses in detail many different tips for organizing your time and creating a schedule that will work for you.

> ### Planning Tip
> Once you start planning your day, you'll be surprised at how much you can get done. By being organized, you can plan your time so you do similar tasks all at one time, which makes things much more efficient—and much faster. Also, having a list of what you need to do means you won't forget things and have to go back to them later, which is also a big time saver.

Making Daily Choices

The small things you do in a day are the actions that will determine whether you achieve your goals. Sometimes people are reluctant to tackle change because at some time in the past they have attempted a major "leap" in their personal or professional behavior and have fallen short. Think about the small steps, rather than the big leaps—steps are easier than leaps. How hard is it to set aside an extra hour for studying, write down a list of six or seven things you need to do the next day, or spend an extra thirty minutes at work helping your supervisor distribute a new shipment of supplies?

Monthly and Quarterly Goal Reevaluation

It's important to review your goals every month to make sure you are still on track. Did you accomplish everything you wanted to do? Most of it? Are some things turning out to be easier than you thought? Some harder? Do you need to shift some priorities? Take a look at your daily and weekly activities and see if you need to make any adjustments.

Then, every three months take a step back and look at the big picture. Assess your overall progress. Are you still on track? Is there anything you can do better? Do your goals still accurately reflect what you want? Remember that your list of goals is flexible—it's meant to serve *you*.

Don't be discouraged if you haven't accomplished everything that you set out to do. Sometimes you may find that you've been overly optimistic about what you can accomplish in a given period of time. Take an honest look at your efforts and don't be afraid to adjust your goals and your time frame if necessary. But be brutally honest: make sure you are adjusting your list to make it more realistic, not because you are unwilling to put in the effort.

Looking at your list critically to see what you can do better is important, but it's equally important to give yourself credit for the progress you've made. Have you achieved one of your short-term goals? Did you get an A on that big test you studied so hard for? Reward yourself by going out to dinner with some friends or by spending an extra hour playing your favorite game.

When you make progress—big or small—be proud of that accomplishment and draw on that success to propel you forward.

Embracing Change

We all have to take responsibility for where we are in life and do something different if we want to change. You are not a prisoner of your past: Examine your choices, priorities, and goals to help make decisions that can change your life. If your path is not working for you, change it. If you are in a job you don't like, look for another job. If you are not the person you want to be, work to be different.

As you work to make meaningful changes in your life, be willing to step outside your comfort zone. If you want to make yourself more valuable within your chosen profession, be willing to stand out by developing an area of expertise. Ask yourself what you need to do to develop expert skills in something that matters to you, and then make the decision to acquire those skills.

Eliminating Fear

Fear often stands in the way of action. People are hampered by fear of many things. Two important fears that can interfere with reaching a goal are fear of failure and fear of success.

Goals represent what you want out of life, and they can help you move forward. Negative illusions only serve to hold you back. The average person thinks over 400 negative thoughts about himself or herself every day. Sometimes, your brain goes into negative overdrive and you start having thoughts like, "I am not smart enough. My hair looks funny. I cannot possibly do that. I am too fat. I am too skinny. I don't make enough money. I don't have enough time. I can't. I shouldn't. I am scared." These fleeting ideas may unconsciously pop into your mind, destroy self-confidence, and diminish potential.

It's important to remember that other people do not share the negative illusions you have about yourself and that those illusions do not take your gifts and talents into account. Instead of thinking about the negative, concentrate on the positive attributes you possess that will help you achieve your goals. Build on your strengths.

Staying Motivated

Motivation is having the energy to work toward a goal. It is made up of the needs and incentives that make us act in particular ways. How can you keep moving toward a goal even when you've reached a plateau? How can you motivate yourself to act in ways that will keep you striving? Setting specific goals helps make it much easier to stay focused and motivated. There will always be times, however, when you become discouraged and wonder when all this work will pay off. For those times, it's important to remember what you are trying to achieve.

Inspiring Images

Start collecting images that represent what you want to achieve so you can use these for inspiration. Do you want a better job? Find an image of an office that you'd like to work in, maybe a corner office with a great view and a nice desk. Add some pictures of how you'd like to be dressed as you sit at the desk in your corner office. Are you working hard to graduate? Find some pictures of students at a graduation ceremony to inspire you. The images you choose don't have to literally represent your goals. They can be images that symbolize what you want to achieve. Collect these images in a notebook, a file folder, a decorative box, or a computer file, and return to them when you need a little extra motivation.

Visualization

Another way you can stay motivated is to visualize yourself achieving your goals. Picture yourself doing what you've always wanted to do. Be specific. Where are you? What are you doing? How are you dressed? What are you feeling? Who else is there? It's important that you feel like you belong in this new role that you've planned for yourself, and the sooner you start seeing yourself as that person, the easier it will be for you to become that person.

Extra Effort

When you are feeling less than inspired, that's the time to put a little extra effort into your day. Take the time to put on some clothing that is a little more polished than what you'd normally wear. Take a little more time with your personal appearance. Stand up a little straighter. Interact with others in a positive way. Find the discipline to pretend that you're confident and motivated—once you start *pretending* that you're inspired, chances are you'll start *feeling* more inspired.

Chapter Summary

- Setting goals helps you define what is important to you.

- Goals can serve as a guide for your future and help keep you on track.

- Break large goals down into smaller steps.

- You should have a variety of goals to reflect all aspects of your life.

- Your goals should reflect things that you want—not what someone else wants.

- Goals should be specific and measurable and have a deadline for completion.

- It's important to put your goals in writing, to create a plan for achieving them, and to evaluate your progress regularly.

To-Do List

☐ Make a list of the top ten things that are important in your life.

☐ Write down something you did this week that provided an external reward.

☐ Write down something you did this week that provided an internal reward.

☐ Think of an activity that provides both external and internal rewards.

☐ Start collecting photos or other images that represent your goals.

☐ Look in your closet and identify two or three items of clothing that make you feel polished and confident when you wear them.

Important Terms

How well do you know these terms? Define them here or in your journal, or look them up in the glossary to help you remember.

intermediate goal   self-assessment

long-term goal   short-term goal

priority

Online Resources

LifeTango, an online collaborative goal setting community
www.lifetango.com

GoalSetting1.com, an interactive goal setting website
www.goalsetting1.com

myGoals.com, a website that provides goal setting tips
www.mygoals.com

MindTools.com, a website that offers career advice, including tips for goal setting
www.mindtools.com/index.html

Exercises

Write your answers in your journal or on a separate piece of paper.

1. Write a paragraph or two in your journal about a time when you accomplished something you set out to do. It can be something big—like a promotion at work—or something smaller—like cleaning out your closet, or saving up for a trip out of town. What made you want to accomplish the goal? What specific steps did you take to do it?

2. Using the goal-setting tips discussed in the chapter, come up with three long-term goals for yourself. Make sure that these goals truly reflect what you want and make sure they fall into a variety of categories, not just one, so that they reflect your entire life. Write the goals down in a notebook or create a computer file that you can use solely for goal-setting activities.

3. Pick a short-term goal, and write a series of daily actions that will bring you closer to that goal. Create a daily task list for what you need to accomplish tomorrow, and make sure you include the actions that will support the short-term goal you've chosen.

Portions of this chapter's content include material adapted from Allyson Lewis, *The 7-Minute Difference* (New York: Kaplan, 2008).

2 | Time Management Strategies

KEYS TO SUCCESS

- Assessing your work habits and time usage each week
- Prioritizing your weekly tasks and commitments
- Identifying commitments and activities that can be sacrificed to make time for your top priorities
- Creating a realistic schedule for your personal, professional, and academic activities
- Developing effective time management techniques
- Recognizing that life rarely proceeds exactly as planned

Take Control of Your Time

One day you open up the newspaper and see an article about someone you knew in high school who is now a successful business owner. You remember this guy as one of the biggest goof-offs in school. The two of you started in the same place, at the same time. How did he get so far ahead of you?

13

The answer isn't what he did year by year; it's what he did hour by hour. Nobody has more than 24 hours in a day. Successful people make the most of their time.

If you want to take the next step in your career—and also have a rewarding life outside of work and school—you'll have to start making the most of your 24 hours each day. Easier said than done, right? It seems like there's always so much more to do than you have time for. The first thing to do is take an inventory of your time and activities.

Assessing Your Day

Certain features of your day are non-negotiable: your work hours, your class schedule, the amount of sleep you need to make it through the day. Not having enough time can be frustrating, but it's the reality you face, so there's no point in getting stressed over it. When your paycheck comes, you know a chunk has been taken out for taxes, but you don't think much about that; you plan what you're going to do with the *net*—the amount actually *in* your check. Consider time in the same way: just think about your after-tax, "net" day.

Taking Stock of Your Goals

First look at your goals. You've already broken them down into smaller tasks and steps. Now work backward until you reach the first step that you can take right away. In a typical week, you'll try to make measurable progress toward a few short-term goals while keeping sight of your intermediate and long-term goals.

Make a list of everything you *have* to accomplish this week—completing an assignment for class, paying your utility bills, getting an oil change for your car. Then review your less pressing goals and figure out the next steps toward achieving each of them.

Personal Time

Take a look at your other obligations for the week—a birthday dinner for your sister, helping your friend set up his new computer, coaching the Little League team. If you have a heavy load of personal commitments this week, accept that you won't get as far toward accomplishment of your goals. That's fine; in fact, it's essential to keep a healthy life balance.

Finally, make sure you think about what you *want* to do this week. If you can't afford to spend an hour in the evening sitting on the couch watching Letterman, or join in the Halo video game tournament Friday night, or go to the mall on Saturday afternoon, then you'll find yourself resenting the goals you have set. This will only make you more likely to drop them.

Setting Priorities

The next step is to assign priorities to all of the things you need and want to do this week. Rank them, from top to bottom, in the following order:

- Things you have no control over: paying the bills, putting gas in the car

- Things you can do now that will spare you time or stress later: keeping up on your coursework rather than cramming the night before a test

- Things that need to be done eventually but can be postponed without becoming harder or more time-consuming: doing laundry, washing dishes

Your personal priorities will mix in with these. Some things you have to do, such as celebrating your sister's birthday (think of all the time you'd have to spend to make up for missing it). Then there are the little things you look forward to every day that make you feel like it's all worthwhile: spending time with your family or significant other, running in the park in the morning, having coffee with your friends after work. Make sure your schedule includes time for the small things that you really enjoy.

Also assess your personal priorities according to how much you will regret *not* doing something. For instance, if that Halo tournament is your only chance to see an old buddy visiting from out of town, that makes it more important than a regular evening sitting in the basement playing video games.

> **Time Management Tip**
> Setting priorities helps you decide which tasks are most pressing. If you have only two hours free on Sunday afternoon, you may have to choose between watching a DVD rental and studying for your pharmacology exam. You'll find that you may have to set aside one or more tasks to achieve the others. In this way planning involves setting priorities.

Creating a Time Management Plan

If there is one message you should take away from this chapter, it is this: You must have a detailed plan outlining the things you need to do each day. If you don't, you'll wind up at the end of the day wondering where all the time went and why you've gotten nothing done.

The most common reason people don't prepare time management plans is that it's just too intimidating. Looking at your obligations for a given week all at once can be discouraging. What's more discouraging, though, is to leave it all up to chance. Then you may end up putting off half of your tasks until the next week, which, combined with that week's duties, will leave you facing an even bigger mountain.

Assessing Your Habits

Nothing shows the benefits of having a plan better than the results of having no plan. Take a week and track how you spend your time. Draw up a grid for the week on paper, with a box for writing down what you do and how long it takes, starting when you normally get up in the morning and ending when you go to bed. Carry the grid with you at all times. Fill it in at least twice a day—at lunch and before you go to bed—and write down everything you've done during the day.

Be brutally honest. Don't report that you were studying from 7:00 p.m. to 10:00 p.m. if you got sidetracked by instant messages at 8:30 p.m. and didn't get back to work until 9:00 p.m. Did you really work until 6:00 p.m., or did you get off at 5:30 p.m. and spend half an hour talking to co-workers before heading home?

Monday	
7:00–7:30	got up, showered
7:30–8:00	ate breakfast, checked email
8:00–8:30	got ready for class, organized books and supplies for the day, finished chapter 4 exercises
8:30–9:00	drove to school
9:00–12:00	attended class
12:00–1:30	had lunch with Tamantha
1:30–2:00	drove home
2:00–3:30	watched TV, read blogs online, checked email, organized and paid bills, did laundry
3:30–3:45	got ready for work
3:45–4:00	drove to work
4:00–6:00	worked
6:00–6:30	ate dinner
6:30–10:00	worked
10:00–10:15	drove home
10:15–11:00	ate snack, watched TV, checked email
11:00–12:00	finished part of chapter 5 reading assignment

Figure 2.1 Sample grid with daily activities tracked

At the end of the week, check your grid for these red flags:

- **Time wasters.** Did you devote big blocks of time to watching TV, reading blogs online, or talking on the phone? There's nothing wrong with any of these activities, but they have no specific goal or ending point. It's easy to keep going until your whole evening is gone—even though you may have intended to spend only half an hour.

- **Long time blocks.** If you spent three hours or more on one task, ask yourself what you accomplished in that time, and if the product was worth the time you put into it. If you had allowed yourself an hour less for the task and really worked at it, could you have made the same amount of progress? If you reach a point where you feel like you're getting nowhere, take a break or move on to something else. Come back later when you can start with a new frame of mind.

- **Gaps.** Are there spaces on your grid showing the times when you were sitting idle in between one scheduled job and the next? Half an hour isn't enough time to do anything, right? Wrong. There are probably a dozen small tasks you could have completed in that time and crossed off your list.

Building Your Schedule

Now that you have a record of how you actually spend your time, look for ways to organize your day more efficiently. Draw up a new grid, and start filling it out by listing your tasks and goals for the week.

This allows you to budget your time and helps you balance your activities. Without a schedule, you can end up spending all your time on the top priorities and

> ### *Practice Critical Thinking*
> Think about how you spend your time during a typical week. Which of the pitfalls described above are the biggest challenges for you? What are some strategies you can try to help you waste less time?

Monday	
7:00–7:30	get up, shower
7:30–7:45	check email
7:45–8:00	eat breakfast
8:00–8:30	organize and pay bills, get ready for class
8:30–9:00	drive to school
9:00–12:00	attend class
12:00–1:00	lunch with Tamantha
1:00–1:30	drive home
1:30–2:00	watch TV, relax
2:00–3:30	do laundry, finish chapter 5 reading assignment and exercises
3:30–3:45	get ready for work
3:45–4:00	drive to work
4:00–6:00	work
6:00–6:30	eat dinner, review exercises and chapter vocabulary
6:30–10:00	work
10:00–10:15	drive home
10:15–11:00	check and answer email, relax
11:00–11:30	organize books and supplies for tomorrow

Figure 2.2 Sample grid with daily tasks planned

neglecting the items that are lower on the list but are still very important. For instance, if you're working on a class project, you could continue to tinker and try to make it better forever if you so desired. A schedule will provide a cutoff point at which you say, "Enough" and move on to other things.

A schedule also helps you to split your time between "hard" obligations—commitments with specific deadlines or due dates—and "soft" ones that you have more control over. If you don't allow time for your soft tasks, they will always get squeezed out by the hard ones.

Setting the Bar

Keep your expectations high but be realistic. A schedule you can't meet is no better than no schedule at all—and can be even worse because of the discouragement that comes at the end of the week when you realize you haven't done half the things you meant to do.

When you achieve specific goals, you engage your brain's reward center; this is what makes you feel so good. Crossing an item off your to-do list gives you the same feeling as sinking a shot on the basketball court or reaching a new level on a video game.

It is also a good idea to reward yourself for taking care of business. You'll be more motivated to finish your income tax return if you make plans to kick back and watch an eagerly anticipated movie when you're done. Nothing feels better than relaxing and doing what you like once you can say to yourself, "I've earned it."

Making Sacrifices

You can't create a workable schedule simply by cutting out inefficiencies. To achieve your goals, you'll have to make some sacrifices.

> **Time Management Tip**
>
> Try not to get distracted by interruptions such as phone calls, text messages, and personal emails. Although a ringing phone may seem to demand your immediate attention, chances are you can take the call later with no penalty. Unless the call concerns something truly urgent, plan to respond later if you are in the middle of a task. Designate a certain time for checking and answering email, rather than being distracted by checking your email every fifteen minutes.

You've taken the first step by prioritizing your needs, wants, and commitments. Now you have to make some hard choices. Think about the amount of time you spend on a particular task and consider whether it's a good investment. Coaching the Little League team is a hard-and-fast commitment: you have to show up for several hours every Saturday, period. But there are a lot of other things you could do with your weekend time. Some are so important to you that you attend to them during the week—but that cuts into your scheduled time for study or other obligations. You have to ask yourself if the coaching gig is something you can afford the time for right now. You can't do everything you might want to do. That's just a fact of life.

Tools for Time Management

Many different tools and methods can be used to put together a schedule. Different ways work best for different people; the important thing is to convert your time management program from a mental construction to a physical form you can actually look at and hold yourself accountable to.

First of all, there's nothing wrong with using paper. You can either draw up a new grid every week with a pencil and a ruler, or print a blank grid from a computer and fill it in by hand. The advantage of using paper is that you can carry it with you anywhere. You can stick it on your refrigerator door or on the wall next to your work area. You can update it just by reaching over and marking it. Filling everything in by hand can be time-consuming, but if it makes your schedule more accessible to you, it's worth it.

On the other hand, your computer offers many useful time management tools, which are loaded with convenient features. There is probably a basic calendar program built in to the operating system; look for it under "Accessories." Some email programs, such as Microsoft Outlook, have built-in calendars for entering appointments and tasks. If you use a free web-based email service such as Gmail, it may also offer an online calendar. You can also build your own using a spreadsheet program like Microsoft Excel.

Personal digital assistants (PDAs) such as Palm Pilot offer an electronic calendar that you can carry on the go. So do most "smartphones," such as the BlackBerry or the iPhone. Just don't get caught up in playing with these devices for half an hour every time you go to check your appointments.

In addition to storing your schedule, many software programs allow you to build a to-do list. A to-do list, prepared each morning or the night before, lists all tasks you want to accomplish that day. The very act of creating the list helps in planning your day and strengthening your commitment. With some programs, you set a due date for a task, and the program alerts you when it's approaching. Combining your calendar with a task list can be of great help in tracking your goals and making the most of your time.

Of course, if you're computer-shy or can't afford all the bells and whistles, low-tech solutions are just as good. Try writing down each of your tasks for the week on an index card. Whenever you find yourself with a chunk of free time—whether it's fifteen minutes or an hour—shuffle through the stack of cards until you find something you can accomplish in the time you have. Update the cards as you make progress, and put the completed ones in a separate pile.

You can also use a planner to create a to-do list for daily activities. Planners are calendars designed for listing daily tasks. Your planner should be your sole source of information about your schedule. Use it to record and schedule all commitments of your time and keep it up to date.

Making an Impact with Your Time Management

In the professional workplace and in school, the difference between people who manage their time well and those who don't is crystal clear. Setting priorities, understanding which tasks need to be done first, and having a plan to complete all of them allows you to stay on top of your obligations. By staying organized and using your time efficiently, you keep yourself prepared for the unexpected. Good time managers rise to challenges, roll with changes, and seize opportunities. They command respect and inspire confidence. They're given greater responsibility in their jobs. Greater responsibility means they get to learn more, which makes them stronger candidates for promotion and gives them an advantage in the job market.

Poor time managers, on the other hand, struggle to keep up with their basic duties, have trouble communicating with superiors, and often have difficulty accepting change. They show up unprepared, and often late, for class. Co-workers learn not to count on them, and when special projects are in the works, they're left out. Because they are poor job candidates, they live in fear of losing the jobs they have, which puts them at the mercy of their superiors. If you don't learn to take control of your time on the job, you may wind up putting in a lot of extra hours doing work of doubtful quality.

Time Management Tip

Sometimes you can't say no to a demanding boss. If you are overcommitted at work and your boss asks you to take on additional responsibilities, don't refuse. Instead briefly outline your current responsibilities and ask your boss for help balancing your competing priorities.

Learning to Say No

There are only so many hours in a day. The effective time manager knows this and has developed the ability to turn down additional projects, responsibilities, or demands when accepting them would mean becoming overcommitted. You need to weigh the demands for your time. Practicing assertiveness and the willingness to say no will help you accomplish your tasks and goals on time.

The Keys to Reliability

The best thing you can do to improve or preserve your professional image and job prospects is to be reliable.

Show Up on Time

The primary thing employers must be able to count on is the presence of their employees. If your boss calls an emergency meeting first thing in the morning and you are absent or late, do you want to be the reason he or she has to repeat the information later, or the reason everyone has to wait to receive important information?

If your workday or your school day starts at 8:30 a.m., plan to get there by 8:15 a.m. This gives you some wiggle room for any of the countless unpredictable events that could occur on the way to work or to school. If a slow-moving freight train is blocking the road you're on, it's nice to be able to just sit and listen to the radio, and not have to worry about how many minutes late you're going to be. Be realistic about how much time you need to get ready in the morning. Is it really worth it to sleep an extra fifteen minutes, if that means choosing between eating breakfast and making your train?

If you're lucky enough to have "flex" hours at work, you should still pick a start time and stick to it every day. Your boss and co-workers will find it reassuring to know that they can count on your being there. Nothing will damage your image at work more quickly than being known as the person who gets there "whenever."

> **Workplace Tip**
>
> Most companies have strict policies regarding employee attendance. Make sure you understand your employer's attendance policy and make it a priority not to be absent or late. Unscheduled time off results in loss of productivity, puts additional pressure on co-workers, and increases inefficiency, which are all very costly to a company. Frequent absences or tardiness may result in termination.

Meet Your Deadlines

A task with a looming deadline jumps to the top of your priority list. If something has to be done by the end of your shift, make that task a priority when you arrive at work. If a supervisor has to ask you for something twice, you can bet the second time will be less pleasant.

Any time you're given a task, ask when it needs to be completed. If there is no deadline, set one for yourself so that you won't forget. Again, you don't want a superior asking you for something twice.

Keep a list of your most pressing tasks, and their due dates, in the most visible part of your work area—stuck to your computer monitor, in your locker, on your bulletin board, wherever you're most likely to see it—and use it as a helpful reminder.

If a deadline is approaching and you know you're not going to make it, you're obviously not in the best situation—but you can still handle it and maintain your reliability. The first step is to recognize when you're in trouble. Next, provide a status update as early as possible. Take responsibility for the situation, but if there's a good reason why you've fallen behind—for instance, the task turned out to be more complicated than anyone anticipated—report it. Explain it simply, briefly, and calmly. Provide an honest, realistic assessment of when you expect to be finished—and make *sure* you meet that deadline.

Remember that spending extra time on one task affects all others. If you have to spend an extra day finishing a project for school or for work, make sure to re-assess the time set aside for other pressing matters, so you won't be late on them also.

ON THE JOB

SCENARIO: Your clinical supervisor asked you to finish entering the new patient information in the database by the end of the day. You're halfway done when your co-worker Lisa, who is checking patients in, is forced to go home to handle an emergency. The clinic is very busy and you fill in for Lisa, and consequently there's no way you can get the database updated by the end of the day.

QUICK FIX: Tell your supervisor what happened. Make sure he knows that you had to fill in for Lisa and it wound up taking up most of the afternoon. You need another hour to finish updating the database, and you'll do it first thing tomorrow morning. If it's really important, offer to stay late to finish, so that it will be waiting for the supervisor in the morning.

Prepare in Advance

If you really want to get ahead, plan your tasks as far in advance as possible. As soon as you know of an upcoming deadline, a meeting or event that's just been scheduled, or a project that's coming down the pike, put it on your calendar.

Whenever you have some downtime at home or at work, use it to prepare for tasks you know are coming up. You can get ahead on your reading assignment for class and reduce your workload for next week. At work you can organize the supply cabinet or take inventory of the office supplies. Not only will this make things easier when crunch time comes, but it will also show your supervisor that you take initiative and plan ahead.

The more you know about your future schedule, the better you'll be able to assess how much extra you can take on right now. You want to say yes to as much as possible, but not to things on which you can't deliver.

By taking control of your time at school or on the job, you'll reduce your stress level, boost your performance, and enjoy improved relationships with your boss and co-workers, or your instructors and classmates. Remember, 80 percent of success comes from just showing up, being there when you're needed, and striving to be an asset rather than an obstacle at your workplace.

Chapter Summary

- The first step toward effective time management is to take a realistic view of how many hours are available in your week. All of your personal, professional, and academic activities should be ranked in priority to identify those that are the most pressing.

- A weekly schedule that accounts for all of your time and necessary tasks is the core of any successful time management plan.

- A task list can help you keep track of the progress you have made toward your goals.

- People who manage their time well enjoy higher productivity, reduced stress, and better relationships.

To-Do List

☐ Make a list of the five biggest time wasters in your typical week.

☐ On your calendar, mark off every day in the next six months that you know is fully or mostly committed, and you won't be able to get anything else done (holidays, family get-togethers, trips, and so forth).

☐ Make a list of everything that you know right now you have to do—even if it's as routine as sending an email or making a phone call. Make your best guess as to how long each task will take, and also write that down.

☐ Practice making sacrifices: make a list of three things you normally do each week that you are willing to give up.

Important Terms

How well do you know these terms? Define them here or in your journal, or look them up in the glossary to help you remember.

hard obligation   **task list**

reward center   **time management plan**

soft obligation

Online Resources

Google Calendar
calendar.google.com

myHours, an online time management, timesheet, and time tracking tool
www.myhours.com

Free templates for planning daily and weekly activities
office.microsoft.com/en-us/templates/FX100595491033.aspx

Articles offering a variety of time management tips
www.buzzle.com/articles/time-management

Exercises

Write your answers in your journal or on a separate piece of paper.

1. Create a grid and track all of your activities for a week, using the procedures described in this chapter. At the end of the week, go through the grid and circle the spots indicating where you spent time without accomplishing anything or fulfilling any personal needs. Also circle places showing where you spent more time on a task than was useful or worthwhile. Tally up the hours you've singled out.

2. Using the techniques outlined in this chapter, prepare a weekly schedule for your activities. Block out your time in half-hour segments. Be realistic about how much time you need for sleep, commuting, eating, and other routine activities. Also make sure to allow for enough personal time so that you can continue to do the things you enjoy. After a week, write several paragraphs in a journal assessing how closely you stuck to your schedule and noting what changes you think you need to make.

3. Use an Internet search engine, such as Google, to research time management tools. Look for software as well as content; maybe you can find some blogs with helpful advice. Write a one-page report on the most useful or promising resource you found.

Portions of this chapter's content include material adapted from Cynthia and Drew Johnson, *Caffeine Will Not Help You Pass That Test* (New York: Kaplan, 2005) and Randal Pinkett, *Campus CEO* (New York: Kaplan, 2007).

3 | Managing Stress

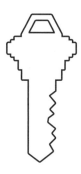

KEYS TO SUCCESS

- Understanding stress
- Learning to identify stressors in your home life and work life
- Discovering your optimum stress level
- Organizing your life and prioritizing daily tasks to manage stress
- Identifying stress relief strategies

What Is Stress?

Stress is a body's natural reaction to danger. It is not a force that is "out there" in the world, existing independently of us. Stress is not the result of "having too much to do." It is not the pressure attached to a deadline. Nor is it the loss of a loved one or the upheaval of a divorce. Such circumstances are all *stressors*, but are not stress itself. Stressors are conditions that trigger a chemical reaction in our bodies. That chemical reaction is stress.

In other words, our bodies create our stress.

Long before humans had jobs, mortgage payments, or weight problems to worry about, stress was the reaction of the body to direct physical danger, such as being attacked by a predator. Also called the "fight or flight" response, the stress response helped the body react with strength or speed—to fight or flee, as the case may be.

Understanding Stress

Question: Do stressors create stress? Answer: No, in response to stressors, the *body* creates stress.

Your body reacts to the psychological stressors of the workplace with the same chemical defenses that were directed at physical threats in prehistoric times. Once triggered, these tense, persistent feelings and urges will continue to afflict you until you relax, just as they once kept our ancestors fighting or fleeing until they were safe from attack.

When you experience stress, your body is responding to something your mind perceives to be a threat. Sometimes the stressor is easy to identify, such as the threat of losing a bonus (or your job) if you fail to meet a deadline. (Note how even the word *deadline* conjures up the image of a mortal threat.) In other instances, many small stressors can combine to create what you experience as an intense level of threat.

No matter what the situation, it is you and not the world that is the source of stress.

Positive and Negative Stress

Much attention is paid to the negative effects of stress, but the pressures of stressful situations can have positive results as well. You might expect that a high-pressure activity such as being a pitcher in a World Series game, with millions of people watching and counting on his performance, would cripple any player with the effects of stress, but some athletes respond in the opposite way, elevating their performance to extraordinary levels. "Clutch" players, as they are called, seem to play best when the stakes are highest. They experience *positive stress*. As the pressure increases, a clutch player rises to the occasion. Other athletes might never face such high-stakes challenges because their stress response to even low levels of pressure traps them beneath a performance ceiling. They experience *negative stress* in response to pressure.

Stress Management Tip

Different situations may provoke different stress responses in the same individual depending on the task to be completed. For example, a person who excels in high-pressure situations on the baseball diamond may come undone when faced with the stressor of having to type eight pages of meeting notes for the supervisor by 3:00. If a particular task consistently causes you stress, practice performing that task. As you develop your skills, you'll perform the task more efficiently, and your increased confidence may help you perform better under pressure.

Researchers who study stress have created a graph to illustrate the relationship between pressure and performance. This relationship is graphed as an arch or an upside-down "U" (see Figure 3.1). As the graph indicates, at low levels of pressure, performance also tends to be low. With no incentive to perform well, individuals become bored and lose focus. But as pressure rises, so does performance. The pressure pushes the individual to perform better. This performance improvement will continue until the pressure has

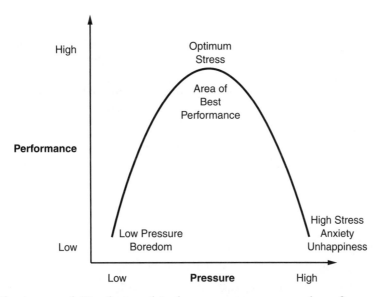

Figure 3.1 The inverted-U relationship between pressure and performance. (*www.MindTools.com, © Mind Tools Ltd., 1995–2010, All Rights Reserved, used with permission.*)

driven the individual to the optimum stress level. Given the ideal amount of pressure, an individual responds with the best performance he or she is capable of. But if the pressure continues to rise beyond this point, the individual's performance begins to suffer. There is a limit to the amount of pressure an individual can withstand, and any pressure beyond this limit brings a corresponding decline in performance. The individual begins to experience anxiety and frustration. If the pressure continues to rise, the stress becomes disabling, and the individual stops performing altogether.

Different individuals, however, experience stress differently. You've probably noticed this when you were part of a team working toward a common goal. If you confront a group of individuals with the same threat, all other things being equal, the individuals will respond with different levels of stress. All will react with a stress response, but the nature of that response will vary from person to person. Some will find the stress overwhelming and perform poorly. Others will be motivated by the stress and raise their level of performance.

Professionalism does not require you to respond to extraordinary pressures with a World Series–winning performance. But professionals are required to handle the natural ups and downs of school and work.

To succeed, companies must occasionally apply pressure to make their workforce respond with a short burst of performance improvement. This pressure could take the form of a deadline, a sales contest, or simply an increase in the amount of work that must be completed by the end of the day. All of these changes put employees under increased pressure. All of these pressures are stressors.

Some people, however, respond to even minor stressors not with performance improvements but with negative stress. For these individuals the optimum pressure level is very low. They may perform well under light pressure, but as the pressure ratchets up, their performance quickly suffers. When other workers are performing optimally, even

Practice Critical Thinking

What kind of a performer are you? At what point does the positive stress from increasing pressure turn into negative stress? Understanding what causes your body to create stress and how stress affects your performance is important to your self-development.

enjoying the excitement of rallying to set a new record for productivity, these performers are faltering and sliding into anxiety and despair.

Most people fall somewhere in between the World Series ace and the worker who cracks under the slightest pressure. Whichever extreme you fall closer to, you can learn to reduce the amount of stress your body creates and help keep your performance near the optimum stress level.

Minimizing Stress

Workplace pressures are not the only source of stress for a professional. People are prey to many kinds of stressors, from all parts of life. Family conflicts, marital squabbles, money problems, legal troubles, and health issues are all powerful stressors that add to everyday stress. As these pressures accumulate, they can push you past your optimum stress level and downgrade your performance—unless you develop strategies for managing stress.

Because stress is created by your body, controlling stress ultimately means controlling your body and the way it creates stress. Many strategies are available to help you scale back the amount of stress your body produces.

Remember that the "fight or flight" response originated as a defensive reaction to imminent physical danger. The response released a flush of chemicals to help the body overcome or escape a threat. The mechanism of stress evolved to help our ancestors defend themselves against predators and other dangers in their environment.

Stress tapers off when the body is finally able to relax. Once an individual is no longer in danger, he or she can stop fighting or fleeing. Stress is no longer needed. Once the caveman had killed the saber-toothed tiger trying to eat him, he could stretch out on his former predator's hide and feel the stress leave his body.

Today, most sources of stress are psychological. Your body experiences workplace pressures as a threat, and this triggers the stress response. Although you may rarely find yourself in a life-or-death confrontation, in the face of continuing pressure, your body still tries to defend itself chemically by creating stress.

So how can you create less stress? Some people look first to removing the sources of their stress, their stressors. They blame their job or their boss, and think, "If I could just land a better position, I wouldn't always feel so stressed."

Others blame forces in their personal lives: "My boyfriend and I are always fighting. If I could just meet someone else, things would be so much easier to deal with."

Still others blame money for their stress: "If I wasn't always worrying over money, my wife and I wouldn't always be fighting, and I wouldn't feel like quitting my job every day."

These are all valid points. A bad job is a more potent stressor than a good job; a difficult relationship causes more stress than a happy one; and bills are less stressful when there is the money to pay them.

But ridding yourself of stressors is not the same thing as ridding yourself of stress. Eliminate your stressors, and new stressors will take their place. And those new stressors will cause your body to produce new stress. You may no longer have the lousy job, or the boyfriend to fight with, or the unpaid bills; but as far as stress goes, chances are nothing has changed: Your new job means new stressors; you dumped your boyfriend, and now he's dating your best friend; and even though your bills are paid, you still never seem to have enough money.

You can never rid yourself of stressors, but you can change how you perceive them.

For example, the one-two punch that many professionals identify as their worst stressor consists of (1) having too much to do and (2) having too little time to do it. Ask most people in a workplace to account for their source of stress, and they will mention one or both of these stressors.

Two simple (although not necessarily easy) strategies can help you change your reaction to these stressors. These measures can change the way you look at what you have to do and how much time you have to do it. By changing the way you look at a stressor, you can change the way your body responds to it.

When you think about what you have to do each day, do you picture an overwhelming mass of responsibilities? Do you see a barrage of obligations, all demanding to be met immediately?

It is almost never the case that everything you must do in a given day is of equal importance. Once you realize this, you begin to change the way you perceive your obligations. The key to managing your to-do list is to prioritize your tasks. Identify those things that you really must do, and do the most important ones first. You might have an impossible list consisting of dozens of tasks, but accomplishing the one or two extremely important items often makes the remaining, less significant tasks far less stressful to manage.

Likewise, if you are more careful in organizing and accounting for your time, you will find that you actually have more of it than you thought. Learning and practicing time management techniques will allow you to see your time for what it is. Chapter 2, Time Management Strategies, examines some strategies for prioritizing tasks and improving your time management skills.

Once you organize your stressors using a workable strategy, you will feel less overwhelmed by them. By taking on your tasks efficiently in order of their importance, you can manage and complete them, perhaps sometimes with time to spare.

How Can Prioritizing Reduce Stress?

By accomplishing your most important obligations first, you eliminate your biggest stressors. You can then complete your smaller tasks free of the stressors from your major obligations.

If you still feel stress even with effective personal organization and management, remember that it is your own body creating that stress. It comes from nowhere else.

Address stress at its source by focusing on its presence in your body and working to remove it. Remember that relief of stress comes with relaxation. Anything that helps you relax helps you relieve your stress. Whether it is going for a walk, reading a magazine, or watching television, if it relaxes you, it lowers the level of stress in your body.

> **Workplace Tip**
>
> Many employers offer discounts on health club memberships. Find out if yours does and if so, ask the health club staff about stress management programs.

Throughout history people have developed practices to help relax their bodies by focusing their minds. Meditation is one of these strategies. The concentration of the mind helps release the body from the grip of stress. In addition to meditation, try enjoying nature, looking at art, listening to music, cooking and enjoying good food, and laughing.

Other strategies to rid your body of stress include using it to do what the stress is trying to make it do. Exercise of any kind, particularly vigorous exercise, directs your stress outward. As discussed earlier, the "fight or flight" response evolved to empower the physical defense of your body. Running takes your stress and puts it to the very use nature intended—the motion of flight. Contact or competitive sports cause the same direct release of stress; sports simulate the muscular expense of effort once reserved for a fight for survival. Whether you are sparring in a boxing ring or fighting for a rebound on a basketball court, physical competition takes the stress response and expresses it through the body, just as nature intended.

Leading a Balanced Life: Taking Care of Yourself

Although it often seems mental or psychological, stress is physical. It is something that happens in and to your body. Chronic stress—stress that affects the body over a long period of time—has been linked to numerous physical diseases, including cancer and heart disease, as well as mental illnesses such as depression. Unrelieved stress places a constant strain on the body. It also makes individuals more susceptible to physically damaging habits such as overeating, drinking to excess, and smoking.

ON THE JOB

SCENARIO: It's Friday and the manager of the office where you work has just given you an important project he needs by the end of the day. You have been having a good week, working hard to meet other deadlines and operating at your optimum stress level. But you have also been under heavy pressure every day, and this new task pushes you past your limit. You work on the project for an hour and get nowhere. You begin to feel anxious, concerned that you will fail and end an otherwise productive week on a bad note.

QUICK FIX: Ask your boss if you can take an early lunch. Then don't eat lunch. Instead, go out and take a brisk walk. If you can, get to a gym and do twenty minutes of vigorous exercise. Focus your mind on releasing your stress. Put all of the things you had planned to work on today out of your mind, and focus on executing the assignment for your boss. Pick up a light lunch on your way back to work, and eat it later at your desk. But for now, tackle that project!

Jaye Lynn Ross

San Antonio, Texas

Attended: Kaplan University—Texas Careers Campus, San Antonio

Area of study: Paralegal program

Employer: Intellectual Property Legal Department, Kinetic Concepts, Inc.

KAPLAN SUCCESS STORY

If you take one thing away from this course, it should be this: Treat each person you meet with respect and professionalism and in the same manner in which you would want to be treated.

Kaplan made it possible for me to obtain a certificate as a paralegal, as well as be eligible to take the national certification examination for my profession. This was all done within a reasonable time frame and under the supervision of knowledgeable and professional instructors.

To treat stress, treat your body. The better equipped your body is to withstand stress, the less damage stress will do. This means leading a balanced life: eating right, getting enough sleep, and exercising. It means finding things to do that you enjoy. You may derive ego satisfaction by pushing yourself too hard and constantly working, but such a pattern eventually leads to burnout, and burnout leaves a professional with unfinished work and unfulfilled ambitions.

Learn to recognize your workplace stressors. Prioritize your work and organize your time. You will find that a prioritized and organized schedule leaves you with less work to do and more time to do it.

Find your optimum stress level and learn how to recognize when you are exceeding it. When you do exceed it and your performance begins to suffer, get away from work—even briefly—and spend some time focusing on your body. Satisfy that "fight or flight" urge through strenuous exercise or competitive sports. Next, direct your mind away from your stressors and toward the things that bring you peace and happiness: your loved ones, art or music, even television. Then relax.

Chapter Summary

- You must understand stress if you intend to be successful in managing it.
- Become aware of what stressors trigger your stress response.
- Learn the positive effects of stress and how to operate under pressure.
- Manage your time and order your responsibilities to keep stressors from overwhelming you.
- Your body produces stress; rid it of stress by exercising, mentally refocusing, and relaxing.

To-Do List

☐ Create a list of what you need to do this week and organize it by priority.

☐ Talk with your friends or co-workers about how they manage stress. Find out what strategies work for them.

☐ Identify the activities that are most relaxing for you and write two of them into your weekly schedule.

Important Terms

How well do you know these terms? Define them here or in your journal, or look them up in the glossary to help you remember them.

chronic stress	stress
optimum stress	stressor

Online Resources

Top 10 Stress Relievers: The Best Way to Feel Better
stress.about.com/od/generaltechniques/tp/toptensionacts.htm

How to Stop Life Stress before It Becomes Severe
stress.about.com/od/lowstresslifestyle/a/dailylowstress.htm

Meditation: Take a Stress-Reduction Break Wherever You Are
www.mayoclinic.com/health/meditation/HQ01070

Exercises

Write your answers in your journal or on a separate piece of paper.

1. Think of a time when you were under great stress and had to perform (finish a job, play a game, complete an assignment, etc.). Create a graph like the one in the text. Draw the inverted-U arc representing how individuals react to stress. Now label the graph according to what was happening in your environment that made your body react with stress. Chart out the course of your performance, indicating when you reached the optimum stress level and when you moved past optimum stress and your performance began to suffer.

2. In your journal, write three paragraphs identifying three stressors that you regularly respond to. Describe how these stressors tend to either improve or worsen your performance.

3. Write down three things you like to do that help relieve stress. Describe what it is about these activities that helps you release physical stress or refocus your mind away from your stressors.

4 | Your Professional Presentation

KEYS TO SUCCESS

- Fine-tuning your personality to fit your profession
- Learning about the corporate culture you wish to join
- Conquering your fear of failure
- Taking responsibility for your successes and failures
- Adopting a professional attitude
- Creating a polished professional appearance

Personality, Values, and Attitude

Your personality makes a lasting impression on the people who work and study with you. More than any other part of yourself, your personality determines the image that people will form of you.

Because personality plays a major role in how people relate to and work with each other, many employers look closely at personality when deciding whether or not to hire a job candidate. Some employers administer personality tests, such as the Myers-Briggs personality inventory, which categorizes a test taker into one of sixteen personality types based on answers to a questionnaire. Long after a hiring decision has been made, supervisors and managers look at personality when choosing employees for promotion. In many workplaces and organizations, personality is a decisive factor in employee advancement. After all, you are more than just a skill set.

Employers care about your personality because it is the strongest indicator of whether or not you are a good fit for the organization. Personality traits signal an individual's compatibility with his or her co-workers and the type of role he or she is likely to take on.

Corporate Culture

Employers also look at your personality as an indicator of how you will fit into what is called the corporate culture. Corporate culture is the set of values, attitudes, and ways of doing things within an organization. In a way, it is the personality of the organization.

An organization's culture typically reflects its founders' vision of what kind of organization it is, what it stands for, and what it believes in. But corporate culture is also strongly affected by other factors, such as the industry the company is a part of; the company's age, size, and location; and how rapidly it is growing. Companies that are new and growing often reflect a culture of adaptation and versatility. Other companies might value stability over flexibility.

Corporate culture indicates what a company values in its employees: some companies reward individualism, while others emphasize teamwork. A company run by an adventurous entrepreneur might reward risk taking, while a family business that has been run for generations by the same investor group might promote stability. In a very large company, different cultures can operate simultaneously within different units of the organization. Some departments of the corporation may emphasize increasing profits (making more money) while units in another part of the organization focus on controlling costs (not losing money). Not surprisingly, groups with different cultures will attract and seek out individuals with markedly different attitudes, values, and personalities.

> **Workplace Tip**
>
> Learn as much as you can about the team you want to join so that you can assess how well your personality fits its culture.

The Importance of Values

Your personal values are the beliefs and principles that you consider important. In the years following the high-profile corporate scandals of Enron, WorldCom, and other corporate giants, organizations have come under increased scrutiny for their values. One consequence has been that in some workplaces greater value is now assigned to the ethical principles you bring with you into the organization. Personalities that exhibit strong moral character, integrity, and honesty align well with a culture of ethical accountability. When your personal values reflect those of the organization, a good decision for you is a good decision for your organization.

Self-Esteem

Self-esteem refers to how strongly a person values himself or herself. It is the level of respect that you have for yourself. Perhaps you were taught the importance of self-esteem when you were younger. Teachers and parents may have encouraged you to take up activities that build self-esteem. The positive feedback and personal satisfaction that comes from successfully meeting challenges—big or small—puts the focus on your strengths and increases your confidence, leading to greater self-esteem. When parents and teachers work to foster self-esteem, their goal is to make those children feel good about themselves. In addition, those who have healthy self-esteem are likely to be realistic about their strengths and weaknesses, willing to take on new challenges, and able to act independently. People who value themselves are also more likely to present themselves in a way that makes others value them.

Self-esteem is important to your role on a team for the same reasons. Individuals with higher self-esteem require less oversight, are more self-motivated, and are more likely to fulfill an employer's expectations.

Strategies for building self-esteem on the job are also great ways to build professional success. Establishing goals and working hard to achieve them is a proven strategy for building self-esteem. At work, offer to take on a new a responsibility or learn a new skill, and approach the opportunity with enthusiasm and a positive attitude. Succeeding at new challenges builds confidence and gives you the courage to seek other opportunities to learn and grow. Few things will please your employer more than working hard to achieve the goals the employer has set for you. The best professionals are goal-oriented and committed to achievement.

If you lack self-esteem, on the other hand, a potential employer might wonder about your work ethic. He or she may have questions about your personality: Is this person reliable? Does she believe she is incapable of success? If she doesn't value herself, then why should I? Don't invite a prospective employer to ask these kinds of questions. Make self-esteem a priority, focus on it, and achieve it!

Dealing with Past Negative Experiences

Ask any very successful person to tell you the story of his or her success and you will almost always hear a story of failures. Failures are opportunities to learn, to improve self-understanding, and to overcome fears—particularly the fear of failure. Only by failing do we learn that we can survive failure. Only by surviving failure, again and again, do we eliminate our fear of it and learn what failure has to teach us.

Don't think about failure as something to fear. Think about fear as something to conquer.

Taking Responsibility

Look back at the successes and failures throughout your life: When you succeed, who deserves the credit? When you fail, who is to blame?

If you answered that you are to blame when you fail, and that you deserve the credit when you succeed, then you have what the psychologist Julian Rotter has called an internal locus of control: you believe that your quality of life rests largely in your own hands. It is your efforts and ability that produce success or failure. You control your own destiny.

If you answered something else—for example, that bad luck is to blame for your failures—then you have an external locus of control. Individuals with an external locus of control generally consider forces outside their control to be responsible for their successes and failures.

True professionalism requires an internal locus of control, and it is no accident that managers and leaders tend to be people with an internal locus of control. People who believe that their success or failure depends on their own ability are going to make the effort to improve that ability.

People with an external locus of control, who believe that their success or failure is a matter of luck, have little motivation to push themselves to get what they want. Why work to learn a new skill if the outcome is out of your hands? Either fate or chance will reward you, or else you will lose through no fault of your own.

Naturally, employers would rather hire people who believe that the quality of their performance depends on their own effort than the person who looks to external circumstance to explain his or her performance. If you believe in your ability to improve your circumstances, you'll be motivated to work hard to succeed. You're also more likely to take responsibility for your actions.

Adopting a Professional Attitude

Eye Contact

Like most social behaviors, eye contact means different things in different cultures. In the United States, eye contact is important to effective communication. Failure to make eye contact during a conversation can convey nervousness, boredom, or even arrogance—as if the person speaking is not worth listening to. Making eye contact during a conversation lets the other person know that you're paying attention.

> **Workplace Tip**
>
> If you're shy and eye contact makes you nervous, try glancing at the other person's forehead or nose instead of looking directly into the person's eyes. It will look like you are making eye contact.

When you are engaging in a conversation with someone, look at the person before you begin. When the person looks back, that is a signal that you have his or her attention and may begin. During the conversation it is natural to look away from the other person—constant eye contact can be make a person uncomfortable—but glance back periodically to reestablish the connection.

Eye contact is also an important factor in taking turns during a conversation. When the other person wishes to speak, he or she will communicate this intention by making eye contact. Avoiding the person's gaze indicates that you don't want to be interrupted. If you look away until you are finished speaking, be sensitive to the fact that you are shutting down the other person's side of the conversation.

When speaking to a group of people, spread the eye contact around. Looking too long at one person signals to the others that you are not speaking to them. Try to move your eyes from person to person to let each group member feel included. This will help you hold the group's attention.

> ### Practice Critical Thinking
> A classroom is a great place to study the importance of eye contact. Observe the other students during in-class discussions. How do people use their eyes to signal their desire to speak? How do they signal that they don't want to be called on?

Expressions

It might seem like stating the obvious to say that your facial expressions tell others what you are thinking or feeling. Everyone knows that a smile typically means you're happy, a frown means you're sad, and a furrowed brow means you are concentrating. But few people have an accurate idea of how their facial expressions look to others. The only way to find out is to ask. Ask someone you trust to tell you how you look. Do you come off as approachable and friendly, or do you look apathetic or distant? When you are not talking, your face is communicating for you. What is it saying? Remember that how you look in a mirror—or in your driver's license photo—is not necessarily how others see you. Others see you thinking, talking, reacting, concentrating, or spacing out. Find someone who can honestly tell you how your expressions make you look.

Posture

Like your facial expressions, the way you sit, stand, and carry yourself communicates a message—a big one. If you walk into a room or onto a job site with your shoulders slumped, your head down, and your hands in your pockets, you will not look like you are there to take charge and make a difference. You will look like you lack confidence and are waiting to be told what to do.

Even if you are a slouch at home and are never happier than when spread across the sofa, in the workplace you must adopt the posture of a professional.

> ### Exercise Tip
> Exercise regularly. Exercise improves not only the appearance of your body but also your posture. To correct a problem posture, perform exercises that strengthen your abdominal muscles. Yoga is an excellent way to improve posture and make you more comfortable standing up straight.

Here is a simple way to evaluate your everyday posture. Stand very straight in front of a mirror with your shoulders back and your head high; then relax and let your body take the position that feels natural to you. Did you just see yourself collapse a little? Does your normal posture make you look smaller? If you observe such a difference, remember this when you are in a professional setting. You want the way that you hold yourself to increase, not to reduce, your presence.

Study your own bearing and develop a workplace posture that is comfortable but that also makes you look confident, capable, and ready to take charge.

Handshake

Once you have improved your posture to where it needs to be, you will need a handshake to match. A weak, limp handshake is the equivalent of a slouching posture and a frightened face.

A professional's handshake should be firm but not overpowering. If you are a strong person with large hands, provide others the courtesy of not crushing their fingers. Clasp the person's hand firmly but gently, give it two quick shakes, and let go. Don't keep shaking someone's hand as you launch into a conversation. First give the person back his or her hand.

Make sure your hands are clean and dry before you shake hands. If they are not, it's okay to say, "Sorry, I need to wash my hands, but it's great to see you!" Just keep the conversation moving: you don't want it to focus on your dirty hands. Never offer someone a visibly dirty hand to shake. You will leave them with a very unprofessional image of you.

Be wary, too, of extending a clammy, sweaty palm. Sweaty palms are unpleasant to shake and indicate nervousness. If you are on your way to a meeting and feeling nervous, dry your palm before it is time to start shaking hands. Carrying a handkerchief or a small pack of tissues is a good idea if this applies to you.

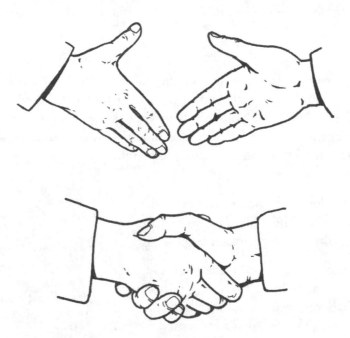

Figure 4.1 Demonstration of proper handshaking technique.

Cell Phone Etiquette

The pervasiveness of cell phones has made cell phone etiquette a staple of professional self-presentation. Although cell phones have made professional communication much easier, they also present opportunities for you to create a very unprofessional self image. Whenever you take a call in a professional setting, excuse yourself politely and hold the conversation in a private place at a low volume.

Cell phone etiquette boils down to a list of don'ts:

Unprofessional conversations. Just because cell phones allow you take calls anywhere doesn't mean you should. Holding personal conversations at work or school, in a public restroom, on the train or bus, or at a restaurant or a reception can cause you to both offend those around you and embarrass yourself. Keep private conversations private. Broadcasting details of your (or someone else's) personal life, gossiping, or engaging in meaningless chatter all constitute unprofessional displays of both bad taste and poor judgment.

Unprofessional volume. Whether it's your ringtone or your voice, turn down the volume if you must receive calls in a professional setting. Use your phone's "vibrate" or "meeting" mode whenever you are at work, at school, or in public.

Unprofessional conduct. *Never* take a personal call during a meeting. Avoid taking personal calls at work in general. If you have to take a call while at work, keep the conversation very brief and go to a private area so you don't disturb your co-workers. Remember that employers are keenly aware that they are paying you for every minute on the job. Avoid wasting a client's or employer's money if you wish to be viewed as a professional.

Unprofessional texting. Never text while carrying on a conversation with another person. Your professionalism requires that you remain focused and considerate. Never text during team meetings unless multitasking is considered acceptable, and even then, keep it professional and brief.

Crafting a Professional Appearance

In your personal life you use your appearance to express your personality. In your professional life, however, your appearance should communicate your professionalism. All aspects of yourself, your appearance included, should be directed toward achieving your professional goals. Anything else you do with your appearance should take a back seat to your professional goals. Leave no doubt in people's minds that you mean business.

When crafting your professional image, keep in mind the message you are trying to convey. You are trying to build the image of a credible, competent professional. Although your outfit may seem "cute" to you, that does not make it professional. Err on the conservative side. Ensure that your clothes are modest, not flashy. Clothes should always be clean, pressed, and well cared for, never stained or torn, and they should fit properly.

ON THE JOB

SCENARIO: One of the technicians you work with has been neglecting his personal hygiene, and clients have been noticing. This inattention to his self-presentation is detracting from your own professionalism. The situation has put you on edge, and this affects your ability to do your own job. Your co-worker, meanwhile, is perfectly at ease and notices nothing wrong.

QUICK FIX: Talk to your boss. It is in your boss's interest to take action and demand that your co-worker clean up his act. If you have a strong relationship with the co-worker, you can address the issue directly yourself. Tell him that you think he could be doing more business if he made a couple of small changes. Tell him that you made similar changes yourself when you were working to improve your own professionalism, and ever since you've been glad you did. If you can deliver the criticism with enough grace and good humor, he might even thank you for it.

If you have questions about the proper attire for your workplace, look at how the boss dresses and model your clothing choices on his or hers (if appropriate to your position). Never try to out-dress the boss.

Workplace Tip

Having fresh breath is a good goal, but consider mints or breath-freshening strips as an alternative to chewing gum. If you must chew gum, avoid making sounds. Loud chewing, snapping, cracking, or bubble blowing is distracting and unprofessional. Think about it: does anyone look his or her best when *chewing?*

Grooming and personal hygiene are as important to your professional image as your wardrobe. Appropriate hairstyles and hair length will vary from place to place, but conservative styles are the safest bet. No matter what the style, hair should always be neat and clean. This includes facial hair, and facial hair includes eyebrows, ear hair, and nose hair. The last thing you want people in a professional setting to remember about you is the hair in your nose.

Your hands should be clean, and fingernails should be kept neatly trimmed. Body odor might be acceptable in some cultures, but in American workplaces it raises a serious red flag. Clean clothes, regular bathing, and use of deodorant will help keep you fresh and odor-free. Avoid heavy colognes, perfumes, aftershaves, or body sprays. Some people are allergic to these products, and others find them irritating. Save the scents for your personal life.

Especially if you work in close contact with people, pay particular attention to your breath. Brush your teeth regularly and don't forget to floss. Because it removes food from between your teeth, flossing is as important to fresh breath as brushing is. Mouthwashes are a useful aid in maintaining fresh breath but are no substitute for flossing and brushing.

Some employers have a dress code prohibiting visible tattoos or facial piercings. If you aren't sure what is appropriate for the situation, remove facial ornaments and conceal tattoos in order to look professional. If you intend to create and maintain a professional image, tattoos should be confined to parts of your body that you can cover. Tattoos on your face, neck, or hands may be unacceptable to employers in conservative industries.

Defining Yourself: Balancing Others' Expectations and Your Individuality

Such a high number of appearance-related dos and don'ts might seem oppressive if you are used to expressing your identity through your appearance. Earning the advantages of being a professional does require a certain amount of conformity. Becoming a professional means ordering one part of your life according to the rules and expectations of the professional world—a world in which you want not only to get by but to succeed and thrive.

> **Workplace Tip**
>
> If you smoke, do everything you can to avoid smelling like your cigarettes. Avoid smoking in your house or in your car, where the smoke will penetrate your clothes and hair. At home, seal your professional clothes in a closet far away from cigarette smoke. If you must smoke, have a breath mint afterward. Smokers often do not smell the smoke on their clothes, skin, hair, and breath, but others may notice and find it distracting.

Chapter Summary

- Choosing a profession that fits your personality starts you off on the right track.

- Knowing your workplace or school corporate culture helps you develop the best strategy for success.

- Failure can be used as a learning experience.

- Look to yourself for the source of your successes and failures, not to others or outside factors.

- If you look, act, sound, and otherwise carry yourself like a professional, you are well on your way to succeeding as one.

To-Do List

☐ Find something about your personality that clashes with the kind of professional presentation you want to achieve. Now work toward changing it. You can start by making a simple list of changes to implement.

☐ Be alert for the next time you blame someone else (or society or fate) for a failure you have faced. Rethink the entire scenario and ask yourself, was there anything I could have done differently that could have altered this outcome?

☐ If you don't know how, teach yourself to iron clothes, polish shoes, and sew on buttons. All of these skills are necessary to maintaining a professional appearance.

☐ If you wear cologne or perfume, ask someone you trust if they think it is too strong or that you wear too much.

☐ If you smoke, try to quit or cut back during business hours. If you can't, do your best to mask its odor.

Important Terms

How well do you know these terms? Define them here or in your journal, or look them up in the glossary to help you remember them.

corporate culture   personality

locus of control   self-esteem

Online Resources

The Eyes Have It: The Fundamentals of Eye Contact
www.bremercommunications.com/Eye_Contact.htm

Cell Phone Etiquette: 10 Dos and Don'ts:
www.microsoft.com/smallbusiness/resources/technology/communications/cell-phone-etiquette-10-dos-and-donts.aspx#Cellphoneetiquettedosanddonts

Workplace Attire
www.helium.com/items/659516-the-importance-of-recognizing-acceptable-workplace-attire

Exercises

Write your answers in your journal or on a separate piece of paper.

1. Write several paragraphs in your journal about a time when you failed at something important to you. Did you fear that you might fail ahead of time? Did you ever try again to do what you failed to do? How did the failure affect your self-esteem at the time? How does it affect your self-esteem now?

2. Write several paragraphs in your journal discussing the culture of your last workplace. How did the goals of the business affect the values, attitudes, and approaches to work that were encouraged among the team? What about your personality was a good fit with that culture? What aspects of your personality did not fit well with the culture?

3. Write a description of what you think it means to be an effective professional in your chosen field. What characteristics would serve well individuals working in this field? Initiative? Teamwork? Independence? Conformity? Creativy? What characteristics might be a disadvantage?

5 | Interpersonal Communication and Business Etiquette

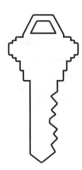

KEYS TO SUCCESS

- Knowing when and how you are communicating
- Understanding nonverbal communication
- Managing nonverbal cues that others notice
- Mastering active communication
- Identifying techniques for getting along with supervisors
- Developing a professional approach to managing social friendships with co-workers
- Adopting standards for dignified and professional behavior at company social functions

You Are Always Communicating

Whether you know it or not, you constantly communicate.

Communication is sometimes defined as the activity of transmitting information. It might be hard to see how you could go wrong with such a basic explanation, but this definition misses an important point about communication. It identifies communication as an *activity*, and an activity (like the related term *action*) implies doing something deliberately, *actively*. When you speak, give a presentation, send a text, or write an email, you *actively* communicate. Communication, however, also happens *passively*. You do things passively when you do them without intending to. For example, if during a class lecture you unconsciously lean forward in your chair and make eye contact with your instructor, you are sending the message that you are interested in the material being presented. You passively communicate information about yourself often without even knowing it—by the way you look and behave. You passively communicate simply by sharing space with other people. The way you look, walk, and act sends information about yourself to others, just as the way other people look, walk, and act reveals information to you.

Anytime you are in the presence of another person, you are sending that person information about yourself—even if you aren't trying to communicate anything. It seems almost unfair, doesn't it? What if you don't want other people to know anything about you?

The truth is, it is impossible to keep from communicating *anything* about yourself because it is impossible to passively communicate nothing. Simply put, you cannot control whether or not you communicate who you are to other people. Communication happens both actively and passively, verbally and nonverbally. The good news is that you have some control over *what* you communicate.

Verbal communication conveys information through speech or writing, and includes conversations, phone calls, speeches, arguments, essays, emails, chats, and text messaging. If you want to communicate nothing verbally, you can stop speaking or writing.

Silence, however, continues the communication even after you have stopped speaking. Silence is, in fact, one of the most expressive forms of nonverbal communication—consider the "silent treatment." But silence is just one form of nonverbal communication. As you will see, there are many others.

Nonverbal Communication

Nonverbal communication includes aspects of how you look and behave: your gestures, your clothing, your posture, your facial expressions, and your body language. These facets of yourself always communicate information to anyone looking at you. And nonverbal behaviors speak volumes about who you are. Fortunately, by actively managing your nonverbal behaviors you can help control what those behaviors communicate.

The Importance of Nonverbal Communication

You've probably heard the term *poker face,* which refers to a facial expression that reveals nothing about a person's thoughts or emotions. Poker players are keenly aware of the importance of actively managing nonverbal communication. Poker players study their opponents' faces, gestures, and postures for clues about what those opponents are thinking. To keep from passively conveying information about their cards, some poker players wear sunglasses to hide their eyes and pull brimmed hats down low over their faces.

Effective poker playing means concealing—not revealing—information. Just as poker players do not want others to know what cards are in their hands, they do not want their opponents to guess the strategies they are pursuing. Successfully managing nonverbal communication can be the difference between winning and losing. Poker players take an active approach to managing their nonverbal behaviors. Winning at poker requires keeping an *active* grip on *passive* communication.

Understanding What Nonverbal Communication Says about You

Poker players have a word for a behavior that conveys information about an opponent's hand. A clue that a player passively communicates about his or her hand is called a *tell*.

But poker players are not the only people who should be concerned with tells. All people have tells. Yours are those aspects of your self-presentation that *tell* others (give information) about you.

If you walk into a building soaking wet when it is raining outside, your wet head tells people you forgot an umbrella. Show up to work at a commercial bank in shabby clothes and scuffed shoes, and your appearance tells customers that you lack professionalism (and that the bank's standards are slipping).

But tells go beyond your clothing and accessories. What if you stand so close to other people when you speak to them that they constantly edge away from you? What if when you speak to other people you never look them in the eye? All of these nonverbal behaviors tell others something about you, and in none of these examples is the news you are sharing good. People who persistently stand too close to others when speaking seem to lack an understanding of personal space, as well as an awareness of how their behavior affects others. Speakers who never look others in the eye make their listeners uneasy and come off as either lacking in confidence or, worse, untrustworthy. Bad table manners not only communicate that a person lacks polish but also that the person lacks self-awareness and a proper consideration for others.

> **Communication Tip**
>
> It's important to be aware of your own tells and to understand what they communicate to others. It's equally important, however, to learn to read other people's tells. Get in the habit of watching other people and paying attention to their unconscious actions that communicate information beyond their spoken words.

Managing Nonverbal Communication

How can you manage your passively communicated information? We all have tried to control one form of nonverbal communication that can easily send others the wrong message: yawning. Whether you are in a classroom, at a meeting, or trying to listen supportively to a friend's lengthy story, you try to avoid yawning; otherwise people may think you are bored, impolite, or simply exhausted from listening to them. The message a yawn sends is rarely one that you would consciously choose to communicate. Stifling a yawn is one of the most common examples of how to control a nonverbal behavior that sends an unintended message. Unless you want people to think you are uninterested in what they have to say (and would rather be home in bed), you try not to let them catch you yawning—at least not when they are speaking.

Just as you constantly passively convey information to others, you constantly passively collect information about others. If asked to describe someone who sat next to you in a meeting or a class, regardless of how much attention you paid to the person, you could probably describe the person's approximate size, hair color, and clothes and state whether or not the person wore glasses. Every day, wherever you are, you pick up this kind of information passively, effortlessly.

If you were asked to think more deeply about the person who sat next to you in that meeting or class, you probably also could recall if the person seemed attentive or distracted, fidgety or drowsy, prepared or disorganized. You might have observed this person for no more than an instant, but in that instant you passively absorbed a great deal of information about him or her. More important, whether you intended to or not, you transformed some of this information into an opinion of the person.

Forming Opinions

You transform information about people into opinions when you decide what that information *means*. Like the passive collection of information, opinion formation is not something you actively think about; it simply seems to be the way that you "see" the person.

Practice Critical Thinking

Think about someone who has recently made a strong impression on you, either positive or negative. Actively identify what led you to form your assessment. What aspects of the person's communication style influenced your opinion? How can you apply that knowledge to your own communication style?

For instance, if the person seated next to you slouched low in his chair and stared at his desk while you sat up straight and followed the speaker's eyes, you might have formed the opinion that the person was not paying attention. Of course, this might not be true. The person may have been concentrating intently on every word. The opinions you form sometimes tell you less about others than they do about yourself, but that does not make opinions any less important.

Most people unconsciously assume that a well-dressed person is successful and respectable. They also assume that a well-dressed person is more trustworthy than someone who is dirty or poorly dressed.

Like your opinion about the attention level of the slouching person seated next to you, the opinion that a well-dressed person is trustworthy is at best a risky guess. However, people venture such guesses over and over, often without realizing they are doing so.

Think about it. Have you ever had a doctor, a teacher, a counselor, or a relative whom you admired, or around whom you simply felt comfortable or assured, for no particular reason? Now reflect on that person's passive and nonverbal communication. Can you find any subtle features of that person's appearance, manner, posture, or gestures that may have contributed to the strong positive feeling?

Tells are not always bad. Passive communication and nonverbal behavior form a large part of what makes a person charismatic or comforting to be around.

Passive Communication in the Workplace

Managing your nonverbal communication is especially important in the professional world. In the workplace, just as at a poker table, passive information is often *actively* collected. People actively observe nonverbal behaviors when they want to learn about a person as surely as they actively listen to and interpret their words. Further, people actively form opinions and make decisions based on this information.

Employers, job interviewers, managers, and co-workers all actively collect the information that you passively convey through the manner in which you behave and carry yourself. They absorb what you communicate, and they formulate judgments and conclusions about you. Based on your nonverbal, perhaps unintentional behaviors, people make decisions about whether you look like a team player, your leadership potential, and the kind of employee or colleague you might be: efficient, lazy, meticulous, careless, confident, untrustworthy, reliable, or a risky bet. When it comes to actively managing your passive communication, the stakes are high.

Communication Tip

When attending a job interview, treat the entire visit as the interview. Smart employers will try to gain insight into a candidate by any means possible, including asking reception staff how the candidate communicated with them and observing the candidate's posture while he or she waits in the lobby. An employer's direct experience of a candidate can leave a more meaningful impression than the candidate's resume or cover letter; it can even be of more importance than the person's actual training and experience. Employers hire people less for what they have done than for what they believe they can do. A potential employer's assessment of you depends on what you communicate, verbally and nonverbally, and whether that communication is active or passive.

ON THE JOB

SCENARIO: During your first employee review at the dental clinic, your supervisor tells you that you need to work on your communication style because patients have reported being unable to follow what you are saying. You are surprised because no patients have informed you of their inability to understand you. Your supervisor asks what ideas you have for improving your communication with patients.

QUICK FIX: Ensuring that your patients understand your communication means paying attention to their nonverbal behaviors. Make eye contact with your patients when speaking and study their faces and body language for signs of understanding. If you usually work while talking to the patient, stop working, sit down, and speak face-to-face with the patient. This will make the patient feel more comfortable asking questions if he or she doesn't understand what you're saying. It also allows you to ask the patient directly if he or she needs to have any information repeated or further explained.

Verbal Communication

Verbal communication is the act of using words to express your thoughts. When you speak, you mix verbal and nonverbal means of communicating. You communicate through the words you speak. But you also communicate through your tone of voice, through your posture, and through any gestures that accompany your words, whether you are aware of them or not. For instance, you might be speaking more loudly or sternly than you realize. If you are standing over a seated person while speaking, the person might be interpreting your passive communication as an emphatic statement of authority, particularly if you are literally talking down to them.

Listeners collect this passive information and add it to your actively communicated information. As long as you are aware of what information your behavior conveys, you can tailor your nonverbal behavior to accentuate the message you are communicating verbally. If you are unaware of what information your behavior conveys, however, and exercise little control over it, your passive communication can seriously distort your message.

Own Your Meaning

Just as with the other forms of passive communication discussed in this chapter, you can help control the information you convey passively through your speech by taking an active approach to managing your verbal and nonverbal behaviors. Through the active exercise of self-control you can better "own" your meaning. Here are some tips.

Be conscious of the speed at which you speak. Speaking too slowly can sound monotonous, and speaking too quickly can make you sound nervous. But at times either slow or fast speech may be appropriate. Fast speech can convey excitement, and slow speech can convey seriousness or build anticipation. Try to maintain an awareness of the speed at which you speak, and vary your speed to suit your meaning.

Be conscious of the volume at which you speak. Particularly if you are discussing sensitive topics in locations where you can be overheard, speaking too loudly communicates that you are unaware of your surroundings. However, speaking too softly, especially when addressing a group, robs you of authority and makes it more difficult for people to listen to you. Avoid making people have to work to understand you.

Speak clearly. Enunciate when you speak. Move your lips and form the words. Mumbling conveys a lack of confidence and suggests that you attach little importance to what you have to say. Consciously enunciating also helps you to accentuate your key points and clearly communicate the parts of your message that you wish to emphasize. Be sure as well that you know how to pronounce your words correctly. If you are uncertain of a word's correct pronunciation, do not use it. Likewise, avoid using needlessly "big" words. Speak simply and directly, or you risk communicating to your listener that you are pretentious, pedantic, or—if you use the wrong "big" word or mispronounce one—ignorant.

Make eye contact. Observe how your listeners are reacting as you speak. If eye contact makes you too nervous, move your gaze between your listener's forehead and nose in a one-on-one discussion. Look just above your audience's eye level when addressing a group.

Because you are not actually making eye contact, you will be less accurate in gauging your audience's reaction to your words, but you will at least convey an appearance of confidence and poise. Speakers who perform a pantomime of eye contact at length often eventually grow comfortable with making real eye contact.

Know what you want to say before opening your mouth. Then say it plainly. Do not be afraid of pausing to collect your thoughts. A pause is a wiser move than a hasty statement. Even though it may not feel that way to you, remaining silent while you decide what to say will make you appear much more composed than if you nervously fill the space between your words with *um* and *ah*. Pauses, in fact, can be very effective in maintaining your listener's attention. Skilled pubic speakers such as politicians, news anchors, and trial lawyers often write pauses directly into their speaking notes.

Inflect appropriately. End your sentences with an upward voice inflection only if you are actually asking a question. Avoid the bad habit of ending a statement with an upward inflection, which can make it sound like you are asking a question. Bring your voice down at the end of a statement with a period, but not one with a question mark. Avoid inviting your listeners to question everything you say by appearing to question it yourself.

Be brief. Never speak longer than you need to. Be wary of "talking to hear yourself speak." Respect other people's time and do not waste it with needless words. The person who can say in a single sentence what for someone else requires a long, rambling speech is the superior communicator. When it comes to words, less is more.

Be considerate. Be sensitive to others who may wish to speak, and listen to them attentively. Use gestures, eye contact, and nodding to convey that you are interested in what they have to say and that you comprehend their meaning.

Getting Along with Your Boss

Developing good communication skills is essential for getting along with co-workers. The most important relationship in your job is the one you have with your direct manager. Your boss is the person with the power to control your day-to-day life at work, and also the one with the most influence over your long-term prospects. Not all bosses are created equal, though. The following sections will show how to deal with different types of managers.

Good Bosses

If you're lucky, you will work for a boss who is in control of his or her responsibilities, sets clear standards, rewards good work, treats all employees fairly, and sets a good example. Some bosses are experts in the area in which their groups work; others are given authority based mainly on their management skills and experience. Either one can be effective; they just have different strengths.

When you work for a good boss, communication will be easy and open—so take advantage of it. Talk regularly with your manager to find out how you're doing at your job, what you could be doing better, and what you could be learning. If you're interested in expanding your responsibilities or would like to be considered for promotion, let your boss know. If you do good work and show professionalism, he or she will protect you, back you up, and reward you as much as possible.

Bad Bosses

Some bosses mean well but just aren't up to the job of leading a team or managing personnel. A manager who is out of touch, flaky, unreliable, or misguided will make your job more difficult. That doesn't mean that you should quit, but you will have to negotiate a balance between doing your best work for the company and respecting the authority of someone who might not be making the best use of your skills or making the best decisions.

The most likely complication in such a situation is that your boss will dictate procedures that make your job harder than it needs to be. The first thing to recognize is that your boss is not trying to make your job harder; there's a reason for doing things this way. If you don't understand his or her reasoning, then ask. It's as simple as saying, "Can you help me understand the goal we're trying to achieve?" There's always the chance that it will turn out to make sense. Or it might simply be a difference in opinion or priorities between the two of you. In that case, it's probably best to let your boss have his or her way. That's what bosses get to do.

If your manager's reasoning is truly flawed, you have some decisions to make. Is it worth trying to change his or her mind? If so, then proceed cautiously. Avoid pointing fingers or criticizing one of your boss's ideas. Find things to praise in the idea. Express your agreement with the basic goal, and suggest ways to tweak the approach to improve the chances of achieving it. Try to express your ideas as simple adjustments of your boss's ideas. Allow room for your boss to take credit for the procedure.

Above all, avoid direct conflict, because nothing good will come of it. You can't make your boss into a better manager. But if you learn how to deal with his or her shortcomings, you might come to be seen as a valuable adviser.

"Ugly" Bosses

Of course, things can get worse. You may work for a manager who is abusive, insecure, or dishonest. In this case, every day at work is like stepping through a minefield as you try to avoid making yourself the target of your boss's wrath.

Depending on how "ugly" your boss is, you may want to simply assume a defensive crouch from nine to five and start looking for a better option. Sometimes the situation is toxic and not worth enduring.

If you don't have the option of shopping around, or if you have other reasons for sticking it out in your job, then you must do what you can to protect yourself:

- **Document everything.** Every time you accomplish something good on the job, write it down. Save every phone message and email you get from your boss. If there's no paper trail for some disputed issue, make one: send your boss an email to confirm that you're doing as he or she asked. If it reaches the point where you decide to bring a complaint up the ladder, or to human resources, you'll be expected to show solid evidence.

- **Don't provoke.** Conflict may be inevitable with an "ugly" boss, but make sure that any dust-ups can't be blamed on you. Do as your manager asks, and don't start fights. Stay polite and professional. If higher-ups are watching, you want them to see that you are the one on the high ground.

- **Watch the gossip.** If your manager genuinely is a problem for the employees or the organization, then it's fine to share information with human resources. Othewise, limit your conversations to those you absolutely trust, or better yet, avoid the topic altogether. You don't want to be viewed by others as a gossip whispering about colleagues.

Relationships with Co-workers

You probably spend more time during the week with your co-workers than you do with your family and friends. They're a big part of your life, and they can have an impact on your career—so it's important to use good sense when dealing with them. Always remain professional and treat everyone with respect.

Social Life and Work Life

Many people make lifelong friends in the workplace. That's great—but remember that your primary purpose there is not to make friends. You're there to do your job and advance your career. Set your sights on being part of a good team. If you end up making friends along the way, fine; just keep your priorities straight.

Remember that once you're friends with someone, you owe each other a loyalty that can come into conflict with your duties at work. What do you do if your friend is doing a lousy job and dragging down the whole team? What if your friend comes into conflict with the boss—or with another friend at work? Be aware of these things as you're getting to know people, and choose your friends wisely.

> **Workplace Tip**
>
> Talking about current events or common interests is a great way to bond with co-workers, but steer clear of any controversial subjects that involve strongly held personal beliefs, such as religion or politics. Instead, talk about the plight of your favorite football team or last night's episode of *Project Runway*. A little good-natured debate is fine, but make sure you keep the tone light.

> ### Workplace Tip
>
> It's great to have a friend at work, but make sure you keep your behavior professional during work hours. Don't talk excessively about personal things at work, and don't spend all your time with just your friend. Make sure your friendship doesn't cause you to inadvertently exclude others in your office.

Issues with Dating

If you get romantically involved with a co-worker, be prepared to deal with some thorny issues. For starters, everything in the discussion above about friends goes triple for romantic partners.

Many companies have policies about employee dating. Some will require you to disclose your relationship, or even declare that you can't both work in the same department. You may consider your love life to be none of the company's business, but private companies in most states can make it their business, and can discipline or fire you for not following their policies.

Consider these points before getting involved:

- **Dating a co-worker is unprofessional.** Even if it doesn't put your job at risk, employee dating cannot easily be defended as *good* for the company or for your work. Having a strong emotional connection with someone you work with is dangerous. You can't be objective about your boyfriend's or girlfriend's work, and your loyalties will be confused at best.

- **People will know.** You may think you're being discreet, but you probably aren't—especially at the beginning of a relationship, when things are exciting and new. You can't control your body language every second of every day. If you don't put your relationship out in the open, be prepared to be the subject of gossip.

- **Perceptions will change.** Both your judgment and that of the employee you are dating will be seen as biased—and rightly so, for all the reasons outlined above.

- **Breakups are tough.** As nasty as ending a relationship can be, doing it with a co-worker is many times worse. You'll still have to see each other every day, you may have to work closely together on a project, and everyone will be watching and talking about you both. The details of the breakup are likely to get around, and co-workers may pick sides and turn against either you or your ex.

Business Etiquette

Aside from responsibly managing relationships with co-workers and superiors, there are some basic guidelines you should follow regarding your personal conduct on the job.

Rules on Company Behavior

Make sure you're familiar with your employer's guidelines for employee conduct. This includes rules about:

- Dressing for work
- Eating on the job—what's allowed, when, and where

- Breaks—how many, how long

- Personal use of company resources—computers, supplies, and other items

- Music and headphones

- Visitors

- Sick days, personal days, and other absences

These guidelines are typically outlined in the company's employee handbook, which you should receive on your first day. However, some smaller companies might not have a comprehensive handbook. In that case, you should ask for the policies in writing.

Personal Business at Work

If you spend the entire business day at work, it makes it tricky to handle calls to your doctor, the bank, your realtor, the plumber, or your kids' school, or to deal with any of the other complications of life that can intrude on your workday. Most employers understand that sometimes you have to deal with personal business while at work, but they expect you to keep it to a minimum.

If any obligation can be handled before or after work or on your lunch hour, do it then. If you must take a call at your desk or access your personal email account, make it as quick as possible. It might be better to take your cell phone outside or to the break room rather than disrupt your co-workers by talking about personal business.

> **Workplace Tip**
>
> Set your cell phone on vibrate, and keep it with you. That way, you won't have to worry about your cell phone ringing endlessly when you're away from your work area. No one likes to listen to the ringtone of an absent co-worker's unanswered cell phone.

Company Social Functions

An office Christmas party or company picnic can be a good time to open up a little to your co-workers, discover common interests, and build productive relationships. Company social functions offer you and your co-workers a chance to see sides of each other that you never see during the workday, and to get to like each other better.

Got that? You want to be liked *better*. So don't treat a company function as a house party. If alcohol is served, feel free to enjoy a drink—not three or four. Loosen up a little, yes, but don't say anything you wouldn't want to hear repeated Monday morning. Avoid any overindulgence, off-color jokes, foul language, and crude or sexual comments.

> **Practice Critical Thinking**
>
> How can you use a company social function as an opportunity to make connections and advance your career?

Should you dance? Participate in karaoke? Well, there are some things that a book just can't tell you. Use your best judgment.

Julie Ann Dannen

Sheffield, Iowa

Attended: Kaplan University Online

Area of study: Master of Business Administration

Employer: Business Manager, Kaplan University—Mason City, Iowa

If you take one thing away from this course, it should be this: Being successful takes patience and the ability to deal with the day-to-day issues that may occur.

Kaplan has given me the courage to complete numerous degrees, from my AAS degree to my BS degrees (accounting and management) and my MBA. I never thought that I would be able to complete all this education, but they gave me the tools and encouragement to succeed.

Chapter Summary

- Understanding the full range of ways in which you communicate will make you a more effective communicator.

- Nonverbal behavior, even when it communicates passively, is often observed actively in the workplace.

- Understanding and practicing your communication behaviors will help ensure that your meaning is communicated intact, which reduces the risks posed by misunderstanding and misinterpretation.

- If you work for an attentive, responsible, effective manager, you have the opportunity to enhance your career prospects by communicating regularly about your job performance and professional goals.

- To deal with an irresponsible or ineffective manager, learn to provide helpful input while protecting your boss's ego.

- When working for an abusive manager, document everything, don't look for trouble, and be discreet about gossiping.

- Making friends with co-workers can be very rewarding, but you need to negotiate a balance between your loyalty to them and your obligation to the company and to your own career. This applies even more to dating, which brings with it many potential pitfalls.

- Your employee handbook should provide you with a basic outline of your company's rules and expectations for conduct on the job. If you don't get a handbook, ask for policies in writing.

To-Do List

☐ Record the nonverbal behaviors that you observe in people you see every day. What do these cues tell you about the person?

☐ Observe the way that service professionals, such as waiters and cashiers, respond to you. What do you think your appearance, behavior, and comportment tell them about you?

☐ Identify one of your tells that you would like to get rid of. How will you go about doing so?

☐ List the three most important qualities in a co-worker and resolve to demonstrate those in your workplace behavior.

☐ List three characteristics that a good boss should have.

☐ Come up with several topics that are appropriate for workplace conversation.

Important Terms

How well do you know these terms? Define them here or in your journal, or look them up in the glossary to help you remember them.

active communication	**nonverbal communication**
business etiquette	**passive communication**
gossip	**personal business**
inflection	**verbal communication**

Online Resources

Communicating and Building Relationships (free PDF download) at Dale Carnegie
www.dalecarnegie.com

Communication Skills Self-Assessment
spot.pcc.edu/~rjacobs/career/effective_communication_skills.htm

How to Get Along with Your Co-workers
hubpages.com/hub/how-to-get-along-with-your-co-workers

Exercises

Write your answers in your journal or on a separate piece of paper.

1. Write in your journal as accurate an assessment as you can of your own passive communication behaviors. What do you do around others that might communicate more information about yourself than you consciously wish to share? (What are your tells?) What nonverbal behaviors might communicate positive aspects of yourself (e.g., that you are a good listener, are patient, or are understanding)?

2. Imagine that you are preparing for an important job interview. Reflect on past job interviews (or other face-to-face meetings at which something important was at stake), and write in your journal three paragraphs about how your understanding of passive and nonverbal communication will affect your preparation for this interview. What will you do differently this time? What behaviors will you change and why?

3. Write down three company behavioral rules that you would like an employer to enforce. Remember, these rules are in place to protect employees and their ability to succeed at work, not just to restrict what employees can do on the job.

6 | Writing Skills

KEYS TO SUCCESS

- Using the "you-attitude" in business communications
- Knowing the differences in writing style between school papers, business messages, and technical reports
- Developing a three-stage writing process that includes planning, drafting, and revising
- Using appropriate grammar and vocabulary in business communications
- Knowing what plagiarism is and avoiding it

Any time you communicate, you need to have the attention of the person you're communicating with. And you want that person's attention on the message you're trying to get across. When you communicate face-to-face, this means that you don't want the person paying attention to unimportant things like the way you're dressed, and you do want to look at his or her eyes and body language to see how he or she is reacting.

When you communicate in writing, your readers can't see how you're dressed, but you can't see them, either. You can't look into their eyes to see if they're paying attention, or study their body language to see if they're annoyed by what you're saying. What you've written has to hold their attention, and hold it in a positive way so that they receive your message and, you hope, act on it in the way you want them to.

Put Your Focus on the Reader

Writing is an important part of many jobs. You may be writing to a customer, to co-workers, or to your boss. Your job of communicating is made easier if you remember that every piece of writing should start by giving your reader this message: "In this business relationship, the most important person is you (customer, boss, or fellow worker), and not me, the writer." This message is called the "you-attitude," and it consists of two parts: (1) putting yourself in the reader's shoes, and (2) having the writing skill to convey your understanding to the reader.

Understanding the Reader

Understanding others, especially if they're customers or co-workers, starts with an understanding of yourself. Do you like to be taken advantage of? Do you like to receive criticism? Do you want people to talk to you as if you were a child? Do you want to listen to other people's problems when they're trying to tell you how to deal with your own? Certainly not—and neither do your co-workers, customers, or other professionals you encounter. It might be a little harder when you're writing to a teacher or a boss, but you do know what they expect of you, and you can be pretty sure that they won't like to have their time wasted by anything that's not necessary to the message or the assignment.

Here are some general truths that apply to most people:

- They expect courtesy—so be polite.

- They respond better to positive statements than to negative statements.

- They want to know what your message is about. Particularly in business communication, get to the point as quickly as you can. If you have a wonderfully clever way to get readers interested in what you have to say, you can do so—but only if the major goal of your message is to provide humor.

- They put their self-interest and the interests of their loved ones ahead of yours; you can't change this no matter how important your message is to yourself.

- They don't like criticism. Anyone's first reaction to criticism is to be defensive and to reject it or try to find excuses. This is true even if the criticism is accurate and even if the reader will tend to agree with it after thinking it over.

- They understand something better if goals and deadlines are defined specifically. How many hours are in a "soon"? How many minutes in "a little while"? When you use time phrases like these, your readers will either put their own idea of "soon" into your message, or they'll know that you're just trying to be vague on purpose.

- They want to be treated as if they're honest and intelligent—so treat them as if they are.

Writing for the Reader

To use your knowledge about your readers, you have to put it in practice when you write. Here are some tips for incorporating the "you-attitude" in your written communication:

- Open with the information your readers are most interested in.

- Organize your overall message in a way that will meet the readers' needs, not necessarily your own.

- Begin and end your message in a positive way: it's important to be as positive as you can all the way through, but it's especially true at the beginning and the end.

  - **Not:** "You cannot use the copy machine in the east corridor between the hours of 9:00 and noon." **Better:** "You may use the copy machines on the second floor before 9:00 and after noon."

- Never start a business message by criticizing your reader, even if you do so politely.

  - **Not:** "Your instructions on the new procedure were not clear." **Better:** "Please clarify your instructions so that the new procedure will go smoothly."

  - **Not:** "You may not be aware that downloading programs without authorization is dangerous." **Better:** "Please help us keep your computer safe by asking for authorization before downloading programs."

- Avoid negative words such as "complaint" or "claim" to describe your readers' actions or statements.

  - **Not:** "We have received your complaint about . . ." **Better:** "Your suggestion that . . . has much merit."

  - **Not:** "Because you failed to meet the payment deadline, your account is delinquent." **Better:** "Your account is past due."

- Use bias-free language, and know and use the language of your co-workers if you are writing to them. (If you can, read several emails from co-workers or bosses on the general subject you're writing about.)

Formatting

An aspect of writing with your readers in mind is to make your message conform to the conventions with which your readers are familiar. For papers and technical reports, you'll usually be given some guidelines by your instructor or your company. For emails, memos, letters, and other business correspondence, you may need to do some research to find out the format that's expected.

Some Rules for Email

1. Always include a salutation, especially if the email is addressed to more than one person.
2. Never "Reply to All" unless you've read every name that the message is copied to and you're sure that you want to send your reply to everyone.
3. You should have a signature that you can use for every email. For business correspondence, your signature shouldn't contain cute quotes or advertisements for yourself.
4. Don't write anything in an email that you don't want a large audience to read.

Once you've figured out the expected format, you'll have more credibility because you'll demonstrate that you know how things are done and that your messages are important. Here are three conventions that most forms of business communication share:

- Use single spacing.

- Separate paragraphs by a blank line.

- Use short paragraphs. They should be especially short for email, which people usually read on a computer screen.

There are many other conventions that apply to different kinds of business communication, and all those rules are focused on allowing the reader to feel comfortable.

Write in Style

Not all of your writing, at least for now, will be for business communication. And no one style of writing is appropriate for all documents or messages. One of the easiest mistakes you can make is to use the wrong style. In the near future, you're likely to be working on three main types of writing projects.

School Papers

In most academic work, you're expected to use a formal, impersonal tone, as though you were writing an article for a magazine that will be read by many people you don't know. Informal writing comes off as disrespectful toward your subject matter, undercutting the substance of your paper.

When writing school papers:

- Avoid contractions (*can't, isn't, didn't*).

- Avoid emotional or judgmental language (*thrilling, appalling, beautiful*).

- Keep *you* and *me* out of it; use *one* instead (*One can detect hints of racial tension in the literature of this era*).

- Make it clear how all of your ideas and statements relate to your assigned topic.

- Avoid exclamation points in scholarly writing.

Business Communication

Remember the "you-attitude" when you're composing business messages. And also keep in mind that in business every relationship is unique, and you should be aware of that as you write. When writing for people you know well, you should consider what tone is appropriate. You should generally be more formal with people you know less, and with people who are above you in the pecking order. That means you should observe the following guidelines:

- Avoid informal figures of speech (*around here, time was, you know*).

- Be cordial but not too familiar (*Welcome back to the office*, not *Long time no see*).

- Address people by title (*Dr., Ms., Mr.*), unless they signal otherwise—for instance, by signing emails with only their first name.

Remember that writing is considered more formal than speaking, especially in a professional setting. Printed messages tend to be taken as more formal and serious than emails, so adjust your tone accordingly.

> **Not:** Holy cow! This has gotta stop! Have we really been paying premium charges EVERY TIME the lab asks for them?!
>
> **Better:** Our bills from the lab have been higher than we normally expect. In the future we need to investigate every added charge from the lab, and negotiate it if necessary.

Technical Reports

When your main purpose is to convey technical information—such as statistics, monetary figures, medical facts, or study results—the most important thing is to be precise, even if it makes your document longer or more complicated. When working on such documents:

- Maintain a neutral, formal tone: state facts, not your opinions on them (unless specifically asked).

- Always compare "apples to apples": don't mix up one set of data with another (compare January's total sales to February's total sales; don't compare January's radio sales to February's pickle sales).

- Define all terms that are likely to be unfamiliar to readers.

- Use abbreviations and acronyms to make for quicker reading (if you use *Monthly Sales Report* ten times in the document, shorten it to *MSR*). Also, define every acronym or abbreviation the first time you use it (*According to the Monthly Sales Report (MSR), we have not met our goals*).

- Consider putting information in the form of a table, chart, or graph; often that will make it easier to follow.

The Writing Process

You want to get your message just right, and you want to focus on the reader. Doing it right can take time. If you find yourself staring at a blank computer screen, or going back over and over to delete what you've written, you might want to pull back for a few moments and consider your approach. Writing isn't just one single task; it's a *process*, made up of several distinct tasks. Once you break it down into smaller tasks, it's really not that intimidating. The three main stages of the writing process are planning, drafting, and revising.

Planning

First, take some time to think about your purpose in writing. Are you trying to convey information, make a persuasive argument, or provoke a certain action? What subjects do you need to address? What information do you need to provide?

If you can't answer all of these questions right away, try brainstorming: Take fifteen minutes to write down every thought and idea that comes into your head. Flag the best and most interesting ideas, and see where they lead.

The planning stage is when you do most of your research. The sources you find may help you gather your own thoughts.

Once you have a good number of ideas kicking around, you should organize them into an outline. Following a strict format isn't that important; what matters is that you put your information and arguments into a logical order that will make it easy for a reader to follow. Remember to organize so that you will present your reader's interests first. Give yourself a blueprint, so that when you're writing you always know where you're going.

Drafting

Once you have your blueprint, it's time to start banging out those words. If you have trouble getting started, try freewriting: For ten minutes just type and don't stop, even if some of the time you're typing nonsense. With a little luck, you'll begin to find your voice and overcome your anxiety.

The important thing during drafting is to not get caught up in the other two stages. If you've done good planning, then you won't have to worry constantly about where you're going with all of this writing. Likewise, don't get bogged down revising your work as you go. There's no point in tinkering endlessly with your sentences at this point, because in the revising stage you may decide to delete them entirely.

Writing Tip

Pretend that you're the person that you're writing to, and read through that person's eyes.

Revising

Once you have a complete draft, it's time to go back and fine-tune your document. If possible, take some time away from it so that you can come back to it with fresh eyes (and more energy). A writer with a good process will spend at least one-third of his or her time on revision.

Make at least three separate passes through your document. The first time, look at the big picture: Are your ideas expressed clearly? Is your argument logical? Have you organized your points in the best way? This is the time for your biggest changes. As before, don't worry about sentence-level issues at this point.

After you've settled on the overall shape of your document, take a second pass through it, looking at the writing. Are all of your sentences clear? Have you overused certain words? Do you repeat yourself unnecessarily? Are there key bits of information that are hard for a reader to find? Edit for clarity, but leave the finer details of grammar and punctuation for later.

> ### *Writing Tip*
> Proofread everything—every written academic or business document should be as error-free as you can make it.

Finally, go through one more time to check grammar, spelling, and punctuation. Correct typos, double-check words like *there, their,* and *they're,* and make sure all of your formatting is correct.

Always run a spell-check, but remember that a spell-checker is just a brainless computer script. You have to make the decisions about which words to fix, and how. You'll still need to proofread with your own eyes, because the computer won't catch misspellings that happen to be real words, such as *roll* and *role,* or *on* and *of*—and it certainly won't tell you if you've left out important words.

Many word processors will check your grammar along with your spelling. Be very careful, though: the English language has millions of rules, and almost all of them have exceptions. Computer grammar checkers are notorious for "correcting" sentences that have nothing wrong with them, and for missing major problems. Always proofread your work.

ON THE JOB

SCENARIO: Your manager needs you to write a letter to customers announcing a new procedure for making appointments at your clinic. It's noon, and he needs it by two o'clock. Even if you drop everything, there's still very little time. How can you make the best use of your two hours?

QUICK FIX: The three-stage writing process is still your best bet, so prioritize your tasks. Take half an hour to read the new procedure and make sure you understand it, note the parts of it that will most benefit the customers, and map out your approach. Do a rough outline in your word processor, putting the customer benefits up front, and then start filling it in with appropriate message text. Be sure to keep the customers' point of view in mind. Save at least half an hour for revision, and be sure to proofread.

Creating the Right Impression: Grammar and Vocabulary

Recall that you want to treat your readers as if they're honest and intelligent. Another important point is that you want them to think of you the same way. When you're talking to someone, seeming honest and intelligent comes naturally. But when you write, your readers will have to judge you not just on your appearance and engaging manner, but also on how well you can follow the universal standards of writing: spelling and grammar. For some readers, reading a message with misspelled words or with poor grammar may be a very minor annoyance that doesn't detract from the importance of the message. For others, however—and these tend to be teachers or managers, people you want to impress—a written communication with bad grammar may send only one message: the writer isn't worth paying attention to.

> ### Writing Tip
> Always write a letter or email that's exactly the right length. And never turn in a written class assignment that's far too long, such as five pages for a two-page paper assignment.

So writing skills *are* important for professional success, but after all those years of English class it can seem as if grammar is a game you can't win, with rules you don't understand. The bad news is that you probably won't ever learn all of those complicated rules and terms. The good news is that you don't have to learn all of them to be a good writer.

Writing for the Real World

In the professional world, the rules for writing can be reduced to three basic principles:

1. **Be clear.** Your sentences should be easily readable from beginning to end. Confine the main information to the subject and verb, and put them at the front of the sentence; then fill in the details. Don't make your boss go back and read something twice just to understand it.

    Difficult to read: Fourth-quarter profits, owing mainly to the Western Division's sales figures, in comparison to the third quarter have moved upward.

    Better: Profits improved in the fourth quarter, mainly because of strong sales from the Western Division.

2. **Project your best self.** Fair or not, how you write will be taken as an indicator of how you work. You should try to appear thoughtful, organized, and engaged, not careless, scatterbrained, or uninterested.

> ### Writing Tip
> Keep in mind that people at work are *busy*. Stick to the point, and don't try to impress people with your command of "business-ese."

3. **Don't waste people's time.** If you're padding your sentences and paragraphs just to make them longer—*stop*. You're not scoring points with anybody. When your instructor asks for a two-page paper, that means two pages of information, analysis, and argument—not a few paragraphs of substance stretched out with a lot of unnecessary words.

In the field of business writing, many people believe that stuffy, formal-sounding phrases like *enclosed please find, as per your request,* and *pursuant to our discussion* make their writing sound more important. But such expressions are just empty syllables that don't say anything. They'll also annoy many readers. Have you ever received a letter or an email from a business that ends "Should you have any questions, please feel free to email us at csr@yourbiz.com"? This sentence does have one piece of useful information: the email address. But it also tells the reader how to "feel," and the over-formal "should you have" makes it seem that the company is talking down to you.

Some Basic Grammar Rules

You don't know all of those complicated rules of grammar? Guess what? Neither does your boss, your co-workers, or your professor. Most self-appointed "grammar cops" really just have one or two pet peeves that they'll never let slide. Unfortunately, they don't all share the same one or two. In fact, if you can learn to avoid a handful of common errors, you can stay out of the headlights of 90 percent of the grammar police out there.

Complete Sentences

A complete sentence contains a subject and a verb. It expresses a single thought, or a set of directly related thoughts. Watch out for sentence fragments and run-on sentences.

A sentence fragment lacks a subject or a verb (or both), or is unable to stand alone as a sentence for some other reason.

No verb: Many people in the office.
No subject: Looking for a lost dog.
Unable to stand alone: Because Rupert was in a hurry.

Run-on sentences are formed by incorrectly joining two or more complete sentences.

Incorrect: Pick up some milk, don't forget to use the coupon.

This is really two sentences (*Pick up some milk* and *Don't forget to use the coupon*). Because both can stand alone, they can't be joined with just a comma.

Parallel Structure

When a sentence contains a list or makes a comparison, make sure that the items listed or compared are parallel in form.

Incorrect: I love skating, bicycling, and to run.
Correct: I love skating, bicycling, and running.
Also correct: I love to skate, bicycle, and run.

Incorrect: To visualize success is not the same as achieving it.
Correct: Visualizing success is not the same as achieving it.

Bulleted lists also need to use parallel structure. Here's a bad example.

Employees are required to:
- wash hands before returning to work
- turn off the bathroom light
- don't leave the water running

In this example, the first two items complete the sentence that begins *Employees are required to*. The third does not. If you rewrite it as *shut the water off*, it will also complete the sentence begun at the top, making it parallel with the other two items.

Modifiers

Modifiers are words or phrases that describe the subject, the verb, or another part of a sentence. Be sure it's clear which word or words your modifiers describe.

Unclear: By accident, she fell off the ladder onto the ground, which was wobbly.

The phrase *which was wobbly* is a modifier, but what is it modifying? The ground was probably not wobbly. It probably describes the ladder, but it's placed too far away from that noun to function properly.

Modifiers are said to dangle when they have nothing to modify.

Dangling: Waiting at the station, the bus drove by without stopping.

The phrase *waiting at the station* can't refer to the bus, which never even stopped. It probably refers to a person—but that person is missing from the sentence. We can solve the problem by simply dropping a name into the sentence:

Better: While Joe was waiting at the station, the bus drove by without stopping.
Or: Waiting at the station, Joe saw the bus pass by without stopping.

Subject-Verb Agreement

Singular subjects take singular verbs, and plural subjects take plural verbs.

Incorrect: Abe don't like his hair cut too short.

The subject, *Abe*, is singular and requires the singular form of the verb, *does(n't)*:

Correct: Abe doesn't like his hair cut too short.

Two or more subjects connected with *and* require a plural verb.

Correct: Joan and Mary are going to the gallery.

Passive Voice

When a verb is active, the subject of the sentence *performs* an action. In a passive construction, the subject is the *recipient* of the action.

Active: The bird ate the birdseed.
Passive: The birdseed was eaten by the bird.

Notice how many more words it takes to communicate the same idea in the passive voice. The active voice is shorter and more direct. Active sentences come across as stronger and more decisive than passive ones. They're also more interesting, because they're about *doing* something.

Note that using passive voice isn't wrong in the same way that the other grammar mistakes listed here are. You can use passive voice if that's the best way to say something—just don't overuse it.

Punctuation

Most sentences should end in a period. A sentence that asks a direct question should end in a question mark. Sentences that express strong emotion or forceful commands should end in an exclamation point.

The comma is a separator: it breaks a sentence into logical chunks so that it's easier for the reader to parse. It should *not* be used to separate two or more complete sentences.

The semicolon is used to separate very closely related thoughts.

> The candidate whom we hired had extensive professional experience; he had been out of school for fifteen years.

The colon serves to introduce quotations, lists, or explanations.

> **Quotation:** Dr. Doernbecher disagreed with his colleague: "This procedure is unsafe!"
> **List:** Be sure to pack the following items: a sleeping bag, a flashlight, and bug spray.
> **Explanation:** I had a good reason for missing work: my car broke down.

The apostrophe has two main uses: to show possession and to indicate omission. Most nouns and indefinite pronouns (e.g., *someone, anybody*) show possession by adding the apostrophe and *s*:

> Uncle Ming's homemade dumplings were the hit of the party.

For singular nouns ending in *s*, add both the apostrophe and *s* unless the pronunciation would be awkward:

> The witness's statement sounded forced.

For plural nouns ending in *s*, add only the apostrophe:

> The witnesses' statements corroborated his story.

The apostrophe is also used when you omit one or more letters from a word. Think of the apostrophe as a substitute for the missing letters. The most common example of this use is in contractions. Notice how the apostrophe is used in the contractions of *cannot, I am,* and *should have* in the following sentences:

I can't believe my good luck.
I'm hoping to get this done before midnight.
We should've left earlier.

Don't use an apostrophe to form common plurals.

Incorrect: We picked up all the item's at the store.

The *s* at the end of the word is all you need:

Correct: We picked up all the items at the store.

Using an Appropriate Vocabulary

Having a large vocabulary is an advantage, but in your workplace it's more important to know the words your managers and co-workers use. You can occasionally make a small positive impression by using a word here and there that your readers don't hear or read every day, but you can sometimes make a larger negative impression if you use words that your readers have to look up.

Do you know what a *paradigm* is? How about a *nuance*? If you do know the correct meaning of these words, you're in a distinct minority. If you don't know what they mean, don't use them just to make yourself look intelligent. However, if you see that several people in your workplace *are* using words that you don't know, it's your responsibility to find out what they mean—either by looking them up or by asking. Then you can use the same words in your own correspondence to communicate more effectively.

Avoiding Plagiarism

Any time you bring other people's information, ideas, or words into your own work, it's critical that you do so honestly and ethically. When you fail to properly identify outside sources in your writing, you commit plagiarism—an act that can get you expelled, fired, or sued.

In the course of a long research project or paper, many people end up plagiarizing without meaning to or even realizing that they have. During your research, you may find another writer's idea so convincing that it becomes part of your own thinking. When you start writing your paper, it's easy to forget that the idea didn't actually come out of your head. You don't credit the original author, so readers assume the idea is yours. You've plagiarized, even though you didn't mean any harm.

> ### Research Tip
> Whenever you cite facts that you didn't gather yourself, give credit to the author or agency that did gather the facts.

The way to avoid plagiarism is to take good notes during your research. As you write down ideas, facts, and quotes, make a note of where they came from. Document all of your sources in full: author(s), title, name of periodical, publisher, date, page and chapter numbers.

When writing, identify where all outside material came from. Exact citation formats will vary, but most of the time you should simply mention the source's author and year within your text, and include a bibliography or list of sources at the end. Remember to give credit for other people's information, ideas, and words.

Information: Prince and Associates' summer survey reported that patients were on average taking thirty more days to pay their bills.

Ideas: Lawrence Bierman (2007) argues that spending on home appliances such as refrigerators and washing machines is not affected by the performance of the stock market.

Words (direct quote): Summers, Harris, and Rosenberg (2003) found "shocking levels of poverty throughout the northeastern part of the state."

Words (paraphrasing): Even given the severe downward trends to the south, Summers, Harris, and Rosenberg (2003) uncovered surprisingly depressed conditions in the state's northeastern tip.

Notice that in the last example above, the writer is still required to credit the original source even though she has changed the wording.

For additional information about research, see the appendix, Effective Research.

Chapter Summary

- To make your business writing more appealing and more effective, focus on what will benefit your reader.

- The appropriate writing style varies depending on the kind of document that you are creating.

- Writing is a process made up of three stages: planning, drafting, and revising.

- Taking the time to learn a few basic rules of grammar and a few new words will have you writing with confidence and style.

- If you use someone else's information, ideas, or words in your writing, be sure to credit your sources. Otherwise you are in danger of committing plagiarism.

To-Do List

☐ Take a look at a recent school paper, business message, or technical report you've written, and see if it follows this chapter's style guidelines. Write down what you think are the three biggest changes you need to make to your writing style.

☐ At the start of your next writing assignment, spend ten minutes either brainstorming or freewriting. See how many good ideas you can come up with after just a few minutes of uninterrupted thinking.

☐ Pick three words you've heard your teacher or classmates use this week that you never use yourself. Then try to use each of them at least once in the next twenty-four hours in your writing or in conversation.

☐ Print out a copy of a paper, document, or message you've written recently. Go through it and underline any fragments or run-on sentences you find. Try rewriting them as complete sentences.

Important Terms

How well do you know these terms? Define them here or in your journal, or look them up in the glossary to help you remember.

draft   **revision**

format   **"you-attitude"**

plagiarism

Online Resources

Writing resources
web.princeton.edu/sites/writing/Writing_Center/WCWritingResources.htm

Online Writing Lab (OWL) at Purdue University
owl.english.purdue.edu

English Vocabulary Library
speakspeak.com/html/d2_english_resources_business_vocab_library.htm

Exercises

Write your answers in your journal or on a separate piece of paper.

1. Browse the online resources listed above to learn about formats for letters, memos, and emails. Compose a list in your own words of the formatting rules for each.

2. Write a paragraph in your journal discussing the first three things you would change or improve about your most recent school paper, if you had the opportunity to go back and revise it.

3. Practice your business writing by composing an imaginary email to your favorite teacher or boss. Using your best "you-attitude," craft a professional email asking him or her to review a policy that you feel could be improved. Make sure you use positive language as you present your request.

Portions of this chapter's content include material adapted from *Sharp Writing: Build Better Writing Skills* (New York: Kaplan, 2008) and *Sharp Vocab: Build Better Vocabulary Skills* (New York: Kaplan, 2008).

7 | Effective Presentations

KEYS TO SUCCESS

- Learning to define your presentation goal
- Analyzing your audience and targeting your argument
- Preparing your research material, building a strong foundation, and speaking with authority
- Setting up your presentation to best engage your audience
- Learning to use visual aids and nonverbal communication to enhance your message
- Using strategies for interacting with your audience

Preparation

You've been asked to give a presentation to your classmates or colleagues: the first instinct is likely panic. Many people avoid every opportunity to speak in front of a group, because public speaking terrifies them. If fear is your main reason for ineffective public speaking, you are not alone. A 1999 study found that only 24 percent of Americans are very comfortable giving a speech or formal presentation.

The best way to address this anxiety is to be prepared:

- Know what you want to achieve.

- Understand who you are seeking to influence.

- Do research in preparation for your presentation.

- Make a concise outline of your presentation.

- Practice your presentation and refine any rough patches.

- Express your message with words, nonverbal cues, and visual aids.

If you've laid this groundwork before your presentation begins, your anxiety will already be lessened, because you'll know your plan, your audience, and your topic. As a result, you'll speak with authority.

Define the Purpose

The purpose of any presentation, written, oral, or visual, is to communicate. To do it effectively, you must state your facts in a simple, concise, and interesting manner.

Your presentation goal needs to be clearly stated to the audience and expressed in a one-sentence statement. Informative presentations fulfill three goals. The audience wants to know, understand, and use information. Persuasive presentations involve the process of influencing another person's values, beliefs, attitudes, or behaviors.

Here are some examples of presentation goals:

As a result of this presentation,

- Team members will understand new procedures for a project.

- Managers will learn the results of a study on employee satisfaction.

- Consumers will understand ways they may invest in real estate.

- The company will adopt a new user guide for a product.

- Potential investors will accept the proposal for funding of an arts program.

- Your client will accept the proposal for setting up new call center procedures.

The first three are examples of informative goals, and the last three are persuasive in nature.

Define the Audience

Once the presentation goal has been set, the second step is to think about what the audience already knows and wants to know. Put yourself in the audience's place: try to understand your listeners' level of understanding and their knowledge of your topic. Once you know what your listeners want and what they can understand, you can figure out how to "sell" the benefits of your topic to them. Take the following facts about the audience into consideration:

- Values, beliefs, and attitudes

- Familiarity with the topic

- Age, experience, and education level

- Number of people in the audience

Once you have this information, you are better prepared to decide what is important to the audience and what issues you should address. More important, you are able to tailor your remarks in a way that will result in a far more effective presentation.

Build a Successful Presentation

If your presentation lacks focus, the audience will stop listening. They will not do your work for you, and they will not struggle to clarify your message. Those confused by your message are seldom persuaded. Learning to build a successful presentation is the key to winning the audience over.

Writing the Outline

Once you have had time to gather information and material and have settled on your overall approach, it is time to develop an outline of the presentation. The outline will over time be revised and turned into the notes and speaking points you will refer to as you deliver the presentation.

Start by restating your overall presentation goal. Here's an example:

As a result of this presentation, the audience will understand the importance of building a recycling center in the downtown area.

Next, develop a central idea, or key points, to be made in the speech, such as:

Concern for the environment and the growing support for "going green" have increased residents' interest in recycling; however, a recycling center is not currently available in the downtown area.

Main Points

Next, develop main points with supporting examples. These are the building blocks that will advance your presentation goal. There are several ways you can approach this:

- You might organize the main points of your speech into categories. For example, a speech on the feasibility of building a community center could be divided into categories such as need, cost, and benefit to the community.

- A step-by-step structure is appropriate if you are talking about things that need to be done in a particular order. A presentation on first aid would break down the steps in terms of what to do first, second, third, and so forth.

- Make your points by setting up a cause-and-effect relationship. For example, because there is no recycling center downtown (cause), some people won't recycle (effect).

- You can divide your main points into two categories: the problem and solution. For example, the absence of a recycling center leads to too much garbage downtown (problem). Providing a recycling center would allow residents to drop off recyclable items rather than rely on city pick-up (solution).

Write an outline of the main points, and build each point by adding supporting examples. This will help you organize your thoughts logically. Main points presented in the speech need supporting material to be effective. Supporting material may be in the form of examples, statistics, survey results, testimonials, and the like.

Introduction and Conclusion

Introduction. The introduction sets the tone for your presentation. You are preparing the audience for the information that will follow in the body of your presentation. Getting the attention of the audience in your introduction is important to your success. A strong introduction does the following:

- Gives an overview of the main points of the presentation

- Grabs the audience's attention through the use of brief quotations, statistics, rhetorical questions, or a short personal story

- Makes clear why the presentation is important

Stay away from the predictable ("Today, I'm here to talk about . . .," etc.). Instead:

- Ask the audience a question.

- Begin with a provocative question, anecdote, or current event—and how it relates to the content of your presentation.

- Set up a problem—and tell the audience that by the end of the presentation, they'll have the tools to solve it.

Here's an example of an introduction using rhetorical questions:

Are you tired of driving fifteen miles to drop off recyclable items? Do you find yourself constantly picking up paper from your apartment courtyard? If the answer is yes, you'll want to learn more about the proposal presented today. The proposal for a new recycling center may assist in lessening these environmental issues.

Wrap up the introduction to your presentation by giving a very brief overview of the main points you plan to convey. Having shared with your audience what they can expect, you can then dive into your presentation, addressing each point in greater detail.

Conclusions. The purpose of a conclusion in a presentation is to provide closure for the audience. It is also a time for the presenter to stress the main points and purpose of the presentation. A strong conclusion will do the following:

- Recap the presentation goal and main points.
- Encourage the audience to respond to the material presented.
- Restate the central idea of the presentation.
- Provide a sense of closure to the presentation.

In addition to providing a summary of the main points of the presentation, leaving a memorable impression on the audience is critical to an effective conclusion. A conclusion can be made memorable in the following ways:

- Use a quotation.
- Pose a call to action.
- Use a personal example that applies to the presentation's central idea.

A strong conclusion ensures the audience will remember the key elements of the presentation. The conclusion should be relatively brief compared to the main points of the presentation. An audience can grow irritated if the words "in closing" are used and the presentation continues on for an extended period of time.

Using Notes Effectively

By constructing your presentation from the ground up in outline form, you might think the eventual goal is to write a word-for-word speech. But in fact, a brief bare bones version of your final outline will be sufficient for creating notes from which you shall speak.

> ### Avoiding Plagiarism
>
> In speeches, you need to credit the source of any thought, idea, or expression that is not your own. Supporting material, such as examples, statistics, and short stories, is often used to enhance a presentation. It is important to verbally state your source if any of this information is not original. Plagiarism can be avoided by stating the source of the information.

Create note cards from your outline. Draft, redraft, and revise them after practicing the delivery. Prepare your note cards based on the key points in the outline. This process will reinforce the presentation in your mind so when you're speaking, you can simply glance down at a word or phrase and that will trigger the next idea or topic. The idea is to speak with ease and from a place of authority.

Never speak while referring to your notes. Maintain eye contact when you speak. Pause, look at your notes, collect your thoughts, and then speak once you have reestablished eye contact with the audience. Always maintain your audience focus.

Use a separate card for any quotes you intend to read. Memorize short, simple quotes, but read from the actual source or a card you have prepared if the quote is long or accuracy is imperative.

Practice using your notes. You should practice your presentation with the same notes you will use during your presentation. Anticipate that you may not have ideal speaking conditions. Think about how you can adapt.

Remember: you *know* what you're talking about. You have practiced giving this presentation. You will be much more loose and engaging if you speak from only a few index cards listing the main points and supportive points from your outline.

ON THE JOB

SCENARIO: A charitable cause you're involved with will be hurt by a recent decision made by your city council. You have been asked to make a brief presentation at their next meeting to explain your position and press for a change to the policy.

QUICK FIX: Read up on recent meeting notes from the newspaper or city website: those decision makers are your audience, and you need to understand where they're coming from. What do you want to accomplish? Consider your presentation goal and your audience as you craft your winning presentation for the council.

Nonverbal Communication

Actions can speak louder than words. In addition to the vocal and visual parts of a presentation, nonverbal communication needs to be considered.

Effective use of nonverbal communication can add to your credibility as a speaker. Eye contact, gestures, facial expressions, posture, movement, and your personal appearance all serve to communicate your interest and enthusiasm in your topic. The impact of nonverbal communication can greatly enhance your professional presentation.

Eye Contact

Making direct eye contact with the audience is a sign of your trustworthiness. Eye contact also can be a sign of confidence, concern, sincerity, interest, and enthusiasm. Lack of adequate eye contact can signal deceit, lack of interest, or insecurity. Give the impression that you are looking at all members of the audience, without staring at individuals. Making eye contact with a variety of audience members can help give this impression.

Gestures

Gestures can help you make the main points of your presentation. Gestures can also help fill a gap between words, providing clarification in your presentation. Find a natural flow and don't force it.

- Practice gestures prior to the presentation.

- Use gestures that are appropriate to the topic and the audience.

- Do not use antagonistic gestures. Pointing toward the audience or shaking a fist will have a negative effect on the audience; try a less antagonistic gesture.

Facial Expressions

Facial expressions are important in demonstrating the emotional side of your message. These expressions are sometimes out of your control because they occur naturally. Wrinkled eyebrows, for example, may be an unconscious gesture based on deep concern. The audience will observe your facial expressions as a sign of consistency with your spoken message. If you smile while talking about the benefits of building a community center, the audience is likely to believe you find this project a benefit to the community.

Posture and Movement

Good posture is a sign of confidence. Posture, which can be defined as the position of the body when an individual sits or stands, is a form of nonverbal communication that is easily seen by the audience. The correct posture to use in a professional presentation involves standing up straight with feet slightly apart.

- Avoid slouching over or shifting weight back and forth too frequently.

- If a podium is used during the presentation, be careful not to lean on it or rock back and forth while holding on to it.

- Do not tap your feet, fingers, or pen, and if you're using a pointer or a mouse, keep it still except when you're using it to point.

Movement, chosen with a purpose, can help the audience pay closer attention to your presentation. For example, movement can signal transitions or underscore key points.

Appearance

Although we all attempt to keep an open mind about the appearance of others, judgments are sometimes made about the presenter based on the way he or she looks. Although it is difficult for an individual to alter body physique, there are elements of physical appearance that you can control.

Clothing and grooming communicate a personal message about you. Dress the part. Jeans and a t-shirt is appropriate for an informal situation. However, this style is not appropriate when presenting a proposal at professional gatherings. Be mindful of the message sent by your clothing and grooming. Err on the side of being conservative, rather than risk being misinterpreted because of casual dress.

Delivering the Presentation

Oral presentations should use simple sentences, familiar words, repetition, and transitions. Use of clear language and strong organization of the presentation will help your audience focus on the main points of your message.

- Be conversational.

- Pay attention to your audience's reaction, and repeat critical points immediately if you sense the need.

- Look at the audience. Try to cover all parts of the room by dividing it into three or four distinct sections. Continue to make eye contact with audience members in each section throughout the course of your presentation.

- Talking is easier if you don't read a speech word-for-word.

> ### Presentation Tip
> Make sure you stay within the specified time limit. Staying within the time limit helps maintain your credibility and shows respect to your audience. Practice and time your presentation prior to the live session.

Engaging the Audience

Your oral presentation will be more successful if it not only provides your audience with information, but also engages them in the presentation. If you are excited by the presentation, the audience can see and feel this level of enthusiasm.

Effectively engaging the audience involves establishing a connection between you and the audience. Being direct is an effective way to demonstrate interest and concern for the audience and involves doing the following:

- Maintain eye contact with audience members.

- Use a friendly, conversational tone of voice.

- Use animated facial expressions, especially smiling, when appropriate.

- Present in close proximity to the audience members.

Controlling Nervousness

Even the most confident speaker may feel stress when anticipating delivering a presentation. The goal of growing in confidence as a speaker lies in controlling your nervousness, not eliminating it completely. In fact, some level of stress can lead to a better public speaking performance. This "positive stress" may take nervous energy and channel it into energy for delivering an engaging presentation.

> ### Practice Critical Thinking
> Think about which kinds of visual aids will be most effective with various topics. Which topics would be best served by models? When would you prefer to use a flip chart rather than PowerPoint? For which situations would marker boards be more effective than an electronic presentation?

Using Visual Aids

Visual aids commonly used for professional presentations include models, objects, handouts, flip charts, posters, marker boards, photographs, slides, transparencies, and electronic/multimedia presentations. PowerPoint, a program commonly used to create computer-generated visual aids, carries with it both benefits and challenges.

Use of presentation aids helps the audience understand the material. Most listeners learn faster when presentation aids are used, which allows you to present information in less time.

Preparing, Structuring, and Organizing Your Presentation

When preparing, structuring, and organizing your presentation, search actively for spots where visual aids can be used for achieving presentation objectives. Many people gain and retain information more easily when it's presented visually.

Preparing and structuring a presentation involves gathering information on the topic. Additional research may need to be gathered, such as statistics, expert opinion, interviews, Internet resources, databases, and other sources.

Use Visual Aids Effectively

Use visuals to enhance the information in the presentation. If a visual does not add to the written text, do not include it. Also, ensure that information presented in the visual is accurate and clear.

- Use transitions between slides or main ideas.
- Explicit verbal transitions need to be used in the presentation.
- Example transitions include *next*, *the third point*, *finally*, and *in summary*.
- Do not just jump from one topic to the next without clearly noting connections.

A Note on PowerPoint

Electronic or multimedia presentations are the most common form of presentation aid used in the workplace. Microsoft's PowerPoint is a common electronic presentation aid. When using computer-generated visual aids, remember the following:

- Less is more. Keep text on your slides short. If the audience is reading, they're not listening to you. If everything the audience needs to know is written on the slides, why would the audience need you?
- Create clear visuals. Be sure that all text, including labels on charts and graphs, can be seen.
- Don't read from the slide. It's a sure way to put your audience to sleep.
- Use standard slide transitions. PowerPoint includes many bells and whistles in slide transitions. Text and graphics can spin, creep in slowly, or fly across the page complete with sound effects. It's best to avoid these effects altogether.
- Likewise, be very selective when adding graphics to a PowerPoint presentation.
- Clipart in particular is generic in nature. The message it sends is generic as well.
- Don't give a presentation in a dark room where the audience can barely see you. You need to be in at least *some* light so that eye contact, your facial expressions, and your gestures are visible to your audience.
- Prepare for technology failure. Bring a hard copy of the outline and slides to the presentation. In the event that technology is not in working order, the presentation can continue. Practice using both a hard copy of the slides and the computer-generated presentation prior to the event.

Crystal Kay Faxon

Omaha, Nebraska

Attended: Kaplan University—Lincoln

Area of study: Business Administration

Employer: Director of Financial Aid, Kaplan University—Omaha, Nebraska

If you take one thing away from this course, it should be this: Professionalism will come natural when you have the confidence to become successful or be a member of a successful team. That confidence comes from education.

After high school, I knew exactly what I wanted to do in life. I wanted to work in the business field and I wanted to be successful. The only problem that I had was not being confident in myself or my abilities. The teachers and advisors at Kaplan University made me feel like I was their only priority. They gave me positive feedback on papers and presentations, and by the time I graduated I had a huge amount of confidence in myself and my ability to be successful.

Responding to Questions

Question-and-answer sessions are common in many presentations. This is an important time when the audience can ask for clarification or additional information on points made during your presentation. Confirm with the person planning the program that there will be time for such a session. Because time is often limited in professional presentations, set aside a block of time at the end of your presentation to address questions.

Think in advance of potential questions that the audience may ask. Write down potential questions and answers on note cards and rehearse the responses. If possible, ask someone familiar with the topic to listen to the presentation, write down questions, and pose questions so you can practice responding.

View the question-and-answer session as a positive experience. This is a good opportunity to clarify information from the presentation and receive valuable feedback.

- Give those interacting with you compliments like "Thanks for that question" or "Excellent question!"

- Look directly at the person asking the question. Demonstrate active listening by maintaining eye contact with the person asking the question.

- Repeat the question asked to make sure that everyone in the audience has heard the question.

- Respond loudly and clearly to the question while looking at all of the audience members, not only the person who asked the question.

- Be honest in your response. If you do not know the answer, it is important to say so; you should not attempt to make up a response.

- Avoid negative responses like "We've already covered that." This discourages further questions and makes the audience think that you don't really want questions.

- At the start of the question-and-answer period, allow the audience members a brief amount of time (ten seconds is a good standard) to think of questions to ask. If there are no questions, bring closure to the presentation by stating, "If there are no questions, this concludes the presentation."

Chapter Summary

- Successful presenters speak with authority because their preparation allows them to understand both their audience and their presentation goal.

- A presentation outline is a vital tool to develop your approach, refine your presentation, and structure your delivery.

- An effective speaker utilizes verbal and nonverbal communication along with visual aids to enhance the delivery of the message.

- An effective oral presentation is one that not only provides the audience with information, but one that also engages the listeners in the presentation.

To-Do List

☐ Watch a speech on television, the Internet, or from the video archives of your local library. List five ways the speaker uses nonverbal communication to communicate his or her message. Which of these nonverbal methods was most effective? Which was least effective? Why?

☐ Read an article from your newspaper's local news or political news section. Consider how you would deliver a brief informative speech on the subject, versus how you would approach the presentation if it was to be persuasive in nature. Write a presentation goal for each version of the speech.

☐ Pretend you will soon be giving a five-minute informative presentation to your classmates. Sit for fifteen minutes and write out a list of possible presentation topics. Remember, you want to speak with authority. Consider topics you already know something about. Consider what visual aids might improve your presentation.

Important Terms

How well do you know these terms? Define them here or in your journal, or look them up in the glossary to help you remember.

audience	persuasive presentation
authority	presentation goal
informative presentation	visual aids

Online Resources

PowerPoint
http://office.microsoft.com/powerpoint

The History Channel (includes an index of more than 100 speeches and verbal messages)
www.historychannel.com/speeches/index.html

Presentation = Speech + Slides
http://inthelibrarywiththeleadpipe.org/2008/presentation-speech-slides

Exercises

Write your answers in your journal or on a separate piece of paper.

1. Choose a topic for an upcoming five-minute classroom presentation. Develop your presentation goal, central idea, and the main points you wish to communicate. Review in small groups with classmates and seek input on how to improve your approach.

2. Visit a library or search online to learn more about your topic. While you research, decide upon some form of visual aid that you can incorporate into your presentation to help convey your message.

3. Prepare an outline for your classroom presentation and practice your delivery. If you have a video camera available, videotape your practice and review. Rehearsing your presentation with a partner or before a mirror can also help you improve your delivery.

Portions of this chapter's content include material adapted from David J. Dempsey, *Legally Speaking*, revised and updated edition (New York: Kaplan, 2009) and Diane Martinez, Tanya Peterson, Carrie Wells, Carrie Hannigan, and Carolyn Stevenson, *Technical Writing* (New York: Kaplan, 2008).

8

Conflict and Negotiations in the Workplace

KEYS TO SUCCESS

- Identifying the needs and characteristics of external and internal customers
- Adopting best practices for providing reliable, high-quality service to prevent conflicts
- Practicing listening techniques for identifying and meeting co-worker and customer needs
- Practicing techniques for resolving conflicts by controlling the situation
- Understanding the unique challenges involved in negotiating conflicts

Depending on your chosen profession, you may be highly aware of the need to develop good customer service skills, or such skills may not be on your radar at all. If you fall into the latter camp, here's some news for you: *everybody* is in the customer service business. The sooner you realize this, the better you'll do in your job.

Every job demands that you deliver services and products to other people, either outside your organization or within it. And every time you deliver these things, there's a potential for conflict to arise. There are two parts to customer service: (1) doing what you can to prevent conflict, and (2) negotiating to resolve conflicts that do arise in spite of your best efforts.

The face that you present to others is the face of your company, your department, or at the very least your professional self. Good customer service skills will make working with others easier, and it will help people feel positive about the work you do.

Identifying the Customer

Let's take a look at several different types of customers you may be working with; some you may not even be aware of.

External Customers

Customers You Sell To

The traditional understanding is that a customer is somebody from outside your organization who comes to you for products or services. This can be a shopper in a drug store where you work, a patient in a hospital where you volunteer, a distributor buying your products wholesale, or a client to whom you provide support services.

If you deal with these sorts of second parties, then you're on the front line of your employer's customer service army, directly representing the company to the outside world. The stakes in these situations couldn't be higher, because a customer's experience with you could determine whether or not he or she will come back and do business with your company again.

In direct customer service situations like these, you're acting as the face of your employer, so you want to present the best impression possible:

- Be courteous, friendly, and attentive. Listen to everything the customer says, even if you think it's irrelevant. Answer the customer's questions—whether smart or (seemingly) stupid—using the same professional manner.

- Make customers feel good about the exchange and about doing business with your company. Explain the benefits of what you're offering or proposing to do for them—and remember the difference between features and benefits, as explained in Chapter 15.

- Emphasize the customer's side. Don't expect customers to care about your operations, costs, or methods. Make it all about them: their needs, their convenience, their goals, their questions.

Customers You Buy From

There are other people from outside your company that you may have dealings with. These are people who are delivering services to you or your company. They may include the mail carrier who delivers to you or the HVAC servicers who maintain your furnace and air conditioners. You might think that because these people aren't buying anything from you, you don't have to treat them the same way you do the paying customers. However, your company has an interest in keeping these people happy as well. They'll do better work if they're treated well—if they can perform their duties without any conflict from you or your co-workers. And replacing suppliers is expensive for your company, which is why companies don't usually switch vendors without very good reason.

Internal Customers

No matter what your relationship with external customers, you will always have to deal with internal customers: your boss, your co-workers, and, if you work for a large company, even workers from other divisions whom you seldom, if ever, see. In a sense, your job—no matter what your job description says in your employer's handbook—is to practice customer service skills with all these people: prevent conflict if possible and resolve it if prevention is impossible.

Many jobs deal exclusively with internal customers: the people you work with. If you provide a support service—electrical, facilities, shipping, payroll, telecom, or some other variety—your job is basically to help other people in the company conduct their business. This is an important thing to remember. Because you deal with the infrastructure, you may have a lot of power. You can shut the lights off, print the checks, or change the passwords. It's easy to fall into the habit of thinking that the responsibility is on the other employees to use your equipment and services in the way that works best for you.

But that's not how it works. You don't make money for the company; you're a cost center. You're there to make the jobs of other workers easier. That doesn't mean you shouldn't enforce rules or make suggestions for improving efficiency, but you must always keep the needs of the business in the forefront of your mind. In every interaction, ask yourself how you can help the customer (that is, your co-worker) carry out the company's mission and increase profits. If you can't fulfill a co-worker's specific request, look for other ways to meet the business need. For instance, if you can't get six photocopiers to the event services department in time for a big printing rush, you might be able to work with IT in networking the print jobs to laser printers in nearby departments.

> **Practice Critical Thinking**
>
> How do you help internal customers—your co-workers— carry out the company's mission and make money?

Again, you don't have to be in a support position to do customer service. Anytime somebody inside your organization asks you to perform a task or help out with something, you're providing a service—making that person's job easier, and in so doing helping the company carry out its mission. Focus on your common goals, as well as the larger goals of the company. Put as much effort into meeting your co-workers' needs as you would for an "official" customer.

Preventing Conflict

Adopting a few customer service "best practices" will help you to deliver the kind of service your company can be proud of.

Reliability

There's no substitute for knowing your stuff. The basic requirement to keep people satisfied with your service is that you do the job right. But reliability involves more than job skills and competence. It requires careful time management and good communication skills.

When you take on a task for any customer—someone outside your company or one of your co-workers—you must know that person's expectations. Make sure both of you understand exactly what you're going to do. Let the customer know:

- How long the task will take

- Any possible complications you foresee

- How much it will cost (if it involves a financial transaction)

Just as with any other part of your job, you must be accountable. Keep the customer in the loop. If a complication does arise, with an external or an internal customer, do the following:

- Let them know what's going on

- Provide them with a revised timetable and stick to it

ON THE JOB

SCENARIO: In your job as an emergency room nurse, you take a basic history for a patient with painful stomach cramps. At the time he's admitted, traffic in the ER is light, so you tell him that a doctor should be in to see him within fifteen minutes. Right after you leave the patient, a large number of victims from a bus crash arrive. As a result, everyone in the ER, yourself included, will be tied up for the next hour. When you finally get back to your stomach patient, he's upset and still in pain.

QUICK FIX: As soon as you reach the patient's bed, you express your regret at having taken so long, and you explain the situation. You ask if the pain has gotten worse or if the patient is experiencing any new symptoms that make his case more urgent. Based on the patient's response, you provide a realistic estimate of when he's likely to be seen, and make a point of checking back regularly to see how he's doing.

If something happens to change the basic parameters—the cost, amount of time, or end result—you should bring the customer into the decision-making process. Explain the situation, and let the customer make the call on whether you should go forward or not. Offer alternative plans, if possible. People don't like to feel like they're being railroaded into something they don't fully understand; they like to be in control. If you respect your customers and keep them informed and in charge, you can usually trust them to make the right decisions.

Listening and Delivering

High-quality customer service requires sound listening skills. Typically, a co-worker or a customer will approach you with a question, a request, or perhaps a completed work order that's based on his or her limited understanding of things. If someone walks into an auto shop and says that his alternator needs to be replaced, a careless mechanic will record the car's make and model, quote the customer a price, and do the work that the customer wants. A *good* mechanic will ask exactly what problem the customer is experiencing, and then examine the car to find the cause. This way, the mechanic avoids doing unnecessary work and the customer won't be billed for something that doesn't fix his problem. The mechanic is also more likely to get this customer's business in the future.

Using good listening habits to know what your customer wants is important, even when dealing with internal customers. You probably know that you need to figure out as quickly as you can what your boss likes and doesn't like, and how to get along with the co-workers you talk with every day. If you work for a large company, though, you may occasionally have to deal with requests from other employees of the company whom you barely know. In such cases, don't forget that you need to ask questions and listen to their answers. For example, the billing department that you usually work with may not need you to provide a detailed history of each client's payment history. But a billing department in another branch of your company may need that information because they use a different system. If you don't find out up front what information the unfamiliar department needs, they may think your branch is incompetent when you deliver what, to them, is incomplete information.

Take the time to talk to your customers and figure out what their needs are. Don't just give the quickest, most obvious answer to the question; determine the best solution to the problem. Don't be satisfied until the customer's needs have been met.

Handling Difficult External Customers

Customer service can be incredibly rewarding. It's basically the art of making people happy, which also makes you feel good. A handshake from a grateful customer makes you feel that you've made a difference and are doing something valuable.

Some people, however, are not so easy to please. They may use customer service providers as their personal punching bags, taking out their anger and frustration on someone whose job, as they see it, is to sit there and take it. People whose jobs consist entirely of customer service have one of the most stressful jobs in the workplace. You may get twenty pleasant customers in a given day, but it's always that one obnoxious character that you can't get out of your mind as you're driving home.

Difficult customers are an unfortunate fact of life, but they're customers all the same. You have to learn how to deal with the bad apples.

Resolving Complaints

First, last, and above all, don't take it personally. If a customer expresses dissatisfaction with your performance, it can be difficult to listen to. You take pride in your work, and this person probably doesn't understand how hard it is and what factors you must weigh in making your decisions. It doesn't help things when he sticks his finger in your face, questions your competence, or talks to you like you're ten years old.

Just remember: He's not unhappy with *you*. He doesn't know you, he never will, and you're probably glad about that. He's simply displeased about his own situation. Resolve the situation, and his anger will likely disappear.

To resolve complaints effectively:

- **Listen.** Treat the complaint the same as you would any request, and try to find out what the customer *needs*—as opposed to what he or she is upset about. Once you direct the conversation toward identifying what you can do to solve the problem, you have begun repairing your relationship with the customer.

- **Be patient.** Let the customer get angry if he or she needs to. If things haven't worked out the way the customer would like, then he or she is going to react with frustration, nursing a big knot of tension. Letting the customer vent for a while may release some of that tension and get everyone thinking reasonably again.

- **Don't take the bait.** The customer may attack your integrity, use foul language, or make ridiculous claims. Just let it roll off your back. Keep your own tone moderate and respond in a reasonable fashion so that you continue to project professionalism. The customer is using volume and aggression to try to take control of the situation. If you allow yourself to get emotional, the customer wins. If the customer's hysterics don't make you blink, you stay in control.

Workplace Tip

After dealing with an abusive customer or stressful situation, take a five-minute break to clear your head so that you won't start out on the wrong foot with the next person who comes to you.

Negotiating Conflicts

You may have to deal with a customer who's unhappy not with your work, but is angry instead with a colleague of yours, or with your company's services or policies. In this case, you're not just resolving a complaint; you're mediating a conflict. On one side is your employer—the answers they've given, the work they've performed—and on the other is the customer, who is asking you to give a different answer or to make good on poor service.

This can get you into dicey territory, because by resolving the customer's complaint you run the risk of making your company or co-worker look bad. You have to perform a balancing act: you're an advocate for the customer, but also a representative of your company.

The key is, as always, to focus on meeting the customer's needs. If a policy is the point of contention, you'll probably have to stand behind your employer—unless the customer has very special circumstances that argue for an exception. Try to find a way to help the customer without violating the policy. If there truly is no way for your company to meet the customer's needs, then you owe it to the customer to explain that fact clearly and considerately. Show that you understand the situation, and end the conversation on a positive note by offering your service any time in the future, when it's more appropriate.

One thing you should be very careful about is apologizing. Be aware that in dealing with external customers, apologizing, admitting fault, or disparaging your company's policies can have major consequences for your employer. Even explaining the reasons behind a policy or decision can give a troublesome customer fuel for further complaints or lawsuits, particularly if you don't completely understand those reasons or haven't been cleared to disclose them. Remember that although you represent your company, you aren't necessarily authorized to speak on its behalf.

Dealing with Difficult Co-workers

Chances are you've lived with, worked with, and been in groups with people who behave in ways that annoy and frustrate you. You've developed ways to deal with such behavior in your siblings, friends, and peers. You may have to find other ways of doing so in a formal work setting, however.

You might find yourself spending part of your day with a co-worker who irritates you, perhaps to the point where your work suffers along with your patience. You may encounter co-workers who won't stop talking about their personal lives, tell off-color stories, shower infrequently, shirk their responsibility to keep the break room clean, park in your personal space, or are just plain rude. How do you cope?

The natural response to irritation and frustration is a display of emotion, which may provide a few seconds of relief but which will do nothing to prevent or resolve conflicts. Instead, observe the following rules:

- Do not take it personally. Whatever your co-worker is doing, he or she is not doing it to annoy you. Responding with anger will likely just make the problem worse.

Negotiating Tip

When negotiating any conflict, it is not as important to "win" as it is to lay the groundwork for preventing future conflicts.

- Do not complain to other co-workers or your boss. You don't want to be seen as a "whiner" or as a "high-maintenance employee."

- Do not try to change the co-worker by leaving an anonymous note. That just generates ill will.

- Do not leave hints for behavior change (such as deodorant on the desk of an infrequent bather).

- Do not sink to the co-worker's level by imitating the problem behavior or retaliating in any way.

If you can't get mad, gripe, or get even, what can you do? Be professional. When you get past the initial impulse to respond emotionally, try your best to act in a calm and rational manner. The first step is the hardest. Here are some other helpful ideas:

Workplace Tip

Whenever you have a conflict with a co-worker, remember to apply your customer service skills. Actively listen to your co-worker's side, to see *why* he or she is taking the position. Maybe you'll be able to change the situation so that both of you win something rather than create a problem where one of you must lose.

- Look at yourself. Are you the only one who is bothered by this person? Do a lot of people annoy you? It may be that you're the one who needs to adjust to the work environment.

- Talk privately to a friend or trusted co-worker. This shouldn't be a gripe session. Present the situation to another person so you can get someone else's perspective.

- Appeal privately to the annoying co-worker. Stay calm. Be pleasant. Be specific about what bothers you, and don't offer a general indictment of the person's personality. Maybe just being friendly will help. A follow-up conversation might also be needed.

- Make a more public appeal with others around. Use a light touch that pokes fun at the situation, not the offender.

If you are unable to make any progress, then:

- Talk to the boss. State the problem in terms of its negative effect on your work rather than presenting it as an interpersonal conflict ("I'm having trouble doing my job because . . .").

- Enlist the aid of other affected co-workers in an effort to appeal to the offending colleague.

- If the situation gets worse and can't be resolved, then

  • Avoid the person.

  • Request a transfer.

  • Look for a different job.

Things should not be allowed to go that far. Civility doesn't just make the world nicer to live in; it is a necessity. Fortunately, consideration and courtesy are often contagious.

Ron Briney, Jr.

Crafton, Pennsylvania

Attended: Kaplan Career Institute—ICM Campus, Pittsburgh, Pennsylvania

Area of study: Information Technology

Employer: Advanced Solutions Representative, Comcast

If you take one thing away from this course, it should be this: I learned that through hard work and sacrifice you can achieve your goals.

Coming to Kaplan saved my life. Everyone at Kaplan treated me very well. They cared, challenged, and dared me to succeed. Every day I had help in many different ways. In my eyes, they didn't come to work for a paycheck; they came to make a difference, and did.

Chapter Summary

- It's your job to practice customer service with all your internal and external customers: do what you can to prevent conflict and do your best to negotiate it when you can't prevent it.

- When supporting internal customers—your co-workers—remember that your job is to help them carry out the company's mission and to make money for the company.

- Reliable customer service requires that you manage the customer's expectations and be accountable.

- Your responsibility is not simply to answer a question or fill a request, but to identify and meet the customer's needs.

- Resolving customer complaints requires that you remain patient, keep a moderate tone, and do everything possible to meet the customer's needs.

- When negotiating a conflict between a customer and your company, be an advocate for the customer but a loyal representative of the company.

- When dealing with difficult co-workers, be professional. Act calmly and rationally, and avoid an emotional response.

To-Do List

- ☐ Write down three strategies you can use on the spot to avoid becoming angry during a conflict.

- ☐ Practice your listening skills. When someone asks you to do something—at work, in school, or at home—listen carefully to identify the need behind the request. What is the person really asking for?

☐ To help you to see things from the customer's point of view, write down three times in the last month when you received poor customer service. What went wrong? How did you feel?

☐ List three occasions in the last month when you've received excellent customer service. What made the service so good? How did you feel?

Important Terms

How well do you know these terms? Define them here or in your journal, or look them up in the glossary to help you remember them.

conflict resolution

customer service

difficult customer

external customer

internal customer

policy

reliability

Online Resources

The Negotiation Skills Company
www.negotiationskills.com

CustomerServiceZone.com: Dealing with Difficult Customers, Angry Customers, and Just Plain Rude Customers
customerservicezone.com/faq/indexangrycustomers.htm

YoungandSuccessful.com: 5 Rules to Improve Customer Service
youngandsuccessful.com/5-rules-to-improve-customer-service-and-personal-life/comment-page-1

Exercises

Write your answers in your journal or on a separate piece of paper.

1. Choose an organization that you are familiar with such as a clinic, bookstore, grocery store, or package delivery service, and try to identify their internal and external customers. Identify as many of their customers' needs as you can.

2. In your journal write a paragraph or two describing a conflict that you have faced or witnessed. Review the tips for preventing conflict. Is there anything that you could have done differently? Write a paragraph or two describing additional or alternative tactics that could have been employed to resolve the situation more smoothly.

3. Recall a situation in which a friend, neighbor, or fellow group member continued to behave in annoying ways. How did you handle the problem? How might you have coped differently using the advice from this chapter?

9

Resumes and Applications

KEYS TO SUCCESS

- Developing a resume that highlights your skills and education
- Identifying transferable skills
- Writing a cover letter that expands on your resume
- Customizing your resume and cover letter to specific job descriptions
- Learning the basics about filling out a job application

Standing Out in a Competitive Job Market

If you're like most job seekers, you want to know what catches an employer's attention. Is it talent? Work history? Education? Relevant experience? And what are the best ways to target desirable positions?

Your resume—a brief written account of your qualifications, experience, and education, generally sent with a cover letter and a job application—is your calling card. A prospective employer expects to review a candidate's resume, no matter who you are or who you know. It's your ticket—actually, a front-row seat—to an interview.

As you begin the resume writing process, think about your career goals. Read up on your industry so you acquire the ability to speak the lingo and be comfortable in your skin. Job seeking can be stressful under the best of circumstances. Some people just muddle through—trying to get it over with as soon as possible. Many applicants copy a resume that suits their needs, plug in the pertinent information, dash it off to a prospective employer, and hope for the best. They don't take the time to discover their skills and accomplishments and how best to match them with what an employer wants.

What Makes a Good Resume?

Resumes need to be not only individually tailored for a particular job but skill-specific and results-oriented as well. It must be immediately obvious to a prospective employer that the job seeker is a good fit for the company and its culture.

Gather Relevant Content about Yourself

Before you begin writing your resume, compile key information—contact information, job objective, employment history, educational background—so that it can be positioned as needed. Prepare a work file at your desk or on your computer where you can keep pertinent information you'll refer to time and again as you craft job-specific versions of your resume and fill out applications.

This information is the raw material of your resume, and you need to spend a good portion of your time developing it and, later, revising it. Not only must it be 100 percent accurate and error-free, but it must also be vibrant and focused. If the key information is faulty, even the best design will fail.

Highlight Your Transferable Skills

Even if you're changing fields, your work history has a lot more to offer than you might think. The key is to identify your transferable skills, that is, the skills that you learned in one situation that can be applied in another. To get an accurate idea of what you really have to offer an employer, don't think about your previous job titles—instead think about what you *did* on the job.

For example, suppose you spent two years working as a checker at a grocery store. Don't just describe who you were—a checkout clerk—but highlight the skills you developed in your position: You gave good (and fast) customer service to a widely diverse clientele. You managed a wide variety of merchandise issues, you worked quickly and well under constant pressure (during shopping rushes and holidays, for example), and you assisted customers with payment issues. *You* were the face customers put on your employer's establishment. Think of these attributes—do they sound like the job description of a checkout clerk to you? How about the job description of an administrative assistant at a legal firm? Or a medical assistant at a busy clinic? By taking a closer look at the skills you mastered in your previous jobs, you'll get a whole new outlook on what you have to offer prospective employers. When you put it on your resume, you'll have potential employers seeing things exactly the same way.

Selecting Your Resume Format

Creating an easy-to-read resume starts with the basics and moves toward the finer points. To begin, you must decide what format works best for your skills and experience. Two primary forms are explained below.

Chronological Resume

Most resumes follow a reverse chronological format: a history of your work experience, beginning with your most recent position. Many recruiters prefer this format simply because it's easy to read. A chronological depiction of your work history allows hiring professionals to see how long you worked for each company. It allows them to quickly track your growth as an employee, and it provides a straightforward depiction of your increasing responsibilities.

> **Practice Critical Thinking**
>
> Consider your skills, your education, and your work history. Which resume format works best for highlighting your particular strengths?

Functional Resume

A functional resume emphasizes your qualifications by presenting a summary of your skills independent from your work history. It works particularly well if you have limited work experience, you have large gaps in your employment history, or you are changing careers.

For example, if you are applying for a medical assistant position and want to emphasize your educational qualifications and the skills you acquired working as a volunteer, rather than your last short-term job as a cashier, the functional layout may be a good choice. The format puts the focus on your education and allows you to mention the skills that you developed, while your work history is less prominently displayed.

Functional resumes have their downside as well, however. Practiced human resources professionals can easily detect any attempt to disguise weak points in your experience. Even if a recent work gap was legitimate, a functional resume can send the wrong signal to some employers, who may wonder if you are hiding something. The good news is that an unconventional employment history can still be transformed into a virtue if the information is presented in a strong, honest, and focused fashion.

> **Optimal Resume**
>
> Optimal Resume is an online resume-building tool you can use to easily and quickly create an impressive, professional resume, which you can share online or download and print. You can build your resume from scratch, section by section, or you can use a sample resume as a starting point and update it with your own information. The site provides examples of a variety of resumes and gives industry-specific tips on developing your resume. Visit https://kheu.optimalresume.com to get started.

Other Formats

Not every work history falls neatly into either a chronological or a functional format. On the contrary, quite a few format variations—the linear, creative, accomplishment, international, keyword, targeted, and curriculum vitae, as well as a combination of these formats—may be suited to your needs. As you become more comfortable putting together your resume, you may want to experiment with different formats.

STEVEN WEEKS

123 Rosewood Avenue
Penbrook, PA 34511

555-555-5555
steven@optimalresume.com

OBJECTIVE

Seeking a position as a medical assistant in a fast-paced environment where helping people with their healthcare needs is a top priority. Adept in both clinical and administrative settings.

EDUCATION

Kaplan Career Institute, Harrisburg, PA
Registered Medical Assistant, 2010

American Red Cross
Certified Nursing Assistant, 2007

RELATED EXPERIENCE

Dewey, Fixem & Howe, Internal Medicine Harrisburg, PA   1/2007 – Present

Certified Nursing Assistant
- Assist patients with bathing, dressing, hygiene, and grooming in accordance with established care plan.
- Obtain specimens, weights, and vital signs of patients.
- Assist doctors and nurses with examinations and procedures.
- Provide pre-operative and post-operative patient care and monitoring.
- Sterilize and maintain bio-medical equipment.
- Support doctors, nurses, and other staff by filing, charting, and documenting.
- Perform billing and coding tasks, create referrals, and schedule appointments.
- Manage supply inventory.
- Take incoming calls and messages while running front desk.

Home Care Providers of Colonial Park Colonial Park, PA   2/2005 – 1/2007

Receptionist
- Answered phones and greeted customers; directed calls to the appropriate designations.
- Demonstrated superb communication skills, both verbal and written.
- Sorted and forwarded mail and performed various errands for the doctors and nurses.
- Assisted with infants and toddlers in the lobby.

VOLUNTEER ACTIVITIES

Volunteer, Habitat for Humanity
Volunteer, Race for the Cure
Fund Raiser, United Way

Figure 9.1 Chronological resume

Lisa Hart

123 Rosewood Avenue
Detroit, Michigan 48201
555-555-5555
lisa@optimalresume.com

CAREER OBJECTIVE

Professional position in accounting or finance

PROFESSIONAL SKILLS PROFILE

One year of related work experience, plus an internship, in combination with strong academic training and credentials in:

- Accounts Payable & Accounts Receivable
- General Ledger & Cash Reconciliation
- Credit & Collections Operations
- Corporate Banking & Asset Leasing

- Financial Analysis & Reporting
- Economic & Demographic Analysis
- Budget & Cost Analysis
- Project & Team Leadership

EDUCATION

Associate's degree – Business Administration, 2010
Kaplan University, Detroit, Michigan

Honors & Activities:
- President, Student Accounting Club
- Member of the Society for Financial Professionals

EMPLOYMENT EXPERIENCE

Bookkeeping Assistant   September 2008 to present
TCI TECH SOLUTIONS, INC.
Flint, Michigan

Part-time permanent staff position with one of the region's fastest-growing telecommunications companies. One of the first three employees hired into the Accounting and Finance Department, which currently employs more than 25. Instrumental in creating accounting systems and procedures to support the company's accelerated growth and nationwide expansion. Earned four promotions in three years.

- Assisted the CFO with designing and automating the company's accounting, financial reporting, cash management, banking, and leasing systems.
- Wrote and produced a 200-page accounting procedures manual.
- Coordinated software upgrades and enhancements with internal IT staff.

Accounting Intern   Summer 2008
GRAYSTONE FINANCIAL SERVICES, INC.
Dearborn, Michigan

Full-time summer position with a financial and accounting services firm. Worked in cooperation with professional staff to prepare journal entries, maintain general ledgers, reconcile bank statements, and prepare financial reports for clients in the transportation, telecommunications, and hospitality industries.

Waitress/Hostess   Summers 2006 and 2007
THE TOWNE MARKETPLACE
Flint, Michigan

Fast-paced customer service position in one of the area's finest restaurants and resorts. Gained excellent experience in public relations, special events planning, and cash handling/reconciliation.

Figure 9.2 Functional resume

Putting It Together

Every resume should provide the following data:

- Contact information
- Job objective
- Professional experience
- Educational background

Avoid listing the following:

- Personal data (height, weight, age, marital status)
- Hobbies
- References
- Salary requirement or salary history

Your resume must accentuate the positive. Save sensitive issues (such as a criminal record) for later.

Contact Information

In the digital age, contact information takes up more and more space on a resume. How much data should you provide? Begin with your name, address, home telephone or cell phone number, and email address. Decide if it's necessary to provide a daytime contact number; if you don't want to include your current work number, a cell number is the best alternative.

> Jason Brown
> 1425 Birch Street
> Anytown, IL 10000
> (555) 674-2000 (home)
> (555) 674-1000 (cell)
> jasonbrown@all.com

Job Objective

The job objective is a brief statement that appears after your contact information. It should list the type of position you're applying for and it may include a brief statement describing your skills. You will tweak this section of the resume again and again, depending on the position you're applying for.

> Objective: To secure a position in the field of law that utilizes my paralegal training

Professional Experience

This section is the heart of your resume. How you list your previous employment experience will depend on whether you use the chronological or functional format.

When preparing a chronological resume, your most recent experience should be listed first, followed by earlier professional experience, presented in descending order by date. List your official title, the full name of the company, the city and state where the company is located, and the time frame that you worked there. In the chronological format, put the emphasis on the professional experience listed in the first entry, as most employers are primarily interested in your current or most recent employment. If it's not obvious what industry you worked for and you are fairly certain the prospective employer won't be familiar with the company, then describe it briefly, either right after the company name or in the description of your accomplishments or duties. The first entry usually gets the most space on a resume.

A functional resume, on the other hand, emphasizes your skills rather than where you worked and for how long (although it is recommended that you give dates and where you worked, just in a less prominent position). The skills that you want to emphasize are typically presented in a section titled "Skills Profile" or "Professional Skills." Your work history follows in a separate section. Sometimes you describe a particular position; sometimes you describe just your skills. The first position in the work history section in the functional format is often reserved for the work experience that most closely relates to the new position you're seeking. Your work history section in the functional format will be more skills-oriented and less specific than it would be in the chronological format.

Educational Background

List your degrees and professional certifications in this section. How much space you devote to your educational background depends on what you want to emphasize in your resume. If you have very little work experience, you may want to expand on your college coursework or certifications here. Here are a few additional pointers:

- A common option for recent graduates is to rearrange the order of the key information and highlight the educational section by moving it to the top of the page, following your contact information.

- Whether you place dates next to your completed degrees is a personal decision. Some prefer not to include these dates because they believe it pinpoints their age.

- If you are fluent in another language or have relevant professional affiliations, you may also include these items in this section.

- If you are in the process of completing a degree or a certification program, list your anticipated graduation date.

- Some career experts recommend that high school information or unfinished college degrees not be listed, although this issue is not set in stone. You need to decide whether mentioning an incomplete degree will further your cause.

Content Is Crucial

Your contact information, job objective, work experience, and educational background form the backbone of your resume. Although there's room for variation in the design of a resume, this information must be correct, readable, and dynamic. The more accessible and straightforward this information, the better the chances your resume will hit its intended target.

Content is still king in a resume, so it's a good idea to determine how best to present your work experience. Employers want to see results, and they are particularly interested in how you contributed to boosting your former employer's bottom line. Make sure your content reveals this.

Style and Vocabulary

Resume writing is primarily about verbs, the actions you performed while working. Examine the verbs shown in the following box to see how they apply to what you did in your former positions and what you want to do in your new job. Your particular profession probably has a few verbs of its own, so make sure you jot them down during your research. It's essential for prospective employers to think of you as a doer—and an insider who uses the specific vocabulary associated with your field.

Action Words: What you can DO for the employer

achieved, acquired, authored, developed, devised, doubled, earned, introduced, invented, led, limited, managed, minimized, motivated, operated, purchased, recovered, recruited, served, streamlined, supervised, trained, wrote

Try to remain consistent in your use of tense. In your professional experience section, use present tense verbs for your current position and past tense verbs for your past experience.

Personal pronouns (*I*) and adjectives and articles (*a* or *the*) should be avoided when writing a resume. Instead of saying "I did this," your sentences should have an implied subject. For example, human resource professionals know you managed the produce department, so to conform to resume style, drop the *I* and write instead, "Managed the produce department." Use bullet points so the material is easy to read.

ON THE JOB

SCENARIO: When you're putting together your resume, you may be tempted to cast your education and experience in a more flattering light than is truthful, in hopes of improving your chances. Should you take the gamble?

QUICK FIX: Absolutely not. Part of a human resources professional's job is to detect exaggerated claims, hype, or downright lies on resumes. No matter what, it is unacceptable to inflate your qualifications on your resume. Don't confuse a positive attitude with dishonesty—there is a difference. It's perfectly acceptable not to highlight your lack of a college degree, but don't say you have an MBA when you don't.

Save the descriptive words—adjectives and adverbs—for your future novel. Those who are making hiring decisions prefer resumes that are concise. Making every word count eliminates the temptation to overhype or exaggerate, too.

Design Elements

What are some of the design elements of an easy-to-read resume? Balance, symmetry, and white space all contribute to the visual impact of a reader-friendly resume. No one should have to struggle to review your material. A good design goes a long way toward easing eyestrain, especially when hundreds of resumes must be reviewed.

> ### Don't Neglect the Basics
> Before sending your resume and cover letter to a potential employer, it is essential that you make sure your information is accurate and error-free. Proofread your resume and cover letter—twice. Run spell-check. For extra insurance, have another person read your material for grammar and spelling errors or inaccurate gaps in your employment history.

- Choose page-width spacing or a column approach to display all your key information in a flattering light.

- As a starting point, allow one inch for your margins—top and bottom as well as left and right.

- Experiment with fully justified or ragged-right margins. Full justification (in which both margins are aligned) may give you more words per line, but a ragged right margin (the right margin has an uneven edge) is faster to read.

- To get a few ideas about indentation, bullets, rules, and columns, take a look at how other resumes are designed.

- Experiment with a few designs to see which one works best for the material you're presenting.

Consistency is a good indicator of a logical mind. Human resource professionals are practiced at noticing inconsistency in the layout of your resume, so spend a few extra minutes taking note of the following:

- **Spacing.** Be consistent in the amount of spacing between lines, between words, and between headings.

- **Spelled-out versus Abbreviated.** If you spell out "September" in one line, don't use the numerical alternative ("9") in the other line. Or if you use the abbreviated version of a state name in one line, don't spell it out in the next.

- **Typeface.** If you use boldface for your job title in one reference, make sure you use boldface in the next. Or if your headings are in a 14-point typestyle in one section, make sure they are the same size in the next.

- **Indents.** Tabs have a way of playing tricks on you, so make sure everything is aligned correctly.

- **Verb Tenses.** If you use past tense in one bulleted item, use the past tense in the next bulleted item. Use present tense for your current job and the simple past tense for former positions.

- **Punctuation.** Consistency is important in punctuation as well. Exercise your punctuation choices correctly and consistently.

Target Your Resume to the Job Description

Your basic resume is a work in progress that will be further refined based on each position you apply for. When you've written your basic resume, you've written a page about your academic qualifications and the job positions you have held in the past. But when you tailor your resume to an employer's open position, you're writing a final copy of your resume to show how you already fit that position.

As you are preparing to apply for a job, first read through the job description for the open position and make a list of the specific qualifications that the employer is looking for. Compare those qualifications to your own background and look for ways to show how you already have these skills. Draw on your work history, you coursework, or your volunteer activities for activities that demonstrate the key qualifications listed in the job description, and revise your resume to include specific examples that show how you have those skills. For example, if you are applying for a job that requires a lot of client contact, emphasize the two years of customer service experience you gained from working at a department store. If the position requires excellent written communication skills, emphasize the writing skills that you developed at school.

The objective on your resume should also be tailored to make it clear what position you are applying for. For example, if you are applying for an executive assistant position, your objective should be "To secure a position as an executive assistant." If you later apply for an office coordinator position, update your objective to match the new target job.

By tailoring your resume for each job you apply for, your resume will clearly indicate what you can do for the employer.

Avoiding Common Resume Errors

Your resume should demonstrate the skills and qualifications that you will bring to an employer. Are you dependable? Make sure your resume reflects that. Read the information you just wrote—make sure it's accurate and straightforward. Are you detail-oriented? Then don't risk letting a single error of spelling or punctuation slip through. Are you a problem-solver? If you send your resume to the wrong department or address it "To Whom It May Concern," an interviewer will have a hard time believing so.

You may bring an impressive array of skills and abilities to a new job position, but the quality of your resume speaks first—and loudest. The following tips will help you avoid common resume errors:

- Keep it brief: Try to limit your resume to one page. A busy human resource professional may not take the time to read a lengthy resume. Keep your resume concise by focusing on the skills and qualifications that are most relevant for the position you are applying for.

- Avoid long paragraphs of text: Use short sentences and bulleted points so your key points stand out. Human resource staffers tend to skim through resumes, so make sure your key accomplishments and skills are displayed in a way that makes them easily noticed.

- Pay attention to the details: Double-check your resume to make sure there are no errors in grammar, spelling, or punctuation. Spell-check will catch many errors, but you still have to proofread your resume yourself. For example, if by accident you write "Panned and coordinated corporate meetings" instead of "Planned and coordinated corporate meetings," spell-check won't pick up the error "Panned." Proofread each resume you send out, and ask a friend or family member to read your resume as an additional check.

- Be easy to reach: Make sure your contact information is complete, correct, and up to date. If your phone number is wrong on your resume or your address is out of date, chances are the human resource office won't take the time to find the correct one.

- Keep it professional: Use a simple, clean design and a standard typestyle. Avoid using cutesy fonts, bright paper, colored text, or clip art.

- Stay focused: Emphasize your most relevant professional and academic qualifications. Don't include hobbies, gender, or marital status. Never include your photograph on your resume.

Cover Letters

A well-written and insightful cover letter can help you stand out above the rest. Think of a cover letter as a means of furthering your cause beyond the resume. What do professionals expect from cover letters?

- They accompany every resume you send.

- They are brief but error-free and accurate.

- All pertinent contact information is included (name, address, telephone number, email address).

- Accomplishments are highlighted in a short paragraph.

- The position being applied for is specified.

123 Rosewood Avenue
Durham, KS 34511

January 15, 2010

Mr. Jonathan Monroe
Human Resource Department
Zenyatta Corporation
201 North Avenue
Durham, KS 34511

Dear Mr. Monroe:

Enclosed is my resume, which I am submitting as a candidate for the executive assistant position listed in the *Durham Daily News*. Having recently graduated with a degree in business administration, I bring to you a unique blend of educational and work qualifications.

While serving as an intern at the Durham Social Services Department, I coordinated a complete workforce training program with the local workforce board. This was a great experience and gave me an opportunity to work independently with no supervision. I am proficient in all core office administration functions, including document preparation, internal and external communications, data and records management, meeting scheduling, and task prioritization. In addition, I am able to quickly adapt to new situations, communicate with a wide range of associates, and maintain a high degree of organization and professionalism.

I would be delighted to have the opportunity for a personal interview and can be available at your convenience. Thank you in advance for your time and consideration, and I look forward to what I anticipate will be the first of many positive communications.

Sincerely,

Maria Vega

Enclosure: resume

Figure 9.3 Cover letter

Format

If your cover letter will be sent as hard copy (rather than by email), use a standard format for a business letter. Various formats are available. Figure 9.3 shows one basic arrangement. Here your address, the date, the employer's name and address, salutation, body, and closing are all flush left.

Examine the format and notice the placement of information: your address, date, the employer's address, the salutation, the body, the closing. Avoid taking short-cuts with this style. Prospective employers want to see, at the very least, that you're familiar with the basics of business correspondence, so include all of this information, and—here's the difficult part—make sure it fits on one page. Time is in short supply, so no matter what, strive to be concise (try not to exceed 250 to 350 words).

Follow these guidelines when you are putting together your cover letter:

- The cover letter should follow a standard business letter format.

- It's centered on the page, with an equal amount of spacing on the top and the bottom.

- Your closing should be followed by four lines to accommodate your signature (in black or blue ink).

- In the address section, use the postal service's two-letter (no periods) state abbreviation; in the body of the text, spell out the state's name.

- In the employer's address, also include a courtesy title or professional title (Mr., Ms., Dr.).

- Using a department name will ensure that your letter gets to the appropriate hiring authority.

- Department names are capitalized in an address. Then on the next line use the full name of the company.

- After the salutation, use a colon, not a comma.

- After your complimentary closing, use a comma.

- Below your name, add the notation "Enclosure: resume" to indicate that your resume is enclosed.

Content

Now let's look at the body of the letter. Your cover letter should be written to a specific individual. (Try not to send a cover letter "To Whom It May Concern.") In the first paragraph tell the employer what position you're interested in, where you heard about the position, and why you're interested in the position. In the next paragraph explain how you are qualified for the job. Use this section to discuss two or three specific accomplishments or qualifications that are relevant to the position. In the last paragraph mention that you're looking forward to discussing the position in person. Include your contact information and thank the employer for his or her time.

Writing a good cover letter ensures that you will stand out. Remember that employers are getting an added look at your communication skills, so the cover letter must be letter-perfect, clear, and concise.

Cover Letter Tips

- Use your cover letter as an opportunity to say something about the company that is offering the position so they'll know you've done your research. Mention a recent success or a particular strength that makes working for the company particularly appealing.

- Your cover letter will touch on skills that are also listed on your resume, but don't repeat information word-for-word from your resume. A cover letter should complement and expand on your resume.

- If you get stuck about what to include in the body of the letter, go back to the description of the position you're applying for and review the specific skills mentioned in the description. Tailor your letter to those qualifications.

- Don't overuse the word "I." It's OK to refer to yourself; just don't overdo it. If you have too many sentences that begin with "I," go back and revise some of them.

- If you are sending a non-email version of your cover letter, don't forget to sign it. Use black or blue ink, never pencil.

Applications

Most employers will have you fill out an application in addition to submitting a resume and cover letter. Sometimes you'll be asked to fill out the application to send along with your resume and cover letter; other times you may be asked to fill out the application when you arrive for an interview.

Applications cover much of the same material that is on your resume, but they typically require more specific information. If you are filling out the application on-site, make sure you arrive prepared. Bring along your driver's license and Social Security card, along with detailed information about your employment history. Be prepared to provide the name, address, and phone number of current and former employers; date range of employment; name of supervisor; and the starting and ending wage for each job that you list on the application. Also bring along contact information for all your references.

Use the following guidelines when filling out an application:

- Read through the whole application before you start.

- Write neatly in black or blue ink (not pencil).

- Follow all the instructions carefully.

- Don't skip any questions: if a question doesn't apply to you, write "n/a" (not applicable).

- If you are asked about salary requirements, write "negotiable."

- Make sure that job titles, dates of employment, and similar information match those listed on your resume.

- If you are asked to list the reason why you left a previous job, always stay positive. Make a general statement about what you were seeking in the new position rather than writing something negative about a previous employer.

- Review the entire application to make sure everything is complete.

Online Submissions

In our increasingly high-tech world, many prospective employers have moved most or all of the preliminary applicant screening process online.

When applying for jobs online, be sure to follow directions to the letter. Those who fail to do so are frequently not even considered for the position. When a company states in a job posting that your resume attachment must not exceed 16,384 characters, do not send one that has 18,000 characters. This may sound simple, but many applicants don't follow basic instructions. Don't be one of them.

On some company websites, you may only apply for open positions. Others allow you to submit a profile or resume for future openings. Again, follow the directions.

Make sure you read the job description thoroughly. The description is usually more elaborate than a classified advertisement. Pick up some of the key words from the job description and put them on your resume as they apply to your experience.

Before sending your resume to a prospective employer, make sure you know the employer's preference for receiving it. If the preference isn't clear in a job posting or company website, then send an email or call and ask. If you're unsure what to ask, consider these questions:

- Should I mail my resume? Fax it? Email it?

- Should I attach my resume to an email?

- What file formats should be used for email attachments? MS Word (.doc) or Rich Text Format (.rtf)? Or pdf (.pdf) format?

- Should my resume be in the body of the email (converted to plain text or ASCII, pronounced askee)?

- Should I go to the company website and fill out an e-form? And whom should I follow up with?

Electronic Cover Letters

If you send an electronic cover letter, plan to follow the same block styles, but there's no need to include your address, the date, or the employer's address. Instead, you need a correct email address, the correct name of the hiring authority (if it's not a general "contact us" submittal), and a topic for the subject line (a job number or position title).

The Attached Resume

Many job seekers prefer to send their resumes and cover letters as attachments to their emails because this method retains their formatting (bold, italics, underscore, bullets, etc.). If you are asked to send your resume as an email attachment, the process is fairly straightforward. The procedure may vary slightly depending on which email program you use, but here are the basics:

- Put the address in the "To" line.

- Put the name of the specific job you're applying for as well as your name (e.g., Equity Sales Trader–John Smith) in the "Subject" line.

- Write a cover letter in the body of your email.

- Attach your resume by clicking on the "Attach" icon in the email menu.

- Scroll down and hit "File," then select your resume file. Once your resume file is highlighted, hit "Open." The file automatically attaches to the email.

- Before you hit "Send," double-check that the email cover letter and attachment are in order.

Application Tip

In the work history section on applications, you are typically asked to explain why you left a previous position. This can be tricky if you quit a job under circumstances that were less than ideal. Remember to keep your response positive. Be honest—but not too honest. If you left your last job because your boss was a tyrant, don't write it on an application. Your boss may well have been a tyrant—but it'll only make you look bad if you say so. A potential employer will be watching for anything that could indicate that you're difficult or hard to manage.

Instead of noting what drove you away from a previous position, consider instead what drew you to your next position and phrase your answer to emphasize something good about that position. So instead of writing, "I hated my boss," you could write, "I wanted a position that would make better use of my communication skills" (or whatever skills you enjoyed using in that position).

Claire B. Schmoll

Lisbon, Maine

Attended: Andover College—Lewiston, Maine

Area of study: Business Administration

Employer: Assistant to the Vice President for Finance & Administration and Treasurer, Bates College

If you take one thing away from this course, it should be this: In any profession, an employee must always exude professionalism. That can be accomplished in a number of ways; however, for me that entails accountability, morality, ethics, and exceptional customer service.

I was able to accomplish my goals by being fortunate enough to have had four great instructors who were willing to listen to everyone and who gave their time and energy to those who requested it. Kaplan was a great place for nontraditional students like me to get back into higher education.

Chapter Summary

- Resumes need to be individually tailored for targeted jobs so it is immediately obvious to a prospective employer that the job seeker is a good fit for the company and its culture.

- A cover letter should accompany every resume you send.

- The cover letter should expand on skills that are covered in your resume.

- Neatness counts: make sure your resume and cover letter are error free.

- In addition to a resume and cover letter, expect to be asked to fill out a job application.

- Before sending your resume to a prospective employer, make sure you know the employer's preference for receiving it.

To-Do List

- ☐ Prepare a personal file at your desk or on your computer where you can keep all the information about your employment history and educational experience so that it is handy to refer to as you complete resumes and job applications.

- ☐ Critique a variety of sample resumes from online sources, books, or classmates. What do they do well?

- ☐ Compile a list of vocabulary words that are specific to your field and start using them now.

Important Terms

How well do you know these terms? Define them here or in your journal, or look them up in the glossary to help you remember them.

chronological resume   resume

cover letter   transferable skills

functional resume

Online Resources

Optimal Resume, an online resume building tool
https://kheu.optimalresume.com

Monster.com, offers resume writing tips and sample resumes
http://career-advice.monster.com

QuintCareers.com, offers resume tips
http://www.quintcareers.com/resume-dos-donts.html

Exercises

Write your answers in your journal or on a separate piece of paper.

1. Prepare both a chronological and functional version of your resume. Work with classmates to critique and improve upon the resumes. In what circumstances would a chronological resume be more appropriate? When would the functional version be more suitable?

2. Create a standard cover letter that you can adapt to target specific positions.

3. Select a specific job at a specific company you'd like to apply to for purposes of this exercise. Adapt your resume and cover letter for this target.

Portions of this chapter's content include material adapted from Brenda Greene, *Get the Interview Every Time*, revised and expanded edition (New York: Kaplan, 2008).

10 | Portfolios

KEYS TO SUCCESS

- Describing the features that should be in every portfolio
- Identifying additional elements to include for your target industry
- Collecting the documents that will go into your portfolio
- Organizing your portfolio in a way that will show a future employer what you've done and what you hope to accomplish
- Assembling your portfolio

You might think that only "creative types" such as graphic artists or journalists use professional portfolios, but in reality, a well-constructed portfolio can help almost any job seeker, in almost any profession. When you hand over your portfolio to a prospective employer, you're instantly accomplishing a few key goals:

- Showing off your organizational skills by presenting a professional, comprehensive, well-organized portfolio

- Demonstrating your skills by providing samples of your work

- Indicating that you're serious about your career and you are willing to take the time to develop a portfolio that highlights your achievements

This chapter examines what should be in your portfolio and provides some tips on how it can be used to your best advantage.

What Is a Portfolio?

A portfolio is a snapshot of your professional accomplishments. It differs from a resume in a couple important aspects:

- It is much more in-depth than a single sheet listing your work experience; unlike a resume that shows what you *have* done, a portfolio gives an employer an idea of what you *can* do.

- It allows you to "show not tell." Your resume outlines your skills; your portfolio backs up your resume by *showing* your skills.

Your portfolio can include any document or work sample that might be important to prospective employers. Examples include certificates of achievement, samples of your work, awards, letters of recommendation, and anything else that helps provide a complete picture of you as a person and an employee.

If you think of your resume as a snapshot of your skills, then you should think of your portfolio as the feature-length movie.

What Goes in a Portfolio?

Throughout your life, you've no doubt received many certificates of recognition and accomplished things you were proud of. There might be trophies or awards from sports you're involved in, scholarship letters, papers you're especially proud of, letters of recommendation, and on and on. So how do you know which parts to include in your portfolio?

Here's the simple answer: think of your portfolio as a story. It's not a random collection of documents, but a cohesive binder that tells a *narrative*. More specifically, it shows how you've grown academically and professionally, what you're capable of and where you're heading, and why you belong in your chosen profession.

Once you start thinking of your portfolio in these professional terms, it will become easier to choose which pieces to include. Maybe your Little League certificate of achievement doesn't belong after all—unless you're aiming for a coaching position.

Components of Your Portfolio

Although your portfolio should be specialized for your industry, there are certain elements that belong in any portfolio. Don't worry if you're still a student or don't have a wealth of professional work samples. Your portfolio isn't meant only to illustrate what you've done; it should show what you're capable of doing in the future.

Your portfolio should contain the following components:

- Title page and introduction. This simple sheet should introduce you and contain a simple, brief statement of your professional goals. Your goals should be broad, not tailored for any particular interview. In other words, your goal shouldn't be, "Land this job," but "Establish a long-term career in the [blank] industry, ultimately rising to [blank] position."

- Your resume. This is not a substitute for handing over your resume, but your portfolio should include a copy of your current resume.

- Contact information. Some portfolios include areas for business cards with contact information.

- Samples of your work. This can include everything from class work to published articles to artwork.

- Transcripts, degrees, and certifications. Include degrees and certification that you've earned and a description of any relevant coursework. You may also want to include your transcripts.

- Awards and honors. This can include any honors or awards you've received for your coursework or outside activities, positive performance evaluations from your workplace, and perfect attendance certificates from classes.

- Reference list. A sheet of references should direct prospective employers to people who can vouch for your work habits and skills. If you have letters of recommendation, include them in this section.

Matching Your Industry

Obviously, the portfolio of a graphic designer will look dramatically different than the portfolio of a dental hygienist—but both individuals can benefit from having a portfolio. The following list gives examples of documents that professionals in a variety of industries can include in their portfolios.

- Business program graduates. White papers, reports, advertising campaigns, promotional ideas and documents, cover letters, brochures, marketing campaigns, presentation outlines or slides, case studies, memberships in professional organizations

- Criminal justice professionals. Research projects and presentations, mock trial projects, fingerprinting work, field experience internships, crime scene work and photographs, memberships in professional organizations

- Allied health professionals. Certificates of training, sample patient records (use fictitious patients to protect patient privacy), HIPAA certificate, research project on diseases and drug intervention, treatment protocols, adult and infant CPR certification, transcription reports, memberships in professional organizations

- Graphic artists. Transcripts, sample projects, published work, letters of recommendation, group projects, multimedia projects, fine art projects, illustrations

- Office administration/management professionals. Speed certificates for typing, certificates for note taking, samples of penmanship, attendance records from school, sample business communication, presentations including slide shows and PowerPoint presentations

- Writers. Writing samples from a variety of media, awards, multimedia projects, research projects

This list is just to stimulate your thinking, but you can see the options are almost endless. In essence, anything that shows mastery of your field or highlights skills you've developed that relate to your industry belongs in your portfolio. Additionally, personal recognition and testaments to your character—such as volunteer work, blood drive certificates, and community recognition—can help a prospective employer better understand what kind of person you are.

ON THE JOB

SCENARIO: You are at your first job interview after graduation, and thing are going very well. You're a little bit nervous but you've easily handled some tough questions. Suddenly the interviewer asks you a simple question about what you liked best about your coursework, and for some reason you draw a blank. You reply that you liked writing best of all, but you struggle to complete your thought.

QUICK FIX: Since you have your portfolio on hand, you offer to show the interviewer an example of your writing. You direct her to the section in your portfolio that has your technical writing samples, and as she looks through the samples, you use the slight pause to regroup. Because you are so familiar with your portfolio, you feel confident talking about your writing samples. Your nerves are back under control, and you use your writing samples as a starting point for discussing your unique strengths as a technical writer.

Gathering Your Documents

For many people, one of the most challenging aspects of assembling a portfolio is gathering the material. Faced with the prospect of job hunting, they launch a mad hunt to find the proper paperwork, assemble it, and pull together a portfolio. While you can certainly build a portfolio this way, you'll almost certainly end up with a better product with some advance planning.

As you progress through your coursework, you should keep a special folder or box titled "Portfolio." This is where you'll put documents that will someday be candidates for your portfolio. For example, if you produce an especially good report for a class, immediately place this in your portfolio folder. You can also get portfolio material from your outside activities. A certificate of recognition, for example, from an organization where you volunteer could also be included.

When it comes time to assemble your portfolio, you will review all the material and then decide what stays and what goes. Remember, not every piece of paper you collect will actually make it into your portfolio. But it's better to have too much to work with than too little, so don't hesitate to build a large database of prospective documents for your portfolio.

> ### Practice Critical Thinking
> What documents do you have right now that you can include in your portfolio? Think about accomplishments you've earned for coursework that demonstrates competence in your field, but also consider recognition you've received for other qualities that are valued in the workplace. For example, a certificate of perfect attendance from one of your classes shows a potential employer that you are reliable and that you take your responsibilities seriously.

Assembling Your Portfolio

Your portfolio is a physical document—the way it looks and feels can say almost as much about you as what's inside it. It's essential that your portfolio is neatly and professionally organized, free from simple spelling and grammar errors, and contains only your best work.

Here are some tips for organizing your portfolio:

1. Use an attractive three-ring binder or, better, a leather portfolio case. The actual binder will vary depending on your paperwork—artists have larger portfolios to accommodate their drawings—but choose the very best you can afford. (Don't worry—a prospective employer will not expect to keep your portfolio, but only review and return it.)

2. Use tabs to separate sections and chapters. Colored tabs, with a matching table of contents, will help employers quickly navigate through your portfolio. You can organize sections according to their content, using such headers as Research Projects, Resume, Awards and Recognition, Education, Letters of Recommendation, Volunteer Work, Slide Shows, References, and so forth.

Portfolio Tip

Building a portfolio is an ongoing process, so when you buy tabs and backing paper, buy enough to last for a while. Your portfolio should have a uniform appearance throughout, and you don't want to have to redo the whole portfolio every time you update your material.

3. Use the highest quality paper and backing material you can. Every document in your portfolio should be individually and professionally presented. Don't simply throw a bunch of article clippings or drawings in a folder; instead mount them on individual pages. If you're presenting reports and longer items, make it easy for the reviewer to access the information. Remove staples and tape.

4. If you cut out articles or sections from reports, use scissors and obtain a clean margin. Don't include anything that looks ragged, stained, or worn. If your certificate of achievement is stained, don't include the actual certificate, only a mention that you received it.

5. Make sure your contact information is current. Every email address, website, and phone number in your portfolio needs to be current at all times. Double-check these before you use the portfolio and update if necessary.

Your Portfolio Online

A basic paper portfolio is still a great resource, but if you really want to set yourself apart, consider creating a simple online presence that works in conjunction with your portfolio. It's fairly easy to build a simple website using an off-the-shelf template from a web hosting company such as Yahoo or GoDaddy. Creating a simple website requires reserving your web address, designing the site, and paying for hosting services (usually about $50 a year, at the minimum).

Optimal Portfolio

The resume-building website Optimal Resume offers a portfolio builder that allows you to easily create an online portfolio. You can organize your portfolio by section and upload documents to include in each section. The site supports a variety of file types, including document, image, and video files. When your portfolio is complete it can be shared online or downloaded as a zipped file. Visit https://kheu.optimalresume .com to get started.

If you choose to build an online companion to your portfolio, make sure to provide the website address in your portfolio and on your resume and business cards. The Internet can only help you if people visit your site.

Using Your Portfolio

Your portfolio is a tool that presents you in the best possible light. It shows employers your past accomplishments, and gives them a well-rounded view of you as a person as well as an understanding of your professional goals. The best portfolios tell a story about you as a person and employee, and make it easy to understand why you would make a great employee.

Your portfolio can be a powerful tool during the job interview process, and there are certain steps you can take to maximize its impact.

First, you should always take your portfolio with you during job interviews. At the interview, you can present the portfolio to your interviewer at the appropriate time. However, don't expect the interviewer to sit and absorb your entire portfolio during the course of the interview. If you hand it to him or her at the beginning of the interview, it can be used during the interview as you direct the interviewer to pages as you answer questions and discuss your background.

If you hand the portfolio to your interviewer after the interview, make sure to include a request that the portfolio is mailed back or offer to stop by and pick it up. It's widely understood that portfolios are not meant to be kept by employers—portfolios often require significant investment in time and money to produce, so it's not reasonable to expect a prospective employee to leave a portfolio behind.

Chapter Summary

- Your portfolio is a collection of documents that gives a detailed history of your accomplishments and an idea of your future goals and direction.

- Include in your portfolio certificates of achievement, transcripts, letters of recommendation, projects, and work samples that give a complete picture of your skills.

- Your portfolio should be matched to your profession and include supporting documents that would interest and engage professionals in your field.

- You can also include documents that show your character, such as volunteer work, community recognition awards, and letters of reference.

- Use your portfolio during an interview to provide examples of your qualifications, or leave it for the interviewer to review, with arrangements to collect it later.

- An online presence, such as a website, can be a powerful tool to help boost your portfolio.

To-Do List

☐ Brainstorm a list all possible documents that will go into your portfolio. Don't worry about organizing the list. The goal is to have a large number of possibilities that you can refine later.

☐ Obtain a box or a folder that you can use to store the documents that will go in your portfolio.

☐ Buy the portfolio material so you'll have it on hand when you put together your portfolio.

☐ Make a list of ten people you can ask for a letter of recommendation.

Important Terms

How well do you know these terms? Define them here or in your journal, or look them up in the glossary to help you remember.

letter of recommendation   **portfolio**
narrative

Online Resources

How to use a portfolio in an interview
www.jobweb.com/interviews.aspx?id=342

Benefits of Maintaining a Career Portfolio and a Current Resume
www.jobbankusa.com/CareerArticles/Resume/ca93005a.html

Portfolios: The Art of Finding a Job
http://alis.alberta.ca/ep/eps/tips/tips.html?EK=151

Exercises

Write your answers in your journal or on a separate piece of paper.

1. Plan the organization of your portfolio. What skills are most important in your field? What sections should your portfolio include to highlight these skills? Create table of contents for your portfolio listing each section.

2. For each section in your portfolio, make a list of documents that you'll need to include in the portfolio. Your list should include documents that you already have and a plan for additional documents to include as you complete your coursework.

3. Assemble your portfolio.

11 | Personal Branding and Networking

KEYS TO SUCCESS

- Tailoring your image to promote your personal brand
- Finding opportunities for networking
- Understanding the guidelines for successful networking
- Using social networking sites and other online resources to promote yourself

What do you want people to think about when they think about you? Your sense of humor? Your designer wardrobe? Your tattoos? Your compassion and intelligence?

Your answer to this question is more important to finding the right job than you might think, because it concerns your personal brand. If you feel that you don't have a personal brand, then it's time to develop one.

What Is Branding?

You are already familiar with hundreds, if not thousands, of brands. It's impossible to go through a day without being bombarded with brand messages. Think about all the messages you're exposed to in the course of a single day. How many are linked to a logo, a slogan, or a particular company or product? Nearly all of them, probably.

This is branding. And branding is pervasive because it works.

One of the most important things to understand about brands and brand recognition is that a brand is built on *perceptions,* which are fundamentally different from product descriptions.

Take two pairs of jeans by different manufacturers. Essentially, both pairs are made from inexpensive cotton denim fabric and have a similar overall design. True, one pair might feature different elements in terms of design and workmanship—it may have buttons instead of a zipper or it may have a darker wash than the other. But fundamentally, these are similar products.

So why can one manufacturer charge $120 for its pair of jeans while the other charges only $35? The difference comes down to consumer perception. The manufacturer of jeans priced at $120 isn't just selling denim—it's selling a lifestyle and attitude associated with the company. And that perception of lifestyle and attitude is created through effective branding.

Personal Branding

But you're not a pair of jeans, right? Unless you're a famous movie star, a political candidate, or a prominent business owner, it is unlikely that someone is going to run commercials about you or develop a catchy slogan around your name. So how can you be a brand? The idea behind personal branding is simple: think of yourself as a total package, and take conscious control of your own image. Make sure that everything about you says exactly what you want it to say.

According to personal branding expert Dan Schawbel, it boils down to this:

Personal branding is how you market yourself to others.

This simple definition sweeps everything in, including your style of speaking, your online persona, your appearance, your goals, your clothing—even something as simple as your email address. All of these elements should be carefully considered and crafted to present the right image for you—in this case, the image that will help you get a job and advance your career.

Personal Branding Tip

Some view personal branding as a form of self-promotion and egotism. There is some truth to this, but that doesn't mean it's a bad thing. Developing your brand makes you a more valuable asset to a potential employer. Don't forget, it's your future we're talking about. Don't you want to make it a success? With effective branding, your career success will translate into happiness outside the workplace as well.

Branding Mistakes

In today's competitive job market, it's not uncommon for a human resource department to get 100, 200, or even 300 resumes for every opening. Most of these applicants can be disqualified right away; in fact, human resource recruiters have to disqualify most of them right away to avoid spending the next month poring over resumes and cover letters.

In addition to broadcasting the skills and qualifications you bring to a prospective job, you need to pay attention to the minor details that make up your overall image. Consider the following examples:

- An applicant responds to a job posting using the email account rebelgurl420@google. net. Will the recruiter bother opening the email? Probably not.

- Twelve candidates are being interviewed for one open position at a leading company. One candidate shows up for the interview five minutes late, carrying a steaming Starbucks cup. What kind of impression does that make? Wouldn't the logical first question from the recruiter be, "Why should I hire you for this job if your coffee run is more important than being on time to your interview?"

- An applicant is among the final three candidates being interviewed for a new position. All three applicants interviewed well, and they all have the required qualifications for the job. The recruiter logs onto Google and does a little searching. A few clicks later, she runs across a fraternity blog displaying photos of one of her candidates. He's obviously severely intoxicated and making obscene gestures at the camera. Assuming all other characteristics of the three candidates are pretty much equal, do you think this person will get the job now?

These examples are neither extreme nor uncommon. In an era of unprecedented competition and lack of privacy, most employers are looking for any reason to disqualify a job candidate, and it only makes their job easier when candidates essentially disqualify themselves. Make sure all of your actions—large or small—are directed at presenting a professional image.

ON THE JOB

SCENARIO: You're confident as you prepare for your interview scheduled for next Friday; you're pretty sure you'll nail it. You've practiced answering all the questions they could possibly ask, and you feel really good about your qualifications. As you're thinking about what else you can do to prepare, you remember that the recruiter said she would be doing a little research into each of the final candidates. You begin to worry about a few photos on your Facebook page. What should you do?

QUICK FIX: Take them down, fast! It's a good idea to review the material you post on social networking sites *before* you begin your job search and make sure that your posts reflect the image that you want to project.

Building Your Brand

You've seen how branding can go wrong, but how do you use it to lead to the kind of career you really want? The answer is: consciously.

Building a career doesn't happen by accident. Those with successful careers—from neurosurgeons to pop singers—did not maintain their lengthy careers by accident. It takes a conscious act of will to succeed in one's chosen field. Think about your intended career in light of the following attributes:

1. **Education.** What kind of education is needed for your career? Whether it's studying as a journeyman plumber or going to a four-year university, your education is the ticket for entry. You'll never get past the first closed door without it.

2. **Industry knowledge.** This is different from education. In today's wired world, it's easier than ever to learn how an industry really works. It doesn't matter which industry. Whether you want to be a cabinet maker or a jet mechanic, you should learn everything you can about what's going on in your industry, including the big names, the most current developments, and the long-term prospects.

3. **Enthusiasm.** Don't underestimate the importance of enthusiasm to your overall success. Without enthusiasm, everything just seems like work.

With these three big-picture elements in mind, consider some other variables:

- **Resumes, cover letters, and business cards.** Use these important job search tools to refine the image you want to present. Emphasize your strongest qualifications on your resume and in your cover letter. Make sure your grammar, spelling, and punctuation are perfect. Use high-quality paper when you print out your resume and cover letter, and invest in professional-quality business cards.

- **Communication.** Your communication style is more than the way you speak. Think about the way you write email. When contacting potential employers, use proper English and avoid slang and "text speak."

- **Appearance.** This isn't about your personal looks—it's about fitting into the field you want to join. For example, men in banking and finance don't wear long hair. There's no rule against it; it's just the way things are. So think about your appearance and presentation. In your field is it appropriate to have multiple piercings, visible tattoos, or an unusual hairstyle? It very well might be—but if it's not, then you should think about changing these things.

- **Presentation.** This overlaps with appearance, but it goes deeper into the overall way you project yourself to the world. This includes your online presence on social networking sites such as MySpace and Facebook, and more obvious things like always being on time and shaking hands.

The most important thing about a brand is its *authenticity*. Employers can spot a fake a mile away. If you're serious about your career, and you love what you're doing, it should show in everything you do. Branding yourself isn't about creating a phony persona to "sell" to employers and the rest of the world. It's about being yourself, but in a tailored, deliberate way.

Networking

Networking is loosely defined as the act of making beneficial contacts. In a career sense, this means meeting and getting to know people who have been in the field longer than you, and who can potentially help you with advice and even leads on job openings. When you enter any career or profession, it can sometimes seem like a closed club. It can be intimidating. You don't know who is who, and worse yet, you don't know how to get inside. How can you get started? By networking.

A number of websites are great for networking, including LinkedIn, Facebook, MySpace, and numerous industry-specific forums and information clearinghouses. If you don't know where to go to meet people, these websites are the perfect place to start. Joining a professional organization associated with your field is another option. Doing volunteer work can also be a networking opportunity, especially if the organization or the work is related to your career goals.

When you're creating a network, here are few reminders:

1. **Be respectful of other people's time.** When you meet someone new, keep your communications appropriate, brief, and on topic. If someone prefers communicating by email rather than by phone, honor that request. Be mindful of the value of other people's time. Time hogging is not just bad manners—it creates the impression that you're either selfish or oblivious.

2. **Be positive.** Remember when you're talking to professionals in your field that they have all been where you are. Everybody had to start somewhere, so complaining about how hard it is to get established will just seem like whining. Instead, let your natural enthusiasm show. People respond to enthusiasm.

3. **Ask questions.** It can be tough when you feel like the only person in a conversation who doesn't know the "ins and outs" of the business. It doesn't matter if you're talking router bits or investment vehicles; everybody has to learn somehow. Ask questions and listen carefully to the answers. People generally like to answer questions—it feels good to be treated like an expert.

4. **Acknowledge acts of generosity and kindness.** When someone helps you, it's always appropriate to thank that person. This can be a simple email thank-you to someone for providing you with another contact, for example. For a more significant act, like recommending you for a job, a handwritten note is appropriate. However you do it, just remember to express your honest gratitude.

Starting out can be hard, but remember: these are the people and companies you hope to work with for the rest of your career. And someday newly minted professionals will approach you—and you'll remember how you started out.

Using the Internet for Networking

If you're serious about launching your brand and your career, you need to understand and use new media tools to help spread the word. Here are some useful online tools that can promote your brand:

- **Social networking sites.** Sites such as MySpace, Facebook, LinkedIn, and Twitter allow you to create your own "homepage" or persona and use it to reach other people. These sites are true networks—you build them by inviting others and, in turn, you are invited to join other people's networks. Social networking sites are the easiest way to reach large numbers of people who know you, including family, colleagues, and friends, as well as like-minded people you'd like to know.

- **Blogs.** A blog is a simple web page that allows you to perform basic publishing tasks, such as writing and posting photos. Blogs are offered through companies like Blogspot and WordPress. These services are very easy to use. You simply sign up, pick your template, perform a few basic modifications, and begin writing your entries. Blogging is best for people who have the time and interest in writing frequently and want to build an audience.

- **Personal websites.** You can build a website using tools intended for non-designers. Companies such as Go Daddy and BlueHost provide easy-to-use templates with instructions for including photos, text, and even animation. Websites are extremely valuable for posting visual information that describes business practices, specialties, expertise, and so forth. However, if you're just interested in posting basic information, such as your qualifications, you may want to keep a blog instead of a website, as blogs are much easier to modify and keep current.

If you're unfamiliar with social networking and personal web publishing, start slowly. For example, you might want to set up a Facebook page and "friend" your family members, and get used to posting updates and gain an understanding of what types of posts are appropriate.

When you have gotten a little practice and feel more comfortable, you can expand your online presence. It's not uncommon for professionals to maintain a variety of online sites, including a blog, a personal website, and pages on a variety of social networking sites. This is a wired world, so use it to your advantage.

Tips for Success with New Media

When you get started online—or when you decide to get serious about building your brand online—the Internet can seem overwhelming and confusing. There are always technological issues, and it might not be obvious how all these social networking tools are helping your career. To help you navigate the online world, here are a few simple tips:

- **Remember that you're in public.** Never post or write anything online that you wouldn't want your whole family, your teachers, and your boss to read or view. This includes pictures, videos, and even comments on other people's websites, blogs, and social networks. If you can find embarrassing or compromising material about yourself, remember that other people can, too.

- **Keep it current.** Regular content updates keep readers engaged and interested. The more often you update your online content, the more likely you are to attract interest from readers and potential employers—which will help you expand your existing professional network.

- **Use humor (within reason).** Just because you're trying to build a professional career doesn't mean you have to be boring. Appropriate humor and funny anecdotes are a good way to attract attention and keep people reading. It's best to be brief, however.

- **It's a conversation, not a monologue.** One of the great things about the online world is the give-and-take of the conversation. Don't be afraid to directly engage commenters and posters. The more engaged you are, the more engaging you will be.

As you get more comfortable, you can branch out from your original pool of contacts. To raise your profile, join online discussion sites such as Internet forums and message boards in your industry. These sites generate discussion by allowing users to post questions or messages and to comment on other posts. Always remember to approach the online world as a professional. This is your career—this is your brand you're building—so make sure that everything you do and say supports your overall message.

Watching Your Own Brand

To protect your brand, you need to pay attention to what is said about you. If you've ever seen one of those daytime TV court shows, you've probably come across a scenario like this: Person A sues Person B because Person B posted something embarrassing, incriminating, or false about Person A online.

> ### Workplace Tip
> Writing is a crucial skill for using the Internet. Proofread anything you post to make sure your grammar and punctuation are perfect. Treat the material that you post online with the same care that you put into your resume and other professional correspondence.

It's unfortunate, but the Internet tends to lower people's inhibitions. People do and say unkind or inappropriate things to each other online that they would refrain from in person, and they have little regard for their long-term effects. Celebrities fall victim to this all the time—videos and pictures showing them not in the best light. Gossip is spread about them. It can happen to you too, so from time to time, search your name and review what turns up. If you discover something unsavory, there are some things you can do about it.

First, however, try to avoid situations that conflict with your career goals. If you find yourself in a compromising situation or engaging in behavior that might threaten your job search or career progress, it's probably worth asking yourself a simple question: "Why am I doing this? What is to be gained from it? What do I stand to lose?"

Ultimately, you're the only person who can provide accurate and damaging information about yourself, through your own behavior.

This doesn't mean that malicious people won't lie about you, or go so far as to doctor photographs, hack into your blogs and social networking sites, or even assume your identity. Whether this is done as a joke or not, this kind of behavior can be damaging, and you should take it seriously. If someone close to you is responsible for the prank, set him or her straight. If you feel that you are being bullied or harassed online, contact the appropriate authorities. These might include police, school administrators, your boss, or even a civil lawyer who can file a small claims lawsuit. The important thing is that you stand up for yourself and protect your reputation.

Winning Through Branding

The modern successful employee treats himself or herself like a mini-corporation. Think of yourself in terms of your skills and strengths. What do you bring to a company? What do you want to accomplish with your life? Your strengths are yours alone, and it only makes sense that you market yourself as the best commodity possible.

Chapter Summary

- Personal branding refers to the way you present and market yourself to others.
- Your professional track record, your style of speaking, your online persona, your appearance, your clothing, and your goals make up your "brand."
- Networking can help you gain valuable contacts in your field.
- Social networking sites, blogs, and personal websites can be used to promote your brand.
- Use caution when posting material on the Internet. Don't post anything you wouldn't want a potential employer to see.

To-Do List

☐ List three important characteristics you want to emphasize in your brand.

☐ List ten small adjustments you can make to your behavior, communication style, or presentation that will support the three characteristics that you selected above. Start making those adjustments today.

☐ Google yourself and see what comes up. Do the search results support the image you want to project?

☐ Identify five places—either online or in real life—where you can network in your chosen field.

☐ Set up a page on a social networking site (or overhaul your online presence if you already have a page).

Important Terms

How well do you know these terms? Define them here or in your journal, or look them up in the glossary to help you remember them.

blog	networking
brand	perception
cyber bullying	social networking sites

Online Resources

Tom Peters, "The Brand Called You"
www.fastcompany.com/magazine/10/brandyou.html

Dan Schawbel's personal branding blog
www.personalbrandingblog.com

Career Hub, advice from career experts on a variety of topics, including networking
www.careerhubblog.com/main

Exercises

Write your answers in your journal or on a separate piece of paper.

1. Identify someone in your field whom you admire—it could be the CEO of a leading company in your industry, or it could be someone you know personally who is working in the field—and write a paragraph or two in your journal summarizing that person's brand. Next, list five specific elements of the person's work, work product, communication style, presentation, or appearance that directly support the brand image.

2. Write down five standard questions that you can ask people in case you get stuck for something to say when you are networking. Form a group with a few students, and practice asking your questions. Remember that your demeanor as you listen to the other person's response is just as important as asking the question smoothly.

3. What can you do to make your brand stand out over the competition? List three unique qualities you have, and write a paragraph or two about each one, describing how you will showcase this quality during your job search.

Portions of this chapter's content include material adapted from Dan Schawbel, *Me 2.0* (New York: Kaplan, 2009).

12 | Preparing for the Job Search

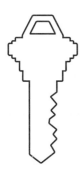

KEYS TO SUCCESS

- Obtaining the documents you need for your job search
- Knowing how to put together a list of references
- Ensuring that your job search documents are accurate, neatly presented, and error free
- Knowing what to expect from background checks and drug tests
- Presenting your information in a way that supports your career goals

In the movies, a job search always begins dramatically: the job seeker opens up the classified ads and circles prospects with a thick red pen, or begins calling companies and asking to talk to the boss.

In real life, job searches rarely work like this. Your job search actually begins long before you read your first job ad or send out that first resume. In fact, the more prepared you are when you start your job search, the shorter your search is likely to be. Doing research before you start sending out resumes will also make it more likely that the job you ultimately get is one that suits your particular skills, personality, and goals.

This chapter isn't about the job search process, but it can help you find work in your chosen career. This chapter is about what happens *before* you start the actual job search. It's about the all-important prep work you need to do so your search will go smoothly.

Your Background

Looking for a job is always challenging, and this is especially true for new graduates and people who are changing careers. That's why it's vitally important to be as organized and prepared as possible. This means assembling the documents that prospective employers will most likely ask for, including:

- **Transcripts.** Transcripts are typically obtained from your school. A complete set of transcripts will list your coursework and grades for your entire time at the school. Transcripts may or may not be requested by a prospective employer, but you should have an up-to-date copy of your transcripts easily available in case they are needed, especially considering that it often takes weeks to obtain them.

- **References.** References are people who can vouch for your character or other personal qualities that make you a good job prospect. References usually consist of instructors or past employers, although it might also be appropriate to include respected community members such as spiritual advisors or leaders of charities or service groups where you have donated time. Family members and friends are not appropriate references.

- **Resume.** Your resume is crucial. This document lists your relevant work and educational experience. Early in your career, your resume should be restricted to one page, free of grammatical errors and typos, and presented in a pleasing format using a traditional typeface. Resumes are discussed at length in Chapter 9, Resumes and Applications.

ON THE JOB

SCENARIO: You'll be graduating soon, and you are already planning the job search process. You can't think of anyone to use as a reference from your current job, because it's not in the same industry that you will be targeting in your search. What should you do?

QUICK FIX: Even if you are planning on finding work in a different field, you can still use current and former supervisors as references. They can confirm your general professionalism and reliability. You can also use people outside of work as references. Think about other people in positions of authority who might make good references, such as instructors, volunteer coordinators, coaches, and religious leaders.

Check and Double-Check

Obtaining all of the necessary information and assembling these documents will take some time, so it's best to begin long before you plan on sending out your first resume—say two months in advance. Keep all the information organized and easily accessible.

Transcripts can usually be obtained from your school's administration office. This is true for both high schools and colleges at every level. To make the process easier, check online to see if your school has a website directing you to the transcript office. Bear in mind that some schools take a while to generate a copy of your transcripts, and there might be a small fee attached.

When you put together your references, try to think of four or five credible individuals to list. Employers typically ask for three references, but it a good idea to have a few more lined up in case someone asks for more. Contact all references and get their permission before you list them; you need to check ahead of time to make sure they'll give you a good reference and to prepare them for a call by a prospective employer. Most people welcome the opportunity to serve as a reference, and it's very rare for individuals to agree to serve as your reference if they plan on giving a bad report. When you put together your list of references, make sure you include each person's name and job title, the name and address of the company where the person works, a phone number, and an email address.

Make sure that all the information in your documentation is absolutely accurate. Never "fudge" your GPA on your resume; in case your prospective employer requests your transcripts from your school, your deception will be immediately exposed. Never fake a reference by asking a friend to cover for you; it's easy for a prospective employer to uncover the truth here as well.

> **Practice Critical Thinking**
> Make a list of your skills and experiences. Which of them do you think are most appealing to your target employers? How can you highlight these most effectively?

Most employers are overwhelmed with job applications for every open position, and inaccuracies—even accidental ones—give the employer a good excuse to throw away your application without seriously considering it.

Drug Testing

Drug testing is a common component of job hunting and employment. Many employers routinely require drug testing for new job candidates. Industries that regularly drug-test include construction and any occupation that requires operation of heavy equipment, health care and allied health care professions such as medical and dental assistant positions, and jobs in education where you'll be working closely with children.

The best way to avoid losing your dream job because of a drug test is to avoid using illicit substances in the first place.

Employers use a number of technologies to perform drug tests:

- Urine analysis
- Hair analysis
- Breath analysis
- Oral fluid analysis

Of these, urine and hair tests are by far the most common. In many cases, samples for these tests are collected on-site, or in a dedicated laboratory, by a certified drug testing technician (DTT), who has experience in collecting samples and administering drug tests. These samples are typically sent to a lab that has experience in analyzing samples. In recent years, labs have grown more sophisticated, returning more positive results for people who attempted to cheat the drug test by some means or another.

Drug testing falls under state jurisdiction, which means there are no federal laws covering drug testing policy. However, most states allow employers to conduct drug testing on employees and prospective employees as part of a "drug-free workplace" policy. According to the Department of Labor, companies typically have "considerable latitude" over their drug testing policies. Most companies will keep a written "drug-free workplace" document that clearly details the company's notification policy and drug testing protocols.

Background Checks

In addition to drug testing, many employers conduct routine background checks. The Internet has made it easier than ever to dig deep into an applicant's background, so if you're worried about anything in your past, it's best to be up front about it. During the interview process, you might be asked to give written permission for a background check; your permission gives the employer legal standing to search records covering a variety of areas:

- Employment verification
- Driving record
- Social Security verification
- Military records
- Workman's compensation claims
- Credit report
- Civil claims
- Criminal history
- Prison record
- Registered sex offender status

You have the legal right to refuse to give permission for a background check, but during the job search process this may mean you won't get the job. If you are worried about a background check, address the things that can be fixed, such as poor credit or outstanding parking tickets, and investigate whether you can erase other black marks on your record.

Marketing Yourself

As you assemble your information and prepare for your job search, you're doing a very important task: you're creating your brand. Chapter 11 examined the concept of personal branding, which means deciding what you stand for in a professional sense and using every tool available to create and reinforce that brand.

As you embark on your job search, it's time to start spreading the word about your own brand. In other words, it's time to start marketing yourself.

The idea behind a successful job search is to convince a prospective employer that you have the perfect blend of personality, education, creativity, and experience to excel at the job you're trying to land. If you want to work as a plumber, this might mean you have attended a trade school or served as a journeyman plumber, you are familiar with the newest plumbing-related products on the market, you understand local building codes, and you're enthusiastic and excited about plumbing.

To accomplish this, you must carefully craft every element of your total package to show you in the best light.

Your skills. Whether you're promoting yourself to an employer through your experience or education, you want to show that you have the skills necessary to perform the job you want. But it's not necessarily a problem if you lack direct job experience. Part of marketing yourself is identifying valuable skills you already have and then showing how they relate to the job you want. For example, if you're hoping to work in the front office of a medical clinic, your experience as a hostess in a restaurant might show that you have the necessary people skills to deal with patients. Always look for ways you can relate your past skills to your present job aspirations, even if it seems to be a stretch.

Your education. Education is the stepping stone into your career. Although there are still occupations that can be obtained with a high school diploma or GED, these are increasingly rare. More and more companies require some form of higher education, whether it's a trade school, a two-year college, a four-year university, or an advanced degree. Make sure to showcase all relevant educational qualifications when you present yourself to a possible employer.

Your extracurricular activities. Just as colleges and universities seek well-rounded applicants, employers often like to know that their prospective employees are active. It's especially helpful if you're a member of one or more organizations related to your chosen career. An example is membership in a woodworking club or society if you want to work in carpentry. You can also use positive travel experiences, such as field trips, to reinforce your appeal. For example, any conventions or seminars you've attended in association with your chosen profession should be listed on your resume. The idea is to demonstrate your enthusiasm by showing that you continue to pursue your career even off the clock.

Volunteerism. A history of volunteering or donating your time in the service of others is always a good thing. In addition, the skills you developed working as a volunteer can be listed on your resume. If you've given a significant amount of time to nonprofits or an organization such as the American Cancer Society, make sure a potential employer knows about it (especially if it is related to your career). Just be careful to avoid political or religious discussions during a job interview.

Researching Potential Employers

Once you've assembled all this information and you've thought about how you want to present yourself, it's nearly time to actually begin your search. This can be an intimidating process, involving a lot of insecurity and nervousness. Job hunting will be covered more thoroughly in Chapter 13, Job Search Resources, but for now here's a good thing to remember:

Do your research before you start sending out resumes.

> **Workplace Tip**
>
> Do your research before you start the job hunt. Know what kind of company you want to work for, and find out all you can about the expectations for employees. Then make sure that you present yourself as the best possible candidate.

Many new job seekers make the mistake of plastering the world with their resumes with little regard for the companies they're actually approaching. It's much better to do the research first and then start your job search. This means finding out which companies you want to work for, and what makes those companies unique or special. Learn the names of the people who run the companies or do the hiring. Check out their products, their recent news, and even their competitors.

Although this might seem like a lot of work, it won't go unnoticed. Hiring managers appreciate a carefully considered and prepared job application, and they're much more likely to call back an applicant who seems well suited for the job.

Shannon Vargesko

KAPLAN SUCCESS STORY

McKeesport, Pennsylvania

Attended: Kaplan Career Institute—ICM Campus, Pittsburgh, Pennsylvania

Area of study: Business Administration Management

Employer: Administrative Assistant to the CFO, YMCA of Greater Pittsburgh

If you take one thing away from this course, it should be this: I do what I can in my 8 hour day, and leave the rest for the next. Prioritizing your responsibilities and staying organized makes this easier to achieve.

Kaplan provided the bridge that guided me to becoming a professional, as well as the opportunity for growth as an individual. Kaplan teachers have real world experience and tips that they share with their class.

Chapter Summary

- It's important to assemble all the information employers might need, including transcripts, references, and resume, *before* you start your job search.

- A reference list should include four or five people who can speak about your professional qualifications. References generally come in the form of instructors or past employers; friends and family members shouldn't be used as references.

- All the materials you use in your job search should be presented in a professional way.

- Pre-employment drug testing and background checks are routinely required by companies.

- Your skills, education, and extracurricular activities should be presented in a way that emphasizes your qualifications for working in your target field.

To-Do List

☐ List five people you can use as references and contact them.

☐ Obtain copies of your transcripts.

☐ Clean up your record where you can to remove references to credit problems and outstanding legal issues.

Important Terms

How well do you know these terms? Define them here or in your journal, or look them up in the glossary to help you remember them.

reference   **transcript**

Online Resources

Monster.com, offers popular job-search function in addition to other job-hunting resources
career-advice.monster.com/job-search/careers.aspx

Job Search Tips (from About.com)
jobsearch.about.com/cs/jobsearchhelp/a/jobtips.htm

Job-Hunting & Business Etiquette Resources
www.quintcareers.com/job-hunting_etiquette.html

Exercises

Write your answers in your journal or on a separate piece of paper.

1. Identify a few companies where you'd like to work and write up a short profile of each company, including its biggest products, its competitors, and who manages the company. Store this information with all your job search material so that you can refer back to it when you begin sending out resumes.

2. In your journal, write about five things you can do to improve your list of references or your non-work background. If necessary, do some research on local opportunities for volunteering.

3. Write a one-page essay about how your job field has changed in the past ten years and how you expect it to change in the next ten years. In what ways do you expect that skills needed to enter the field will have to change?

13 | Job Search Resources

KEYS TO SUCCESS

- Identifying companies where you'd like to work
- Keeping detailed notes on companies you are interested in
- Using a variety of job search resources to locate job openings
- Expanding your career network
- Preparing a one-minute "elevator pitch" to use as a quick introduction
- Being persistent and staying positive

You're finally ready to begin your job search. You've got your resume and all your documentation in place. You've got your transcripts and references lined up. You've been practicing the way you present yourself and you've been researching your industry.

Now what?

Finding good leads on desirable jobs can be a daunting prospect. This chapter will help direct you to the best resources to track down good job openings. Finding the right opening at the right time is at least half the battle; in show business, they say that timing is everything, and the same might be said for job hunting.

Doing the Research

The first step is to start collecting information on the companies and industries you're interested in. This means answering some pretty big questions:

1. What's the best way to get started in your career?

2. Which are the best companies in your target industry?

3. Who is hiring right now, and which positions are open?

4. Are you willing to relocate if necessary? How important is geography in your job hunt?

Gathering the answers to these questions requires not only careful thinking about your own goals, but also research and an organizational system to keep track of your findings. As you dig deeper, you'll discover the best places to unearth information on your target companies.

Most companies maintain a strong online presence; important information about a company can be found on its website. The first place to look is the "About Us" description, and then check press releases or the media area, where you may come across annual reports and economic data on public companies. Many companies have a career page on their website where they post job openings and current opportunities; if so, you are in luck.

Other resources include the library, where you can consult comprehensive reference books on industries and companies, your local newspaper, and job placement agency documents.

As you're doing your research, you'll uncover a great deal of information to keep track of and organize. There are many ways to organize this type of information. You can set up a folder on your hard drive and save documents to that folder. You can also create a physical folder, using a simple filing system with manila file folders to store printouts and copies. If you're looking at several companies, consider setting up a file or folder for each company.

Job Search Tip

As you research companies, use the following checklist to make sure you've covered the basics:

- Products or services the company offers
- Size of the company
- Names of the company's competitors
- Company's rank in the industry
- Company type (public or private)
- Key people
- Relevant information pertaining to your particular position

Your notes should contain detailed information covering these items for each company.

You also need to develop a system for keeping track of the jobs that you've applied for. Document the name of the company, the position that you applied for, the date you applied, and the name of the person you contacted. Save copies of your resumes, cover letters, and applications as you submit them.

Finding Your Ideal Job

The best place to start your job search is online, usually by checking the following resources:

> **Practice Critical Thinking**
> Human resource departments that advertise online often receive hundreds of applications for every opening they post, so it's very important to make sure you stand out from the competition. What are some things you can do to make yourself stand out, in a positive way?

- **Monster.com.** Monster.com is one of the largest job search engines on the Internet, with job postings all over the country. You can tailor your search in a number of ways, including by salary, industry, geography, experience level, or some other parameter. However, Monster offers more than classified ads. You can also post your resume on Monster, read job search tips, and access additional resources on the site, such as information about companies.

- **CareerBuilder.com.** Like Monster, CareerBuilder is a large, national job search engine. CareerBuilder also allows you to narrowly target your job search to specific regions, industries, companies, and salary levels. You can post your resume on CareerBuilder, sign up for alerts, and access the site's tips on job searching and resume building.

- **HotJobs.com.** HotJobs.com is another national job search engine that allows carefully tailored job searches and resume posting, as well as tips on job searching plus company and industry information.

- **Craigslist.org.** Craigslist is a national site that posts classified ads, including job listings. You can search job listings by city and also by industry.

- **Indeed.com.** Indeed.com is an aggregator, meaning that it reposts job information from a wide variety of sources, including newspaper classifieds, company websites, job boards, and other places on the Internet.

- **LinkUp.com.** LinkUp posts jobs from company websites, including small, medium, and large companies. The postings are automatically updated whenever the company updates its website.

- **SimplyHired.com.** SimplyHired posts job information from a wide variety of sources, including company sites, job boards, and classified ads.

Tips for Maximizing Your Online Job Search

There's a reason people turn to online job searches: they're extremely effective. The Internet allows you to quickly locate huge numbers of classified ads and narrowly target your job search. But even with this tremendous power, there are still things you need to do to maximize the effectiveness of your online job search.

ON THE JOB

SCENARIO: You want a new job, but you're not sure where to start looking. Every time you try to use a job search engine, you get hundreds of results, but not the ones you want. What should you do?

QUICK FIX: You probably aren't narrowing your search enough. Try sorting your search results by keyword, industry, city, or salary level. Precisely targeting the kind of work you want can save a lot of time.

First and most important, keep checking. In fact, you should check your favorite sites every morning, and immediately respond to any promising ads. Don't just check a site once, send off your resume, and then wait for something to happen. Keep looking.

Online job boards are updated on a daily basis, and often the newest ads will yield the best results. These are the companies that have just begun actively looking for new people. If you're among the first to respond, your application will be among the first they'll seriously consider.

> ### Job Search Tip
>
> Don't sit back just because you sent one resume to a prospective employer and you're dead set on getting that particular job. Continue your efforts. That way, if your dream job doesn't materialize, you'll have other options (and less disappointment).

Second, don't limit yourself to one or two sites. True, you'll probably see some overlap among the various sites; some of the sites pull classifieds from the same sources. But you should still make it a point to visit multiple sites when you're job hunting. You don't want to miss that perfect job because you checked only two or three sites. Bookmark the top five or six and visit them all daily.

Finally, establish a presence on the job sites. Create a profile and post your resume so that potential employers can view it. You never know when someone will be looking.

Your Career Network

Now it's time to find out how online networking can actually help you land the job you want. Chapter 11 examined social networking sites and other online resources that can be used for networking with professionals in your field. As you saw, online networking is a great way to build your brand, learn more about your target industry, and receive career advice from those currently working in the field. It's also a great job search asset.

The importance of a healthy career network is hard to overstate. People in your network might not be hiring, or might not work for companies that are hiring, but if you stay active in your network you'll be more likely to hear about openings and get insider tips on companies you want to work for. Referrals are a great way to find a job—so leave yourself open to as many referrals as possible.

There are some basic rules for using a career network online. First, you have to pay attention to your network. This means keeping updated contacts and continually adding new people you meet.

You also need to remain active on your site even when you are not looking for a job. You know that annoying friend who calls only when he or she needs a favor? You don't want to be that friend. It's a bad idea to reach out to your network only when you need something. Make sure to drop in every so often, if only to update your status, send a quick "hello" email, or post interesting articles and news items related to your industry.

> ### Practice Critical Thinking
> If you want to get into a different field, what are some ways to expand your career network to include people who are working in your new target industry?

Ultimately, online networking is a two-way street. If you continue to pay attention to your network when you don't need it, and you show your willingness to help the people in your network, they'll be much more likely to help you when you are looking for a job.

Career-Oriented Networking Sites

Of all the social networking sites, perhaps the most rewarding for prospective job hunters is LinkedIn.com. Unlike Facebook, Twitter, and MySpace, which mix in social interaction and can be used for business networking, LinkedIn is purposely designed to be a tool for business people.

Once you sign up for LinkedIn, you can post your current position, search by name for people you know, and make online connections with people at target companies and through referrals. Increasingly, companies are turning to LinkedIn networks to find applicants and referrals. This is happening because LinkedIn provides instant recommendations and resumes for anyone in the network.

If you plan on joining only one career-oriented networking site, LinkedIn is probably the best choice. But of course, it's a good idea to spread your networking efforts among several networks—the higher the profile you maintain, the more likely you are to be discovered.

Offline Job Hunting

Plenty of people still find work through newspaper ads and traditional job search venues. In fact, newspaper ads are often the best place to find part-time or local jobs; some local companies avoid the big online job search engines because they don't want to get swamped with resumes from across the country. Other traditional sources for want ads include professional journals and trade magazines.

Beyond the want ads, there are a number of ways to look for work without ever turning on a computer. One of the most popular methods is to attend job fairs, also known as career fairs. These events are designed to bring together employers and prospective candidates. They are typically advertised ahead of time in local newspapers, on radio stations, on television, and online. If you are uncertain where to find a local job fair, search online for the keywords "job fair" and your city or location.

Job fairs are often targeted at particular types of employees—for instance, college students, health care workers, construction workers, or women in the workforce.

The idea of attending a job fair can be intimidating. They are often crowded and noisy, with people lined up for brief face-to-face meetings with company representatives. It can seem like choosing the rollercoaster at a theme park: an hour of waiting for one minute of adrenaline and activity. And it can be scary to think about what it will take to distinguish yourself among the crowds of people.

But people find work at job fairs all the time—and you can too. Here are some tips for a successful job fair experience:

Job Search Tip

A job fair can be an excellent opportunity to polish your interviewing skills. Instead of sending out resumes and waiting to be contacted, attending a job fair guarantees that you'll be able to speak to company representatives on the spot. Consider attending a job fair even if your dream employer is not participating in the fair. Start with employers that you are less interested in, and use this as an opportunity to practice answering standard interview questions.

- Bring multiple copies of your resume, paper and pens, and business cards if you have them. The whole point of a job fair is to get your information into the hands of hiring companies, so make sure you're prepared.

- Dress professionally, but wear comfortable shoes. You'll want to project a professional aura, but keep in mind that you'll probably be on your feet for a long time, so make sure you're wearing shoes that won't blister your feet or ruin your disposition.

- Prepare a one-minute "elevator pitch." At a typical job fair, one minute might be all the time you get. So imagine you're in an elevator with a hiring representative from the company of your choice, and you have only that elevator ride to convince him to hire you. Practice this speech prior to the job fair until you have it memorized and can deliver it comfortably and flawlessly.

■ Be assertive. Sure, the crowds can be intimidating, but the only way to get noticed is to be in the right place to get noticed. But don't be rude, pushy, or angry. Job fairs can be long, exhausting ordeals, filled with tension and nerves. But never let your sour mood show. Present yourself as an enthusiastic, friendly person with goals.

Employment Agencies and Headhunters

Employment agencies, search firms, and headhunters are professionals or companies that help people find work. There are, however, differences in the way they operate.

Employment agencies are companies that typically fill low- to mid-level jobs. Some employment agencies charge the job seeker, while others are paid by the company. In general, most job search experts recommend against paying an employment agency to help you find work. There are too many ways to find work on your own to justify paying someone else to help.

Like employment agencies, search firms are companies that help people find work. Search firms differ in the way they are paid. Some are paid only when their candidate is hired by a company. These kinds of firms often collect huge databases of resumes and send large numbers of them to companies in need of new employees. It's a good idea to file your resume with search firms that specialize in your target industry.

A second kind of search firm typically aims at higher-level jobs. These search firms are known as "retainer firms," and they are hired by companies to fill executive-level positions. Retainer firms are often hired to fill specific positions, and they are typically paid a percentage of the position's salary, whether or not they fill the position.

Finally, the term "headhunter" is used to describe an employment specialist who helps people find new jobs. Headhunters often work for search firms. The best headhunters are like career coaches—they can help position you to get the best jobs, negotiate salaries, and alert you to new possibilities in your industry. Often, headhunters specialize in particular industries and become intimately acquainted with the companies and people in their business specialty.

Using Temporary Agencies

A temporary agency, or temp agency, is a company that fills short-term positions, often office jobs. Some temp agencies also specialize in the trades and can help fill temporary openings in skilled trades such as HVAC, carpentry, and plumbing.

Companies call upon temp agencies for a variety of reasons. A permanent employee may have gone on an extended medical leave or on maternity leave. Perhaps the company has a major project that must get done, or is experiencing a one-time surge in business that requires extra help.

Temp work can be an important part of your career plan. First, temp agencies provide paying work that can be added to your resume for future applications. Additionally, companies are often willing to provide good references for skilled and effective temps. If your resume is

> **Job Search Tip**
>
> Although consulting company websites is a key part of any job search, it's a good idea to keep a broad job search strategy. Surfing haphazardly through innumerable company websites and job boards can be counterproductive if you neglect other strategies. Aim for balance: add job fairs, networking, and employment agencies to the mix.

thin, a temp agency might be a good way to start getting experience and building your resume and references. Second, more companies are using temp agencies to find permanent employees, or "temp-to-perm" positions. Many times, excellent temps are offered a permanent job in the company, and their employment is transferred from the temp agency to the company itself.

Internships

For students in particular, internships are a great way to get a foot in the door, gain valuable experience, and begin to build a career network. An internship is typically a low-paying or non-paying temporary stint with a company. Interns are often assigned relatively low-skill tasks in the field, but an effort is usually made to expose interns to the actual workings of the business. Internships are a great way to see how real companies operate and to get a feel for the type of work that takes place in that industry.

More important, for many students internships are the only real-life work experience they get in their field immediately after graduation.

Finding open internships is often as easy as contacting your school's placement office or checking with a faculty member in your department. Businesses typically maintain close relationships with colleges as a way to locate good interns.

The major drawback to internships is financial. Many students struggle in internships because of the low pay (or lack of pay). However, if you can manage it, internships are an excellent way to land a full-time job—it's not uncommon for companies to hire good interns after the internship is over.

Professional Organizations

Professional organizations are large groups dedicated to particular industries. These organizations are often supported by membership dues. Professional organizations provide a number of services to their members, including publishing trade magazines and professional journals, hosting conventions and trade shows, and lobbying the government on behalf of the industry.

But professional organizations are also excellent resources for job seekers. Most organizations maintain a website with job boards. In addition to using job search engines, you should visit the job boards of your professional organization. Professional organizations are also great networking venues. The whole organization is composed of people in your field, many of whom are experienced professionals with excellent contacts throughout the industry.

The downside to professional organizations is cost (there are often member's dues), and in some cases membership is restricted to people already working in the industry. If you can't join the organization, you still might be able to access the job boards, and it's also a good idea to look for student memberships. Many professional organizations allow students to join at reduced rates, despite a lack of industry experience.

Michael Earl Ball

El Paso, Texas

Attended: Career Centers of Texas—El Paso, Texas

Area of study: Electrical Technician

Employer: Apprentice Electrician

If you take one thing away from this course, it should be this: Take responsibility for your actions, for in anything you try, if the job is going to get done, someone must take the responsibility.

Kaplan gave me the tools necessary to succeed in locating a job as an apprentice electrician. The college also gave me the tools for problem solving, not only as an electrician, but in my day to day life.

A Final Tip

As you look for a job, remember to be resourceful and persistent. This means preparing yourself beforehand, using all the tools available, doing research into your chosen industry and local companies, staying organized, and networking with people who already work at the job you want.

Chapter Summary

- Before you start sending out resumes, think about your goals and target the kind of company that you are interested in.

- Online job search engines are powerful tools, allowing you to locate thousands of job openings and narrowly tailor your search to include only those that are most relevant.

- Classifieds and ads in trade journals are excellent resources.

- Networking is a great way to learn about openings that may not be posted on job sites or in the classifieds.

- Temp agencies, employment agencies, and job fairs are other resources to consider when you are looking for a job.

To-Do List

☐ Check out all the major job search engines. Construct a profile at each and post your resume.

☐ Research major professional and trade organizations in your industry. Find out how you can join.

☐ Try to make five new career contacts every week and expand your career network.

☐ Visit the library to see which trade magazines and journals in your field are available there.

☐ Research upcoming local job fairs and write down the dates. Make preparations to attend.

☐ Research local employment agencies. Call a few to see if they're a good fit for you.

☐ Create a system for keeping track of all the jobs that you have applied for. Document the name of the company, the position that you applied for, the date you applied, and the name of the person you contacted. Save copies of your resumes, cover letters, and applications as you submit them.

Important Terms

How well do you know these terms? Define them here or in your journal, or look them up in the glossary to help you remember them.

employment agency

headhunter

internship

job fair

temporary agency

trade journal

Online Resources

JobSearch.About.com, contains links to major job search engines, as well as tips for job hunting at all levels
jobsearch.about.com

Job-Hunt.org, offers links to employers, state agencies, and classified ads, as well as resources for job seekers
www.job-hunt.org

The Art of Career and Job-Search Networking, offers tips about networking and many links to tools for networking
www.quintcareers.com/networking.html

Exercises

Write your answers in your journal or on a separate piece of paper.

1. Create an online profile that you can post to various job search engines.

2. Visit all the major job search engines and create a list of the strengths and weaknesses of each, including which features they offer and how customizable their search is.

3. In your journal, list ten people you would like to include in your career network, and write a short paragraph describing how you might reach two of those people and form a connection.

Portions of this chapter's content include material adapted from Brenda Greene, *Get the Interview Every Time*, revised and expanded edition (New York: Kaplan, 2008).

14 | Interviews

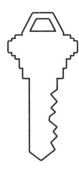

KEYS TO SUCCESS

- Identifying your strengths and planning ways to express them during an interview
- Researching questions that are typically asked at interviews
- Developing answers to standard interview questions
- Researching nonstandard interview questions and developing answers to those questions
- Practicing your answers until you can deliver them smoothly and confidently
- Knowing how to respond to a job offer

So the phone has finally rung. All that work—preparing yourself, tracking down leads, and sending out applications and resumes—has finally paid off, and you've landed a job interview.

Suddenly, everything seems possible . . . you might have a new job in just a matter of days. And you can head into the interview with a measure of confidence: Out of all the resumes they looked at, all the job candidates that made it across the hiring manager's desk, yours was one of the best. Time is too precious for companies to waste time interviewing job candidates they aren't serious about, which means you've got a real shot at getting this job.

Up to this point, you've only been a set of facts and qualifications on paper. Your resume and cover letter have done all your speaking for you. At the interview, by contrast, the company isn't just looking at your qualifications. It will be looking at *you* and trying to decide if you're a good match with the company's goals, direction, and philosophy.

Your task now switches to interview preparation and performance. The better prepared you are, the more likely you are to make it over this final hurdle.

A job interview is not a place to "wing it." Imagine you are interviewing people to work on your house. The first group shows up with detailed knowledge of your neighborhood and local building codes, carefully listens to your requirements, then proposes a detailed plan for getting the job done.

The second group shows up late because the driver got lost on the way over. Once they get there, the basic attitude is, "Don't worry about it. We'll take care of everything." When you ask specific questions, the contractor provides vague answers and reveals that he doesn't know much about the neighborhood or the local codes and doesn't have much of a plan for getting your job done.

Which one would you hire?

The same thing happens in job interviews. Anybody who has interviewed large numbers of job candidates inevitably has stories about poorly prepared candidates, wildly inappropriate interview behavior, and applicants who completely misrepresented themselves on paper. You don't want to be one of these stories.

Job Search Tip

Once you start sending out resumes, expect that you will be getting phone calls not only from friends and family, but also now from people who are interested in hiring you. Make sure your voice mail message is appropriate—this is not the time for cute songs or funny messages. A simple message stating your name or your number along with a request for the caller to leave a message is fine.

Preparing for Your Interview

Hopefully, your preparation began long before you actually got the interview. With any luck, you'll already be familiar with the company you're interviewing with, so you'll have a pretty good knowledge base to start from. But even so, here are some steps you should take before the interview:

1. Do your research. Check the company's website and news reports to see if anything significant has happened since you sent in the application. If it's a public company, you can also check the stock price. Ideally, when you walk into the interview, you'll be current on what's happening at the company, including any major leadership changes, new product launches, and noteworthy business activities.

2. Plan your interview strategy. Once you become more familiar with the company and the job you're applying for, you can begin to work on your interview strategy. You want to highlight the specific strengths that you bring to the company.

3. Practice, practice, practice. You'll definitely want to work on your interview presentation, from handshakes to answers to tough questions. Don't go in unprepared!

Types of Interviews

When most people think of job interviews, they think of the traditional individual or group interview. But those aren't the only kinds of job interviews. Your interview might take any of the following formats:

- **Individual interviews.** Your first individual interview will usually be with someone from the company's human resources (HR) department. If that interview goes well, you will meet directly with a hiring manager or the supervisor to whom you will report.

- **Group or panel interview.** There are two kinds of group interviews. In the first kind, you will meet with a representative group from the company. Common attendees from the company include human resource staffers, department supervisors, and employees from the department you applied to. In the second kind of group interview, job applicants are interviewed in a group to move the process along faster.

- **Dining or social interviews.** In this kind of interview, you will meet with company representatives in an informal social setting, possibly at dinner or lunch. These kinds of interviews tend to last longer and have a less formal air than an individual or group interview.

- **Video interviews.** Some companies conduct interviews by video teleconference. During a video interview, you might be asked to go to a local videoconferencing facility, where you'll interview with company representatives over teleconference. This interview style is convenient and less costly for employees who don't live nearby, but presents a challenge because it lacks the personal factor.

- **Phone interviews.** Phone interviews are common as the first step in the interview process because they allow companies to screen a large number of candidates fairly quickly. Many companies prefer to conduct quick phone interviews before calling candidates in for physical interviews. Frequently a human resources manager will make the call, not necessarily the hiring manager. Phone interviews are the most convenient, but they are the least personal. They do have some advantages, however. During a phone interview, you can spread out your resume and your prepared answers in plain view to help prompt you during the interview. Also, you can easily and freely take notes during the interview. Even though phone interviews are typically pre-interviews, prepare for a phone interview just as you would an in-person interview—if you land a personal interview, you'll have a chance to use all the preparation again.

Traditional Interviews versus Behavioral Interviews

Interview formats are not the same from company to company, so be prepared for whatever kind of interview the company prefers. In traditional interviews, job applicants have been asked questions such as, "What is your greatest strength?" or "Where do you see yourself in five years?" By answering these questions, the applicant reveals his or her background, goals, and ambitions.

A newer kind of interview is the behavioral interview. During a behavioral interview, the company is less concerned with your specific background and more concerned with your skills and actual job experience. Behavioral interviews are based on the idea that previous performance is more important than aspirations, so candidates are asked specific and detailed questions, such as, "How have you reacted to a major crisis at work?" or "Tell us how you handled an intraoffice conflict."

Unless you know for certain what kind of interview you'll be facing, it's best to prepare yourself for any and all kinds of interviews. During your interview practice sessions, make sure you include both traditional and behavioral questions.

Staging Mock Interviews

One of the best things you can do to prepare is to set up mock interviews before you actually interview. During a real job interview, it's normal to be nervous and perhaps forget what you're planning to say. But if you've already practiced your greeting, handshake, and answers beforehand, it'll be much easier to remember once the pressure is on.

During a mock interview, it's important to act as if the real interview is actually taking place. Dress as you plan to for the real interview, take along your resume, notepad and pen, and present yourself just as you plan to during the actual interview.

Choose an interview partner who is willing to take the task seriously. Beforehand, you can provide your interview partner with a list of possible questions, and encourage him or her to ask hard and unexpected questions also. Ideally, your practice interview should be tougher than the real interview—there's no harm in being overprepared.

The most common questions asked at interviews—and the ones that you should be totally prepared for—are:

What would you like to tell me about yourself?

Why do you want to work here?

Your response to the first of these questions should take less than 60 seconds, and it should highlight your positive qualities. This response should never be about your dislikes, only what you do like and what you're enthusiastic about. For the second question, include at least one specific fact that you know about the company. Also include at least one specific fact about the kind of work you think you'll be doing.

Other typical interview questions might include:

1. Why did you leave your last job?

2. What did you like or dislike about your last job?

3. Why are you looking for a new job?

4. What major challenges have you faced at work and how did you overcome them?

5. What was your relationship like with your last supervisor?

6. What was your relationship like with your colleagues?

7. What do you hope to get from your work experience here?

8. What are your long-term goals for your career?

9. Have you ever been fired? Why?

10. What are your greatest strengths and weaknesses?

11. Are you willing to work weekends and nights if the job demands it?

12. What is your view on the balance between work and family?

13. What do your friends say is your best quality? Your worst quality?

14. Are you a team player, or do you prefer to work alone?

15. What are your salary requirements?

16. How much did you make at your last job?

And these are just a few examples. There are hundreds of questions that might come up during interviews. You might have heard stories about silly interview questions, too, such as "What kind of animal do you most strongly identify with?" Although they're not standard, questions like this do crop up from time to time.

Your goal during mock interviews—and during the interview itself—is to handle any question thrown at you. Some interviewers like to try to throw off their interview subjects to see how they react to the unexpected or surprising. The best way to handle this is to be carefully prepared for even the most difficult or unexpected questions.

> ### Job Search Tip
> Go into an interview prepared with a 60-second story about yourself. It should include your experience, your skills, and your cultural fit with the company. It might also include a brief recollection of how you got interested in your field or how you heard about the company.

Handling Tough Questions

It's a virtual guarantee: if you go on enough job interviews, a question will pop up that doesn't have an easy answer. Or there may be some events in your past that are difficult to explain and don't reflect well on your status as an employee. Such events include firings, criminal convictions, harassment issues, or serious conflict with previous co-workers.

You have to be prepared to answer these kinds of questions. With modern background checking (see Chapter 12, Preparing for the Job Search), employers can quickly and easily find out a tremendous amount of information about your past. Legal issues are typically a matter of public record and can be easily obtained. Bankruptcies can be quickly discovered during simple credit checks, and problems with your previous employer can be sleuthed out during reference checks.

And if you refuse to provide references from a former employer, be prepared to explain why.

The first thing to know when you're dealing with tough questions is to always tell the truth. You have to assume that your potential employer is likely to find out the real story, and lying during the interview is a sure way to lose the job.

Second, tackle the issue head-on. Tell the story, along with any repercussions or consequences that resulted. There are always two sides to every story, so make sure that you calmly and politely explain your perspective. But don't make excuses for yourself or become accusatory. This is the time for an explanation, not an excuse.

> ## Practice Critical Thinking
>
> What would be a tough interview question for you? How will you respond to the question if it's asked?

Finally, don't dwell on the negative aspects of it. If you learned a valuable life-lesson from a previous job conflict, let your interviewer know that. Let the interviewer see your integrity and your ability to learn. Instead of viewing the event as a negative that must be hidden, view it as an opportunity to show how far you've grown and how your current goals and ambitions have been shaped and tested by events in your past.

Remember, no one has lived a perfect life, and chances are, your prospective employer will relate at least on some level to your past situation and respect your effort and courage in viewing challenges as opportunities for growth.

Asking Your Own Questions

With all this on your mind, it's easy to forget that your job interview is a two-way conversation. During the interview, the company isn't only measuring you to see if you are a good fit, it's also your chance to get a good look at the company and see if you really want to work there. No matter how badly you need a job, taking a job out of desperation at a dishonest company or signing on in a hostile work environment can only be a negative in the long run. Just as companies are trying to weed out unfit applicants, you want to weed out negative companies.

Potential employers welcome questions during the interview process. An applicant who has detailed knowledge of a company and asks perceptive questions about the company's culture, market, and goals is more likely to get the job than a candidate who seems incurious about the company.

Here are some of the questions you might consider asking:

1. What would be my various responsibilities?

2. Whom would I be reporting to?

3. What are the opportunities for growth in this position?

4. How would you describe the culture of the company?

5. Why is this job open? Where did the previous employee go?

6. What kind of management style does the company believe in?

7. Does the company prefer to advance from within?

8. How long will it take for you to make a hiring decision?

Once again, these are just a few of the possible questions you might consider asking. Be careful, however, in what you ask—even curiosity has its limits, and the job interview is a place to be enthusiastic, open, and ambitious. During the interview, don't try to bargain for immediate vacation time, schedule changes, telecommuting, or other privileges that are usually reserved for long-time employees. The only situation in which it's acceptable to bring these issues up is if they are deal-breakers, such as being unable to work after 5 p.m. because you have to pick up your child from daycare.

Questions That Cannot Be Asked

Although the purpose of a job interview is to match potential employees with employers, there are certain questions that cannot be asked of a prospective employee. Federal and state laws have identified a number of areas that are considered private and not connected to your qualifications to perform the job (see Table 14.1). These include questions about race, color, age, religion, marital status, citizenship, disabilities, and birthplace.

Employers who ask these questions are likely breaking antidiscrimination laws. If you are asked an inappropriate question, you can answer it, or you can try to avoid it. Be aware that if you refuse to answer the question, it might cost you the job—but intrusive personal questions are usually a symptom of an underlying mindset at the company and should be seen as a red flag.

If you believe that you were asked inappropriate personal questions during an interview, and you lost out on the job because of those questions, you can file a discrimination claim against the company after the interview is over. This is a sensitive legal area, however, and will likely require the assistance of a lawyer.

Table 14.1 Illegal vs. Legal Interview Questions

Topic	Illegal Questions	Legal Questions
Race	Any question asked to indicate race is illegal.	Employer can ask about race for statistical purposes *only* after hiring.
Age	Any question about your age or date of birth, or any question with an answer that would indirectly indicate your age.	If hired, can you give proof of age? (if hiring depends on being an adult or being less than retirement age)
Religion	Any direct questions about religion, and questions on whether you can work on religious holidays.	Employer can tell you what hours are required for the job and ask if you can meet them.
Marital status	It's illegal to ask about marital status, number of children, pregnancy, or child care arrangements.	Employer can tell you what hours are required for the job and ask if you can meet them.
Citizenship/birthplace/ancestry	Are your parents native born or naturalized? What country are you a citizen of?	Are you a U.S. citizen? If not, do you intend to become one?
Disabilities	Questions about disabilities are legal *only* if the employer can prove that those questions are directly related to the performance of the job.	

Interview Tips

Although asking and answering questions forms the heart of your job interview, a job interview is much more than a laundry list of questions about your background, ambitions, and skills. In fact, you are being judged as a potential candidate from the moment you are introduced to your interviewers—and even if interviewers aren't consciously aware of it, their perception of you as a future employee will be shaped by many nonverbal clues.

These are some of the things that you should avoid during an interview:

- **Poor communication.** If you need a few seconds to carefully consider your answer, go ahead and think it out before answering. There's nothing wrong with looking thoughtful and deliberate. However, poor communication skills are almost certain to cost you the job. You should avoid slang, swearing, mumbling, or talking too fast. Try to present yourself in clear, declarative sentences.

- **Unsuitable attire.** Interview attire should be professional and not call attention to itself. Although proper attire varies from industry to industry—interviewing for a job on a construction crew might not require a suit or a tie, but rather dress pants with a neatly tucked-in, long-sleeved dress shirt (don't forget the belt, and polish those shoes)—there are certain standards for business dress you should observe. And if you're not sure, err on the side of being overdressed. Things to avoid wearing to an interview include jeans, revealing clothing such as short skirts or skimpy tops, visible underwear or bra straps, your favorite "joke tie," flip-flops and sandals, and tight or low-cut pants or skirts that expose the midriff. The best option is often to choose a classic, dark-colored business suit. If you don't have one, this might be a good time to make the investment. You can wear it to all your interviews.

- **Poor intrapersonal skills.** Intrapersonal skills determine how you relate to other people, including your interviewers. A strong, confident communicator has excellent intrapersonal skills. He or she looks people in the eye during introductions and conversation, shakes hands firmly but not aggressively, listens attentively, answers in an even tone of voice, smiles easily, and sits upright and comfortably. Try to avoid slouching, leaning back, crossing your arms, laughing too loud or uncomfortably, wiggling and nervously fidgeting, interrupting your interviewer, and grimacing or frowning at questions you don't like.

- **Offensive odors and bad habits.** Smell is a surprisingly important element in the way people relate to each other. Besides the obvious—being clean and showered—there are a few odors or habits that will reflect poorly on you. If you smoke, abstain before arriving at the interview if possible—most companies are smoke-free environments, and the smell of tobacco is strong and off-putting for some. Avoid heavy fragrance and meals loaded with garlic or other strong spices just before an interview. Do use breath-freshening mints *before* you enter the building for the interview. Never interview with anything in your mouth.

- **Being late.** Avoid being late at all costs. Some companies will even refuse to interview job candidates who show up late to their interview, thinking that if you can't be bothered to make the interview on time, why would you show up for work on time? It's best to arrive ten or fifteen minutes early. If you have to wait in the lobby or parking lot because you're a little bit too early, take the time to practice your answers and relax.

Controlling Your Nerves

Job interviews can be nerve-wracking, even for experienced professionals. Employers expect some nerves, and it's not going to sink you if you flub a couple words or show a few signs of nervousness.

But serious nerves will not help. In a sense, the job interview is a performance, and you're the star. Signs of nervousness include sweating, shaking, and stuttering. Nervous people are also less likely to pick up on subtle social cues and are more prone to making mistakes like laughing at inappropriate times or drifting off and not retaining the last few sentences that were said.

Interview Tip
It'll be less stressful if you know where you're going before you head off for your interview. Make a practice run ahead of time so you know the exact location of the company where you're interviewing. Check out the area and think about things that could cause delays. Will there be a lot of traffic? Will it be easy to find parking? Plan accordingly.

If you're worried about nerves, take a few steps to control your nerves.

- Memorize a few standard lines. This is where practice comes in handy. When people are nervous, they sometimes reach for words but come up blank, which only increases the nerves. Before the interview, memorize your answers to standard interview questions, especially if you think the questions will be asked early on. This will help you get through those first hard moments.

- Practice your breathing. Deep breathing works. If you start getting nervous, take a few deep breaths. Breathe in through your nose and out your mouth. Imagine your nerves flowing out with each exhale.

- Eat a good meal before the interview. Don't go in hungry.

- Avoid too much caffeine. A morning cup of coffee might be a good thing, but don't load up on an unusual amount of caffeine. It will only aggravate your nerves.

- Get a good night's sleep. The night before the interview, make sure you get a solid night's sleep so you're well rested at the interview.

Discussions of Salary and Benefits

At some point during the interview, the subject of salary and benefits will arise. Obviously, this is a critical issue for both employers and employees. You should include this all-important matter in your research. Before the interview, research how much similar positions typically pay in your area. You can perform this kind of research online (see the Online Resources section for a link to a salary wizard).

Once you've done your research, and you head into the interview, there are a few important things to keep in mind. Don't bring up salary; wait for the interviewer to mention it. Employers are interested in you because you're qualified and enthusiastic and can perform the job they need done. If you make it seem like you're only interested in money, you put yourself at risk to lose the job.

In fact, it's a good idea to avoid a salary discussion until an actual job offer is made. In many companies, the people conducting the interviews are not the ones who determine the salary. You might be interviewing with your future colleagues and supervisor. The job offer might come from a senior manager, a company owner, or even a human resources executive. They will include salary and benefits information as part of the job offer.

Salary is a sensitive issue for any employer. Most companies go to great lengths to keep salary information confidential—nothing will destroy morale in a company like people finding out that certain co-workers make more money or have a better benefits package. This is why you should only discuss salary once they bring it up, with the appropriate person. And it's never right to share salary and wage information about other people in the company, even if you happen to have this information.

Benefits offered by the employer are usually standard, applying to all employees, and you usually can't negotiate them. It is a good idea, though, to find out about retirement plans, health insurance, time-off policies, and other benefits. (See Chapter 19, Managing

Finances, for more detail.) All these benefits are worth money, so you need to take them into account in any negotiations.

Salary negotiations can be tense, so keep your cool and don't make hasty decisions. Through your research, you'll have an idea what you're worth before the interview and what comparable jobs offer. Once a job offer is made, you no longer have to worry you're a qualified candidate—they've already decided you are. It's always a good idea to take some time to consider the offer. You can say, "Thank you so much. I need a little time to think about it." Then, be prepared to settle on a day to get back to them with your decision. Don't make them track you down.

Once you have a job offer, you have three options: you can accept the offer, you can reject the offer, or you can present a counteroffer. At this point in the process, the power subtly shifts. You are operating from a better position than when you were just a resume or just one of several candidates. If you feel that the salary or benefits package is too low, you may after careful consideration want to make a reasonable counteroffer (for example, ask for more money or better benefits), based on your qualifications and the job title.

If you decide to negotiate, focus on the value you will bring to the company, not on what you need. Restate your interest in the position, mentioning a few ways you look forward to contributing to the company's daily operations. Express your desire to be an asset to the company over the long term, not merely for a short time. Then present your counteroffer. Be sure to emphasize once again your interest in the company, and thank the company representative for making you an offer and for considering your counteroffer.

> **Interview Tip**
>
> The best way to handle salary questions is to be prepared. Do some research to find out what the salary range is for the type of position you're applying for, and at all times—even before an interview is set up—be prepared to answer the question, "What are your salary requirements?" Some companies call to screen candidates before setting up an initial interview, and they often ask up front about salary expectations. This isn't a time to negotiate a salary—at this early stage in the process, the potential employer has the upper hand—but you should be prepared to give the interviewer a savvy answer. One way to handle this is to give the interviewer a rough idea of the salary that you'd expect—name as broad a range as possible, but be honest about what will work for you—and qualify your answer by referencing other considerations that are important, such as the quality of the position, opportunities for growth, and the company culture.

After you present your counteroffer, the employer has three options:

- Accept the counteroffer
- Reject the counteroffer
- Present their own counteroffer

If your counteroffer is accepted, congratulations! Be proud of your negotiating skills and accept the position with enthusiasm.

If your counteroffer is rejected, you must decide whether to accept the original offer or continue your search. If you really want the job and salary is not your primary consideration, accept the offer and be thankful. Make sure you are graceful, not grudging

---

ON THE JOB

SCENARIO: After you walk out of the interview, you smack yourself in the forehead. You forgot to mention your volunteer work in the same industry! You know it would have been an important point in your favor. What now?

QUICK FIX: Don't worry! Go home and immediately write a thank you note and mention in a sentence or two that you've volunteered in this industry and you're looking forward to working with this company, if they should give you the opportunity.

---

when you accept. The same professionalism is required if you decide not to accept the offer: make sure you decline politely. Thank the employer for the offer, express regret at being unable to accept, and mention that the decision was difficult to make.

If the employer presents their own counteroffer, you can once again ask for some time to consider the offer. Your options remain the same: you can accept or reject the offer or you can present another counteroffer. Be reasonable, however, if you present another counteroffer. Think about what you want but also consider what you are willing to give up. Prepare to be flexible. Negotiating often involves compromise: the goal is to create a win-win situation in which both parties are happy with the outcome.

After the Interview

Whew. The interview is over, and you're leaving the office or job site. All that preparation paid off, and you presented yourself as a professional, with clear goals and strengths and passion for your career. You answered the questions carefully and fully, and you feel like you have a pretty good shot at landing this job.

Congratulations! This is a big achievement.

But the process isn't quite finished yet. There were likely other job candidates who came in before you, and there may be more who come in after you. The last thing you want is to leave the office and immediately be forgotten. So it's often appropriate to follow up after a job interview by sending a brief thank you note for the opportunity. A follow-up note should come as soon as possible after the interview. You can send a quick email, or drop a note in the mail. If you've collected business cards during the interview, you should have contact information for everyone you spoke with. Remember to thank everyone you met, including all the people who interviewed you.

When you're writing a thank you letter, remember these pointers:

- Express your interest in the job.
- Point out a few reasons you'd be a good match with the company.
- Direct them to any information that might be helpful, such as a personal website or blog.

Finally, keep your thank you brief—no more than a paragraph or two. The thank you note isn't the time to redo your interview, just an opportunity to remind them of your interest and hit on a few high points.

If You Don't Get the Job

Receiving a job offer is a wonderful moment, and unfortunately, its opposite—finding out you didn't get the job—can be devastating.

If you don't hear back from a company after your interview, it's appropriate to let some time pass and then follow up. Candidates who reach the interview stage should be informed of the company's final decision, so feel free to check in with your contact at the company to find out the status.

Don't expect detailed reasons why you didn't get the job. This is a sensitive area, with legal implications, and it's very unlikely that a hiring manager or company will give you a reason why you didn't get the job. You're likely to hear, "We've decided to go with another candidate," or "We're going to promote from within." The exception is salary issues. If your asking price is too high, you might hear, "We'd love to hire you, but we can't afford you so we've gone with another candidate."

Any kind of rejection is hard to deal with. It stings. But it's important not to get angry or become accusatory with the employer. You might be in this field for a while—you never know when you'll run across the same company again or another opportunity will open up. Don't burn a potentially valuable bridge just because your feelings are hurt.

Instead, take a moment to gather yourself, and then let the feelings wash through you. Don't get discouraged—don't give up. Your job search isn't over just because one company said no. In fact, just getting an interview and making it all the way to the final stages of the process is a good sign. It's an accomplishment by itself, and it likely means that you will find another company that sees the same potential in you.

Use this event. People often learn more from their failures than their successes. Michael Jordan, one of the all-time greats in basketball, once remarked that he missed many more game-winning three-point shots than he ever put in. If you saw a highlight reel of him missing the crucial basket, it would look like Jordan was an awful basketball player. But these aren't the events that defined his career. Jordan is remembered for the baskets he did make—and there were plenty. He used failure as fuel to become a better player.

A setback is just that: a setback. It's not game over. So let it sting, then pick yourself back up, and get back on the job hunt. Later on, you'll be glad you did.

Chapter Summary

- Preparation is the key to a successful job interview. Before the interview, research the market, the company, and new developments in the industry.

- Practice is also essential. Stage mock interviews in a variety of formats and practice handling all sorts of questions, from both traditional and behavioral interview formats.

- Don't lie about tough issues in your background. Instead, be up front about the issue if asked, and use the situation to show how you've grown.

- Ask questions about the company during the interview—you're interviewing them too.

- Don't ask about salary until a job offer is made. This is a very sensitive topic.

- When responding to a job offer, use careful consideration if you decide to negotiate. Remain professional at all times and negotiate with the goal of making the outcome a win-win situation.

- Interview red flags include poor communication, unsuitable attire, poor interpersonal skills, and lateness.

- Don't be discouraged if you don't land the job. Failures and missed opportunities are a part of life, so use the experience to become a better interviewer.

To-Do List

☐ Compile a list of twenty-five questions that are typically asked during an interview. Answer all the questions and practice rehearsing your answers.

☐ List five things you feel will be weaknesses in an interview and list ways to overcome them.

☐ List five strengths you have that you will be able to count on during an interview.

☐ Look through your closet and plan what you'll wear to an interview. List any items you'll need to buy.

☐ Set aside time for ironing, shoe polishing, fingernail grooming, hair cut, and other activities related to presenting a good appearance.

Important Terms

How well do you know these terms? Define them here or in your journal, or look them up in the glossary to help you remember them.

behavioral interview

group interview

practice interview

traditional interview

Online Resources

Salary.com, offers salary reports based on occupation and region
www.salary.com

Employment Digest, provides strategies and tips for job hunters
http://www.employmentdigest.net

Interview Strategies.com, which has a lot of good free information about interviewing
http://www.interviewstrategies.com

Exercises

Write your answers in your journal or on a separate piece of paper.

1. In your journal, list the five skills or qualifications you have that you feel are the most important for success in your field. For each one, give an example of a time that you used that skill at work or at school. Give specific details about what you did and what the results were. Think about the best way you can work these examples into a job interview.

2. Pair up with a friend or another student to do mock interviews, taking turns being the interviewer and interviewee. Use both traditional and behavioral interview questions, and practice personal presentation.

3. Write a sample thank you letter after your mock interview, expressing interest in the company and thanking the company for the opportunity.

15 | Standard Company Organizations

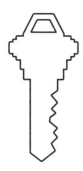

KEYS TO SUCCESS

- Learning and supporting an employer's mission and values
- Identifying the key benefits of a company's products or services
- Understanding an employer's profit strategy
- Understanding the organizational structure of a company and your place in it
- Working effectively with other groups and departments within a company
- Respecting the chain of command

Knowing Your Employer

Every business, from a family-run storefront to a multinational corporation, has an organizational structure, dictating who does what and who answers to whom. Day to day, many employees deal only with a small piece of their employer's overall structure.

However, it's important to understand how a company works as a whole. Knowing your employer's mission, values, and structure can be the difference between being seen as a hired hand who just does the assigned tasks, or as a serious professional who adds value to the organization.

Mission and Values

Most companies have a mission statement—a paragraph or brief document that outlines what it is in business to do, how it does it, and what makes it unique or exceptional in the marketplace. For instance, a general contractor's mission statement might state a goal of providing the best labor value for the money by working with customers to assess their needs and pursuing low-cost, high-impact solutions.

Choose any large company you admire and look up its mission statement: It may be on the company's public website or you may be able to get it from the human resources department. Read it over a few times and think about how it might apply to an employee. What image is the company trying to project to the public? What are its overall goals? What could an employee do to support these goals?

> ### Practice Critical Thinking
> What do your selected company's mission and values tell you is most important about the working environment there?

Many companies also have an official statement of their organizational values—guiding principles for their operations, or traits they expect employees to display. Some examples would be "Customers first," "Rewarding performance," and "A greener office." Knowing a company's core values will help you to know what it looks for in an ideal employee. For example, you might know the technical parts of your job backward and forwards, but if "Service with a smile" is a core value of the company, you could still find it hard to get ahead without focusing on your people skills.

Products and Services

A company's business can be boiled down simply to one of a few things. It either:

- Manufactures or markets a *product*—such as cars, industrial piping, or sports equipment

- Provides a *service*—such as computer repair, plumbing, or health care

- Does some combination of the two—such as a restaurant, which both makes food and hosts guests and events; or a photographer, who stages and takes pictures and then sells prints

A company's reputation is built on some aspect of its products and services. BMW is known for top-quality products. Taco Bell's reputation is built on fast service and low-cost food. FedEx stakes its business on reliability.

Each company is selling specific benefits to its customers—some way in which its products will make the customer's life better or easier. A high-quality luxury car provides comfort, enjoyment, and status; fast food offers convenience at a low cost; reliable shipping can bring peace of mind. Don't just know the features of a company's products and services; know the benefits that it's selling.

It's also important to understand how a company makes its money. Maybe its most popular product line is offered at a very low profit margin, in order to entice customers to buy other, more profitable products. An auto repair shop might offer a bargain on an oil change with a free check of fluids, filters, and belts, in the hope of selling additional parts and services as a result. Knowing how each product and service helps to drive profits will keep you focused on the thing that matters so much to an employer: the bottom line.

Organizational Structure

Depending on its size and the range of products and services it offers, a company may have a fairly simple organizational structure or a very complicated one. It may also be constantly changing. Understanding your place in the overall structure will help you work better with people in other departments.

Common Organizational Patterns

The two most basic patterns of organization are functional and divisional. A functional structure is based on areas of expertise, skills used, and tasks performed. A dedicated information technology (IT) department is a functional business unit: All of the company's network administrators, computer programmers, and help desk technicians report up one chain of command. Other functional units of the company might include engineering, marketing, manufacturing, and sales.

A functionally organized company has the advantage of keeping all its specialists together to share information, pool their knowledge, and develop companywide solutions. It allows for resources and people to be moved around as needed among projects, products, and geographic areas.

A divisional structure is based on product line, service type, market segment, or geography. If a company has offices in four cities, each with its own director, human resources manager, sales staff, help desk, and so forth, then it uses a divisional organization. For example, an electronics company might have separate divisions for car audio, home theater, and computer accessories, each with its own director, human resources department, IT department, and so on.

> **Practice Critical Thinking**
> Think about any group, club, school, or organization that you belong to. Is it organized functionally, divisionally, or a mix of both ways? How does the organizational structure affect how you fit in?

Divisionally organized companies allow each individual division a lot of flexibility in tailoring operations to its own market or region. Divisions function as complete and unified teams, and are able to adapt quickly to local or market changes.

A company may fit one of these two basic patterns, or it may blend aspects of both. For instance, many companies will have an overall vice president in charge of a particular function, but with divisional managers overseeing operations in each individual market, product line, or office.

Departmental Differences

If you work in just one department of a larger organization, it's easy to develop a kind of tunnel vision, where you lose sight of the goals and priorities of other departments. Loyalty to your closest co-workers is one thing, but avoid adopting an "us vs. them" attitude about other parts of the company. Neither your group nor any other is the end-all, be-all of the business; you all work together to achieve common goals.

> **Workplace Tip**
>
> Get to know people working in other departments. Becoming familiar with their daily responsibilities and challenges can lead to greater respect for their contributions to the company.

In any kind of organization—functional, divisional, or a mix of both—different groups develop different cultures. Even with a strongly shared set of core values and a well-defined company mission, it's unavoidable. An office in a cold, crowded East Coast city will have a different atmosphere and general pace of life than one in spacious, sunny southern California. HVAC engineers have a totally different professional background from construction site supervisors.

To work productively with other departments, you have to learn to respect their cultures. Collaborative teams have to compromise and find some middle ground between different ways of working. If you're from a bottom-line-driven, time-is-money manufacturing division, don't lose patience with the free-thinking, easy-going types in the creative department. High-five the sales guys, if it makes them happy. Let the technicians check everything three times. You need each other, and you need them to be able to work in the way that allows them to do their best job.

Levels of Management

All companies are organized according to some kind of hierarchy—a chain of command, running from department supervisors all the way up to the CEO. The first thing to understand is the overall shape of the hierarchy. What are the organizational units of the company? For instance, you might be part of a team, which is part of a group, which is part of a department, which is part of a division.

The Chain of Command

Another way to put this is that there's a pecking order, and you need to know your place in it. You know that when your boss tells you to do something, you do it. But you may also get requests from your boss's boss, from managers of other departments, or from members of other teams.

It's a good idea to learn who the most important people are in your company. Certainly you should know the names and faces of the CEO, the vice president who oversees your part of the company, and everyone in the direct chain up from your boss to the top. But also make a point of knowing who is in charge of key support services, like IT or facilities; who's in charge of personnel or human resources; and who's leading major projects. Take note of who the problem-solvers are when you need help with something like your computer, the phone system, invoices, travel, or supply ordering. If you can, try to get to know them.

ON THE JOB

SCENARIO: You're working on your assigned tasks when the regional manager calls your cell phone. He asks you to put aside your regular duties and instead take care of an urgent issue for your biggest customer. He called you personally because he knows you're an expert in this type of problem. You understand the importance of keeping this customer happy, but you know your direct boss will be upset if you don't complete your assigned tasks.

QUICK FIX: There are a couple ways to handle this. If you're comfortable with the regional manager, you might say, "Yes, of course," but also ask that he call your direct boss and let her know, so someone else can do your regular assignments. Or, you might simply answer yes, then call your boss yourself and explain the situation. Either way, you need to get your boss into the loop as soon as possible.

Do your best to put faces to the names. Maybe your company's Intranet—its website for staff—has a directory with pictures. If somebody important shows up unannounced with a request, you'll want to know who that person is.

Good Relationships at All Levels

In the workplace it's important to respect the chain of command and avoid going over people's heads. Your boss won't like it if you take an idea straight to the department director. That can easily be seen as an insult, which can make your life a lot harder.

If your boss's boss approaches you and asks you to do something, you should do your best to comply. Make a point, however, of bringing your boss into the loop. As early as you can, let your boss know what you're doing and make sure it's alright. The last thing you want is to be caught in the middle of a power struggle between people above you.

Don't bother big people with little things. If you have a question about a routine task or your group's daily operations, first see if one of your peers can answer it. If not, then ask your manager. Don't take it further up the ladder, even if it seems like a high-level policy issue. Follow the same practice when dealing with other groups and departments. Always ask the person closest to your level first. If that person can't provide an answer, he or she can direct you to someone who can.

Some departments may have specific systems that they expect you to use when contacting them with questions or requests. The IT help desk may ask that all issues be logged through an online reporting system; travel services may have a central phone line to call where a coordinator will connect you to an agent. Respect those policies. Don't show up at an IT tech's desk unannounced, and don't call a travel agent's direct line. If you do, it puts them in an awkward situation, where they have to choose between helping you and following procedure, and either one could get them in trouble.

Respect the higher-ups; follow procedure; know your way around the company. Doing these things will help ensure that when you're noticed by those above you, it's in a good way.

Lisa Diane Arnett

Pittsburgh, Pennsylvania

Attended: Kaplan Career Institute—ICM Campus, Pittsburgh, Pennsylvania

Area of study: Business Administration: Management

Employer: School Management Assistant, Board of Education

If you take one thing away from this course, it should be this: To know more, you must stay open to learning more!

Kaplan was very instrumental in preparing me for the work force. They strengthened my weak areas in writing and interviewing and gave me the confidence I needed to apply for jobs that I would have otherwise bypassed due to inexperience.

Chapter Summary

- An understanding of your organization's mission will help you add value to the company by working to support the mission.

- In a functionally structured organization, employees are grouped together by the type of work they do; in a divisionally structured organization, employees are grouped by market, product line, or location.

- Different departments of the same company may have different cultures; to work together effectively, groups must respect each other's cultures.

- To maintain good relationships at different levels, learn the names and faces of important managers and key partners and problem-solvers.

To-Do List

☐ Write out a mission statement for your ideal company.

☐ Describe the kind of organizational structure that would fit that company (and you) best.

☐ Describe the culture of that company. How would that be good for you?

Important Terms

How well do you know these terms? Define them here or in your journal, or look them up in the glossary to help you remember them.

culture	hierarchy
divisional structure	mission statement
functional structure	values

Online Resources

What Is the Purpose of Organizational Structure?
http://www.ehow.com/facts_5154174_purpose-organizational-structure.html

Missionstatements.com, includes mission statements from a variety of industries
www.missionstatements.com/company_mission_statements.html

"Getting Along with Your Boss," general tips including the importance of respecting the chain of command
http://vocationalpsychology.com/essay_17_boss.htm

Exercises

Write your answers in your journal or on a separate piece of paper.

1. Earlier in the chapter you identified a company you admired and found its mission statement. Now, write a personal mission statement for a job you might have with that company. Write one to two paragraphs describing how you plan to support your company's goals in your day-to-day work.

2. Identify organizations you know that have different cultures, or different cultures within the organization, as described in the chapter. Assess why these cultures may have developed as they have.

3. Write several paragraphs describing an instance when you had a conflict with someone else in a group or organization that might have been due to its structure or your roles. How might what you've learned in this chapter help you understand and resolve the situation?

16 Understanding Diversity and Treating Others with Respect

KEYS TO SUCCESS

- Understanding what diversity means
- Learning why it's important to get along with people from diverse backgrounds
- Recognizing how labeling, stereotyping, and prejudice are related
- Being sensitive to your words and actions
- Identifying your own biases and eliminating them
- Knowing what to do if you witness discrimination

You may have heard or read about "diversity" and "diversity training" in the news and wondered what all the fuss was about. Diversity isn't something we need to "practice," right? Maybe and maybe not. It turns out that many people do need to.

What is diversity, exactly, and why is it so important?

Diversity Defined

Put very simply, diversity means difference. There are many kinds of diversity. For example, a diverse population has people from many different ethnic groups. In biology, diversity means lots of different species. For example, a rain forest is a very diverse ecosystem.

With regard to school or the workplace, you probably think of race or gender when you hear a reference to diversity. But diversity can also be used to describe differences of opinion, life experience, job title, educational level, and even income level. The fact is, no two people are the same, no matter how similar their backgrounds. Diversity is a fact of life.

Nevertheless, diversity can be unsettling. It is sometimes hard to relate to people who have experiences or viewpoints that are strikingly different from your own, and it can require patience and understanding to manage relationships with people very different from yourself.

But it's worth it. The fact is, diversity is a strength—that's why universities and businesses have worked so hard to diversify their student populations and workforces. Everyone benefits from diversity, because each person has things to learn from others. And the most important qualities—hard work, loyalty, creativity, intelligence, dedication, and sound values—aren't unique to any one group of people.

Diversity at Work and School

There is no question that the American workforce is becoming increasingly diverse. According to the U.S. Census Bureau, the United States population in 2006 was

- 74 percent white
- 13.5 percent African American
- 4.4 percent Asian
- 14.8 percent Hispanic/Latino

The majority of Americans live in the ten most populous states, and in these states people continue to flock to big cities and their outlying suburbs. The result is the concentration of many different kinds of people in relatively small regions, all working together.

This leads to issues on the job that are sometimes unexpected. People from different cultures celebrate different holidays, they may view issues such as privacy in different ways, and there may be fundamental differences in the way they view leadership and teamwork.

Rather than view this as a source of conflict, companies increasingly understand that diversity is a strength. People from different backgrounds are able to view the same problems from different angles. A group of people with vastly different life experiences has a greater pool of collective knowledge than a group of people who are more similar. This pool of knowledge is a reservoir of good ideas that companies can draw from.

This explains why diversity training has become a standard feature of working life—even small companies can benefit from drawing on the various strengths of all their employees.

Schools and universities also have made a great effort to recognize and adapt to the diverse nature of the American population. Beginning in grade school, students are exposed to various cultural traditions as part of their education. This kind of education may involve learning about different holidays or studying the cultural traditions of various minorities.

> ### Practice Critical Thinking
> You're probably familiar with many examples of negative stereotypes ("women are bad drivers," "young people are irresponsible," etc.). But what about *positive* stereotypes? What if you assume that all women are better than men at communicating? Or that all men are good at math? Think about the ways that such positive stereotypes can be harmful.

Labeling, Stereotypes, and Prejudice

For all its strengths, diversity can be a difficult topic. Some people are uncomfortable with change, and may have been raised with viewpoints that are offensive to others. In some cases, people might not even be aware that certain terminology is offensive, perhaps because they are unaware of the historical context of the words.

People can offend one another in a variety of ways:

- **Labeling.** Labeling is hurtful because it reduces a whole person to a single, often derogatory, label. When members of some group are identified by a single characteristic, they are diminished as whole people.

- **Stereotyping.** Stereotyping is the awkward cousin to labeling. A stereotype is a generalized assumption that is made about members of a particular group. Stereotypes are often associated with labels, so by identifying someone as a specific "kind" of person, you are assigning that person the stereotype associated with that label.

- **Prejudice.** Prejudice is defined as an irrational dislike of or opposition to a person based on the person's external characteristics or background. It is the final step in the labeling chain of hurt. More often than not, stereotypes are negative, so that a person who is assigned a label, and is thereby associated with a negative stereotype, is being singled out for derision and often mockery.

Everyone knows that words can hurt. But you may not always be aware of the hidden or historical meanings of your words. It is surprisingly easy for people to slip into offensive ways of speaking and acting, and in many cases they aren't even aware of the hurt they might be causing others.

The subject matter of the following example may not be pleasant, but it illustrates how language matters and how a simple word can signal a much deeper problem.

ON THE JOB

SCENARIO: You're new at your workplace, and during a lunch break one of your co-workers tells a joke that you find offensive. No one else seems to notice that you didn't laugh, and no one asks if you were offended. What do you do?

QUICK FIX: Find a way to politely mention to the person who told the joke that you find such things offensive. If possible, make sure your boss is aware of what's going on. It's possible that the whole company stands to benefit from sensitivity and diversity training.

> **Example:** As employees prepare for lunch, Jennifer offers to drive out and pick up meals for her colleagues. "Uh oh," says Jim. "A woman driver! We'll probably never get our food!"

In this example, Jim first labeled Jennifer a "woman driver." He might have thought he was joking, and Jennifer might have tried to laugh off the slight, but let's peel back a few layers and see what's going on under the surface. In fact, Jim was playing on an old stereotype that assumes women are dangerous drivers. This stereotype originated in the early days of automobiles, when cars had to be hand-cranked and required a full-time mechanic to maintain them. At the time, it was considered improper for a woman to get dirty working on cars; these were also the days when women had to ride horses sidesaddle because they were considered delicate and weak. Thus, in a single thoughtless phrase, Jim has recalled an entire history of prejudice against women and belittled Jennifer's offer to pick up his lunch. For all Jim knows, Jennifer's driving record is considerably better than his own.

These examples don't apply only to women. Variations can be found for every ethnicity, religion, sexual orientation, age group, and gender. And it only takes a few words.

Diversity Awareness

It's unlikely that Jim in the previous example knew the historical context of his joke, and therefore he might have been completely unaware of the implied insult. The same is true in many situations—people may be exhibiting basic prejudices completely unaware of the effect it's having on their co-workers.

To avoid this situation, here are some pointers:

1. **Never generalize about "types" of people.** Each person is truly a unique individual. When you identify someone as primarily "black" or "gay" or "deaf," you are reducing that person's individuality and, depending on the circumstances, you may be conveying a more serious insult.

2. **Ask questions and show curiosity.** The very best defense against offending and hurting people is to try to understand them. This is the underlying principle behind modern diversity training. And it benefits you, too. By educating yourself about the issues faced by people different from yourself, you become a more rounded, more aware person.

3. **Apologize if you inadvertently offend someone.** If you accidentally offend someone, and you realize it afterward, find an appropriate way to apologize and seek to understand what you did that caused offense. It might be hard at first, but this is the best way to help everyone move forward.

Defeating Your Own Biases

Few people will freely admit to harboring biases or prejudices. But in truth, most people have preconceptions that they use to measure and judge other people. This doesn't make you a bad person. It just makes you human.

The key to understanding your own biases is to recognize their root. Biases are rooted in fear—not necessarily fear of the person who is a target of the bias, but fear of the unknown. People who look different and who act and think differently represent the unknown. Fear of the unknown is a natural human reaction with ancient origins.

Nonetheless, it's important to identify your biases and take action to overcome them. Becoming aware of your biases is usually a straightforward process—no psychotherapists required. It is a matter of practicing the art of observation and evaluation. The following steps can help you identify your internal biases:

- Observe your thoughts.

- Analyze your thoughts.

- Measure the emotional content of your thoughts.

- Observe your attitudes toward human difference.

Pay careful attention to your own thoughts—and be honest. When a biased idea pops into your head, instead of pushing it away and pretending it never entered your mind, stop and examine the idea. Realistically assess how strongly you believe in it and analyze it in relation to your opinion of differences in general. Is this a real bias, a concept that you believe to be true, or is it an older generalization that you no longer take seriously?

> ### Workplace Tip
> Some biases are deeply rooted. Every time you think you have overcome such a bias, it comes wandering back like an unwanted houseguest. Fortunately, there is a way to counteract this: disown the bias, and act as if it doesn't influence you. The Greek philosopher Aristotle believed in this approach. He knew that attitude determines behavior, and with respect to bias he would support the modern dictum "fake it till you make it."

By doing this, you drain the bias of its emotional power. You reduce it to a mere notion that doesn't really match up with your belief system and that has no place in the reality of modern life. Over time, these thoughts will diminish in power until they vanish altogether.

When You See Bias in Action

Unfortunately, prejudice and out-and-out racism are still common problems. You may hear statements at work or school that you know are wrong or offensive. What do you do in these cases? Do you speak up and oppose them right away? Do you wait until later? Do you report them anonymously?

In such cases, the best defense is a good offense. A few words, such as "That's really not cool," can defuse the situation. However, this can also attract hostile attention to yourself.

Every workplace should have a policy regarding discrimination and should make help available to employees with bias problems through official channels, sensitivity training, or conflict resolution. If you know of a problem at your workplace, you should promptly make your superiors aware of it.

The Benefits of Diversity

There are many benefits to creating a diverse environment at the workplace. Here are just a few:

1. **Access to different viewpoints allows better solutions to emerge.** If everyone thought the same things or had the same experiences, the opportunities for truly revolutionary breakthroughs would be limited.

2. **Diversity is unavoidable.** We live in a diverse culture, no matter how similar or uniform the workers in a particular office or job site may be.

3. **Diversity makes you a more well-rounded, worldly person.** Exposure to different peoples and cultures, as well as to people with different abilities, broadens your world and makes you a better person.

Diversity training can be controversial, and many people have strong feelings about some of the issues associated with diversity programs. Ultimately, however, all people have the same goal: to live a productive, meaningful life in harmony with one's fellow human beings. Achieving this goal means understanding, appreciating, and valuing every individual for the unique person he or she is.

Chapter Summary

- Honoring diversity means celebrating the differences between us, including differences of ethnicity, sexual orientation, religion, gender, and ability.

- Words matter. Using labels to categorize people can be highly offensive, whether or not you intend to offend or are fully aware of the reasons why a label is offensive.

- Practice sensitivity by being open, asking questions, and avoiding the use of generalizations and labels with regard to other people.

- Diversity is good for the workplace: the more viewpoints that are represented, the greater is the collective pool of knowledge and experience.

To-Do List

☐ Make a list of experiences all people share, no matter what their background.

☐ Think of the ways in which the casual use of labels has hurt you in the past. What labels do you use that might be offensive or insulting to other people?

☐ Practice openness: ask questions about people's lives and take a genuine interest in their stories.

Important Terms

How well do you know these terms? Define them here or in your journal, or look them up in the glossary to help you remember them.

bias   prejudice

diversity   stereotype

label

Online Resources

Diversity Resources, a publishing company devoted to promoting and understanding diversity issues in the workplace
www.diversityresources.com

Corporate Culture and Diversity, with links to many corporate diversity websites
www.ethnicmajority.com/corporate_diversity.htm

Office of Minority Health, a government website with information on working with diverse cultures
minorityhealth.hhs.gov/templates/browse.aspx?lvl=2&lvlID=11

Exercises

Write your answers in your journal or on a separate piece of paper.

1. Research a historical figure who fought prejudice and bias, and write a short essay about his or her efforts to promote diversity.

2. Think of some negative stereotype about the ethnic or gender group that you belong to. In your journal, write about how this stereotype has affected your life. If it hasn't affected your life, write about why it hasn't.

3. Choose a negative stereotype that applies to an ethnic or gender group that you don't belong to. In your journal, write about how you believe this stereotype came into being. How could this stereotype harm persons in that group, and how could it be harmful to someone who believes in the stereotype?

Portions of this chapter's content include material adapted from Sondra Thiederman, *Making Diversity Work*, revised and updated edtion (New York: Kaplan, 2008).

17

Teamwork and Leadership

KEYS TO SUCCESS

- Identifying the elements of a successful team
- Identifying the qualities of a good team member
- Understanding and using team-building exercises
- Learning how to become part of a successful team
- Identifying the elements that make a good leader
- Learning how to gain leadership skills

Teamwork and leadership are two of the most important, but hardest to define, elements of a successful career. You might have heard that any army can only march as fast as its slowest soldier. The same is true for teams in the classroom and workplace. The whole team is only as good as its weakest link—and you don't want that to be you.

Leadership, too, is an essential element for success. If you've ever worked under an ineffective leader, you know exactly how it feels. Poor leadership can demoralize a whole organization. Workers and students feel bitter or belittled. No one wants to take any risks, and fear runs rampant, making it harder for team members to communicate with each other.

This chapter is devoted to developing these critical skills. You'll learn how to be a more effective team player—which will make you more valuable to any organization (including your school)—and, when the time comes, you'll be equipped with a basic leadership philosophy to help you get the most from your team.

What Is a Team?

What's the first thing you think of when the word *team* comes up? A sports team, perhaps, with a strong coach, an on-the-field leader, and players who each have specific jobs? Or maybe a working team, with a manager and an easily defined objective?

These are both good examples of teams, but they're just two forms that teams might take. Your study group is an informal team. Your youth group is a team. A good definition of a team is "A group of individuals working together to accomplish a common objective."

Although a team is a group of people, not all groups are teams—and it's important to know the difference. Groups are not organized, and they are not designed to accomplish an objective. A group can be anything—a field trip is a group of people, but unless the field trip is meant to accomplish something, it is not a team.

It's no accident that our definition of team includes the word *individual*. Modern coaches and corporate team leaders understand more than ever the value of prizing individuals within the team environment. Each member of the team brings different strengths to the table.

A good team identifies each member's strength and uses it appropriately. If you were a football coach, you wouldn't ask your kicker to quarterback the team, right? And you wouldn't ask your quarterback to kick a field goal.

Diversity: The Glue for a Successful Team

Diversity has become a common catchword in workplaces and classrooms across the country. In that context, it's usually understood to mean inclusion of people from different backgrounds. Where teams are concerned, diversity means something slightly different. A diverse team is one that has individuals of complementary—but not identical—skills and strengths, working together to achieve the stated objective. These team members might have the same backgrounds, or they might be from different continents.

Consider, for example, a major car company that wants to bring out a new model line. Think of all the skills needed to bring this new car to reality. The company will draw upon the skills of engineers to design it, artists to conceptualize it, marketing and advertising professionals to help convince the public to buy it, and salespeople to sell the car. And this is only a tiny fraction of the people actually involved in such a complex undertaking. But you see the point: teams are successful because they are diverse and they draw upon the complementary talents of many people.

But sometimes, the other kind of diversity—the kind meaning people of different backgrounds—is also important. Imagine how poorly a team would function if team members were secretly resentful of their colleagues, or if one team member held a baseless prejudice against another team member.

In some settings, where people of many backgrounds are working together, it might even be appropriate to bring the team together first, before the work starts, for a day of bonding and sharing. This is the essence of modern team-building, and even if it seems like time wasted because no real progress is made toward the actual objective, it's actually very helpful.

Becoming a Good Team Member

It's not hard to picture lousy team players. They're the ball hogs or the credit-takers. They're the ones who speak out of turn, who ignore or shout down others, and the ones who insist that they're always right. But what makes a good team player? Is it possible to learn these skills?

Good team players aren't born—in many cases, they're made. Look down this list of attributes of a good team member and see how many you have:

- Honest

- Trusting of other team members

- Open to new ideas

- Enthusiastic

- Effective communicator

- Willing to share credit

- Encouraging

- Supportive

- Dependable

ON THE JOB

SCENARIO: You're a member of a small team that is introducing a new office procedure at your company. You find out that another member of your team is very much against the new procedure, because it will be less convenient for him. When you confront him about this issue, he says that if the new procedure is implemented, he'll quit. He's a good worker, and you don't want to see him leave, but you also want to do what's right as a team member.

QUICK FIX: Go higher up—to your team leader. You can voice your concerns anonymously, if necessary. Even if you're not sure about the negative impact of the new procedure, your team leader should know about your co-worker's concerns. And if your team leader doesn't know about this, there's not much chance that the team will do its job well.

Team-Building Exercises

Team-building exercises are often part of the routine for any company that consists of more than a couple of people. Although it might feel embarrassing at times, team-building exercises are a very effective way to quickly create team cohesion and identify the various personalities of other team members.

Examples of team-building exercises include:

- Simple communication games, such as telephone or blindfolded search-and-find games, with one team member directing other team members to perform a basic task while blindfolded.

- Cooperation games, such as coordinated games of catch or simple construction projects with interlocking pieces.

- Trust games, such as the blind fall, when one team member falls backward and must rely on teammates to catch him or her.

The point of team-building exercises is to introduce team members to one another in a low-stress environment that's fun, but still fits the classic definition of a team situation (e.g., a group of people working together to achieve a common objective).

These kinds of exercises are used to different degrees in different organizations. Some large corporations believe very strongly in team-building exercises and send their employees away to off-site locations to participate in team-building seminars under the supervision of professional consultants. Other companies don't believe in them at all and don't do any sort of team-building exercises.

Creating a Successful Team

Believe it or not, all successful teams have a few things in common. It doesn't matter if the team is a professional sports franchise or the customer service division of the local cable company. If the team is a winning team, then more often than not, it will have the following qualities:

- **Clearly defined areas of responsibility.** This is essential for effective teamwork. Even if a few areas overlap, it's absolutely critical that all team members know what their responsibilities are, and what they will be expected to do to meet them.

- **A clear goal that is understood by all team members.** This is true whether your team consists of five people or five thousand. All members of the team need to know what the goal is and how it's going to be accomplished. Equally important, they need to understand how their contribution will ultimately help the team successfully accomplish its goal, whether it's a huge task like sending a rocket to the moon or a small task like completing a school project on time.

- **A clear decision-making method.** It's not enough to announce a goal and responsibilities and then send team members on their way. As work progresses, decisions have to be made on how to spend resources (such as time or money) and how to manage the various elements of the project. An effective team will have a clear decision-making process. This doesn't mean that one person will necessarily have total control over the team. In fact, effective decision-making is often a collaboration between various team members. But however it's structured, there needs to be a clear-cut method to brainstorm ideas, arrive at decisions, gain support from various team members, and then act on those decision.

Benefits of Effective Teamwork

You've no doubt seen effective teamwork. A winning sports team, a victorious political campaign, a blockbuster movie—you might not think about it at first, but these are all examples of highly effective teamwork. In each case, hundreds, and sometimes thousands, of people come together to accomplish an objective.

So the first and most obvious benefit of effective teamwork is accomplishing large goals that individuals alone might not be able to reach. Consider a busy medical office: the staff is made up of doctors, nurses, medical assistants, and administrative staff. A single individual would struggle to fill all those roles, but a team working together, with each member contributing his or her talents, makes it possible to successfully treat hundreds of patients a month.

In addition to efficiency, being a team member has personal benefits as well. They include:

- **Personal growth.** By learning to cooperate and communicate, individual team members learn valuable life skills.

- **Stronger connections.** Don't underestimate the power of making connections. Having a common goal is a great way to bond with other people and form stronger connections.

- **Confidence.** Being part of a winning team helps people believe they can go on to accomplish their own personal goals.

Being able to work effectively on a team is an integral part of succeeding in the workplace. A typical workplace includes many different kinds of teams, ranging from entire departments to smaller teams put together on a temporary basis to work on a particular project. In all situations it's important to be seen as a good team member, someone who is reliable and who can work cooperatively with others.

When something unexpected happens at work, co-workers often turn to one another for assistance. Sometimes a formal team is created to work on a challenging project, or an informal team is created on the spot to meet a looming deadline. You may be asked to pitch in and make copies so a crucial proposal is mailed on time, or you may be asked to lend your expertise to

Practice Critical Thinking

Think of the last time you participated on a team, either a formal team, such as a group assigned to work on a project for school, or an informal team, such as friends working to complete a complicated task. Now think about what would have happened if you had been performing the task alone. Could you have accomplished the same result on your own? How would the process have been different?

a large project involving a new client. Whether it's big or small, treat each situation as an opportunity to show that you are someone others can count on. You want your co-workers to be able to depend on you. And you, in turn, want to be able to depend on them.

Teams and Leadership

Although teams are highly collaborative, leadership is one of the essential elements of any successful team. A team might have many leadership positions, or there might be one leader who assumes responsibility for the team's performance. Ultimately, the leader is responsible for making sure the team is efficient and effective and that it's continually focused on achieving its goals.

Good leaders are encouraging, and they strive to create an environment where team members can work most effectively. This includes procuring the needed resources (again, such as time and money), allowing each member to contribute to the best of his or her ability, and ultimately, enforcing the rules that team members agreed upon from the beginning. Leaders do not steal credit, but share it. They do not overrule their team members, but listen for good ideas and implement them. Good leaders don't *make* people work. They make people *want* to work. Leaders are flexible when necessary, but tough when they need to be. And leaders are not cynical, but believe in the goal and work hard to help achieve it.

The list below contains qualities necessary to be a good leader. How many do you have?

> ### Workplace Tip
>
> You can practice being a good leader even if you don't have a managerial position. In fact, if you want to move up the ranks, now is a good time to start practicing the qualities that make a good leader. Review the list of leadership qualities on this page and the next. Which ones come naturally to you? Which ones need a little work? Write down three of the characteristics that you'd like to improve, and think about actions that you can take to improve in these areas.

- **Vision.** A leader understands the final goal and never loses sight of it. This is true even when the leader didn't develop the goal him- or herself. In a class project, a project leader probably didn't write the assignment, but the project leader must intimately understand it and have a clear vision for accomplishing it.

- **Discipline.** Good leaders don't merely pop in and say, "Do this. Do that," and then go off for lunch or a nap. Leaders inspire by working just as hard as anyone else on the team. They lead by example. Leadership means having the strength and discipline to contribute to the goal while also leading the team.

- **Integrity.** Leaders have to earn the respect of their team members, and the best leaders do this by gaining trust. People with integrity are predictable, because you know they will do the right thing. Leaders with integrity don't lie, have tantrums or outbursts, or act phony or fake.

- **Humility.** Good leaders understand that teams require every person to accomplish his or her goal. You've heard the expression, "There is no 'I' in 'team'"? There is no "I" in "leader," either. Leaders are quick to give credit where it's due, and they are slow to accept personal recognition for the accomplishments of the entire team. Good leaders are not afraid to engage their team members and take the best ideas, whether or not the leader came up with them.

- **Creativity.** Leadership requires creativity. The fact is, few projects ever go exactly as planned. Good leaders expect the unexpected and are not afraid to look for creative solutions for unanticipated problems. Leaders use their creativity to look at the same problem from different angles and come up with the best way to move forward.

- **A sense of justice.** Good leaders are fair to everyone on the team. This means they are fair with their time, as well as with the team's resources, and equitable about recognition. Good leaders don't leap to conclusions based on partial evidence or on the word of their closest colleagues and friends. Good leaders listen to all the facts, then act.

- **Assertiveness.** Assertiveness is the other side of the humility coin. Good leaders are not afraid to stand up to anyone in the group, and they do not hesitate to enforce the team's rules. Leaders also defend the team against outside forces that might undermine the team's effectiveness. Few qualities generate loyalty as quickly or completely as a team leader who aggressively defends his or her team members.

- **Humor.** Surprised to see humor on this list? Don't be. Humor is frequently an essential part of leadership. The truth is, the world is an imperfect place. Things go wrong. People act out. Resources are lost sometimes. Good leaders don't explode with anger or recrimination. Good leaders keep their team focused and relaxed by keeping the atmosphere friendly and fun, even in the most intense work environments.

Leadership by Experience

Some people seem like born leaders—and it's true that leadership skills come more easily to some people that others. But anybody can learn basic leadership skills, and it can only be good for your schooling and career.

The very best way to learn leadership skills is to volunteer for leadership positions whenever possible. This means offering to lead study groups, classroom projects, and work projects.

As you're gaining leadership skills, probably the most important thing to remember is to remain open to the experience. The best way to become a good leader is to really listen to the people you're leading. If you create an environment based on trust and mutual respect, people will often be happy to give honest feedback. This is invaluable, especially when leadership is still new to you.

Over time, it will become easier, and as you gain experience, you'll gain confidence in your own leadership. You'll gain the trust and loyalty of the people you're leading, and you'll be better positioned for every kind of success.

Stephanie Jean Bivens

Hagerstown, Maryland

Attended: Kaplan University—Hagerstown

Area of study: Business Administration—Emphasis in Accounting

Employer: Bookkeeper/Bookstore Manager, Kaplan University—Hagerstown

If you take one thing away from this course, it should be this: Always remember that you are a part of a team effort, and in order for this effort to work you have to be positive no matter what the job at hand is.

Kaplan has helped me by giving me the opportunity to work with them. I have always known education is very important, but working with Kaplan has taught me how to reach this out to others. No matter what happens with your job no one can take your education away, and Kaplan has been able to teach this to many.

Chapter Summary

- Teams are groups of individuals, all working toward the same goal or objective.

- Teams use strengths from all their members. Good teams are diverse in terms of their members' strengths.

- Communication and vision are essential to good teamwork.

- Leadership skills can be learned.

- Leaders don't force people to work, but inspire people to perform by embodying the desired traits.

- Leaders lead by example.

To-Do List

☐ List five qualities of a successful team and explain each.

☐ Research three simple team-building exercises that you could do in class or on the job.

☐ Find a formal team in an area of interest. Join it.

☐ List the qualities of a successful leader and explain why each is beneficial.

☐ Write down the names of three people you know who have good leadership skills.

Important Terms

How well do you know these terms? Define them here or in your journal, or look them up in the glossary to help you remember them.

leadership   **team**

motivation   **teamwork**

Online Resources

Dale Carnegie Training, offering leadership training for almost 100 years
www.dalecarnegie.com

Action Centered Training, team-building exercises
www.corporateteambuilding.com

The Leader's Institute: Free Team-Building Games
www.leadersinstitute.com/teambuilding/team_building_tips/index.html

Exercises

Write your answers in your journal or on a separate piece of paper.

1. Using the list of attributes of a good team member included on page 181 in the chapter, conduct a self-assessment to determine how many of the characteristics you have. Indicate which traits you possess or lack, and add any additional traits you believe to be important. Then, for each trait, write a one or two sentence account of how having or lacking that particular trait could positively or negatively affect your ability to work on a team.

2. Write a short essay (one to two pages) describing a successful team that you admire. Remember that the term *team* can be broadly applied. The team you choose could be a corporation or a sports team, or it could be a more informal group. The important thing to focus on is that a team is made up of many individuals working toward a common goal. In your paper, identify the various strengths of the individual team members and write about how each team member contributes to the success of the team.

3. From the list of three people you know who have good leadership skills, from the to-do list, choose one person. Then, in your homework journal, list the qualities that make him or her a good leader. Write a paragraph or two about what you can do to improve those qualities in yourself.

Ethical Behavior and Confidentiality

18

KEYS TO SUCCESS

- Recognizing the difference between illegal and unethical behavior
- Understanding your own decision-making process and how you can improve it
- Creating a strategy for assessing the outcome of decisions that you make
- Recognizing the importance of confidentiality

Let's say you're in a convenience store, preparing to buy a small item like a protein bar. Unfortunately, at the last moment, you realize that you're 25 cents short on the price, and you don't have the money.

However, the clerk has to step away from the counter for a moment, and you see the "Leave a Penny, Take a Penny" dish is full of pennies and nickels—easily enough to make up your shortfall. You reach for the dish to scoop up a handful of change, and then stop and ask yourself, "Is this the right thing to do?"

Congratulations! You've just crossed into the world of ethics.

What Is Ethical Behavior and Why Does it Matter?

The exact definition of ethical behavior may vary from industry to industry, country to country, and even state to state. But all large organizations and communities have ethical standards that are enforced either informally (by societal pressure, for example) or formally (with a rebuke from a professional organization like a union or professional accreditation association, for example). Broadly speaking, ethics is defined as the study of right and wrong.

This is a big topic, and few areas of modern life can provoke more debate than what is ethical versus unethical. It's important to note, however, the difference between legal and ethical issues. Legal behavior is clearly defined by laws and statutes. Illegal behaviors carry penalties such as fines and imprisonment, and they can expose you to civil action such as a lawsuit. An example of an illegal behavior is stealing resources from your workplace, such as permanently "borrowing" tools, raw materials, or even money.

By contrast, unethical behavior is not illegal. Instead, it is generally frowned upon, and may even be professionally sanctioned, but you won't go to jail or get arrested for doing something unethical. An example of unethical behavior might be accepting gifts from grateful clients, despite company policies banning such practices, or taking credit for someone else's work on a big project.

Although there are few legal ramifications for unethical behavior, ethics are nonetheless crucial in modern business settings. Offices and companies can only function effectively when all the employees can be trusted, both with each other and with company secrets such as information, practices, and client lists. Unethical behavior in the workplace creates a climate of suspicion, hostility, and fear as employers worry about their companies, workers worry about their colleagues, and even customers worry about their privacy and safety.

The Golden Rule: Ethics Made Simple

Most professions have organizations that develop and enforce an ethical code. In the trades, such as carpentry and construction, labor unions serve this purpose. In the allied medical professions, such as nurses and therapists, professional accreditation organizations enforce ethics codes.

These written ethical rules governing each profession make it easier to figure out whether any particular behavior is ethical or unethical. But the answers might not always be so clear-cut. In some cases, particular behaviors might not be covered by any professional standard. So what should you do in that case?

One of the easiest guidelines to help determine what is ethical is also one of the oldest. You might know it as the Golden Rule:

Treat others the way you want to be treated.

If you're concerned about the ethics of any particular situation, simply flip the scenario and imagine yourself on the receiving end. Would you want your medical information shared around a medical office without your consent? If you ran a small business, would you mind if your employees shared clients' names and ordering information with competitors? If you ran a parking service and advertised "Free Valet Parking" to customers, would you want your employees to accept tips?

ON THE JOB

SCENARIO: At work, you go out to lunch with a few other employees. The lunch runs late, and you don't get back to the office exactly on time. When you get back and check your messages, you see that your boss called three times while you were at lunch and needs your help immediately with an important client. What should you do?

QUICK FIX: Call your boss right away and get to work on his or her problem. That's the most important thing. Later, after the client has been handled, apologize for running late, give an honest reason for why you were late, and promise that it won't happen again—and follow through on your promise.

Making Good Decisions

Ethics serve a very valuable role in day-to-day life: they help guide decisions. Decision-making is a fundamental skill, and the ability to make good decisions will help you advance in any career.

Many people never spend any serious thought about their own decision-making process. In 2005, author Malcolm Gladwell published *Blink*, a book that gained international recognition for its bold premise that "gut" decisions are often the best decisions, that the more time people spend agonizing over decisions and the more information they collect, the worse the eventual outcomes.

However, Gladwell's book was not a defense of rapid and sloppy decision-making. Rather, he wrote about the power of expert judgment, experience, and people's ability to form accurate decisions from very little information. In other words, Gladwell was writing about the good decisions made by experts who, in the blink of an eye, can correctly interpret a situation.

One day, we can all hope to be experts in our fields. But until then, decision-making skills need to be practiced and honed. Various models exist to help people make good decisions, but one of the simplest is the risk-to-benefit ratio.

Have you ever seen someone draw up a list of pros and cons when contemplating a decision? This is what's known as a basic risk/benefit sheet. By listing possible outcomes, both good and bad, you can measure the outcome of a decision in terms of its possible benefits weighed against its possible downsides. If you've ever tried this yourself, you might have found that you sometimes don't even need to finish your list before you know what to do. Once you analyze the decision in terms of pros and cons, the answer becomes clear.

When you're making decisions at work or in school, here are a few pointers to help you arrive at the best decision:

- Draw up a pro/con list to weigh benefits versus negative outcomes.

- Ask other people who have more experience what they have done in similar situations, but don't blindly follow advice.

- Trust your conscience—let your decisions be guided by your ethical sense.

- Don't agonize over your decision once you've made it.

When the Results Are In

The best approach to improving your decision-making skills occurs after the decision is in the past—it's when you assess the outcome.

Workplace Tip

When you finish a project at work, get in the habit of taking the time to analyze your results. This kind of analytical thinking allows you to make note of the things that you did well, and it also gives you the opportunity to identify things that you can do differently next time.

Every decision you make in life—which school to attend, what kind of profession to pursue, how to spend your weekends—has an outcome, or impact, on every other portion of your life. So the best way to measure the results of your own decision is to look at your life and career right now. Is it working for you? Are you where you want to be? Remember that the answers to these questions directly result from decisions you made, even if you made them years ago.

So, when it comes to assessing your own results, here are three important things to keep in mind:

1. **Be honest about the results.** Doctors know that when people report on their smoking status or weight loss, they routinely goose the results. They say things like, "Sure, Doc, I only smoke three cigarettes a day," or "I lost ten pounds, and I'm only eating salad now." The tricky part is that these people often aren't conscious liars—they may believe the things they're saying, even if they're actually smoking ten cigarettes a day and have only lost two pounds. So be careful to use accurate information when you're measuring decision results—this is the only way to increase your decision-making skills.

2. **Don't leap to a snap judgment.** This is a tough one. Many people leap to conclusions about their own decisions long before the results are in. Human resources experts often say that it takes about a year to figure out whether you're really a good match with a new employer. So, unless there is some extraordinary circumstance, don't evaluate your new job in the first two weeks. Give it some time.

3. **Don't beat yourself up over things you can't change.** Good decision-makers take responsibility for their own decisions, but they don't waste time criticizing themselves for what has already been done and can't be changed. Even bad decisions have something to offer, and many top business leaders, artists, and sports figures say they learned more from their own failures than they did from their successes.

Confidentiality

Confidentiality is related to ethics and decision-making as a core value that allows you to gather the best information possible and earn the trust of your co-workers and colleagues. Simply put, confidentiality is about trust and private information.

Some forms of confidentiality are legally protected. This includes legal and medical matters. Employees in dental offices and medical offices are legally obligated to protect patient confidentiality, or they face severe legal penalties. The same applies for paralegals and employees in law offices. In these settings, handling sensitive information is guided by local and federal laws. If you plan to work in any of these areas, part of your education will be learning how to protect this form of confidentiality.

But confidentiality extends far beyond specific, legally protected information. It might include salary and payroll information, family issues, intrapersonal issues in the workplace or at school, or even lifestyle issues such as religion or sexual orientation.

> ### *Practice Critical Thinking*
> Can you give an example of a workplace scenario in which confidentiality is both a legal *and* an ethical issue? Can you give an example of personal information that you wouldn't mind sharing about yourself, but someone else might not want to share?

If you come into possession of confidential information, or if you're unsure that information is confidential, follow these simple guidelines.

1. Check with your company or profession's code of ethics. Does it cover this situation?

2. Check yourself against the Golden Rule mentioned earlier. Would you want this kind of information shared about you?

If there's any doubt in your mind, then it's probably a good idea to keep the information private.

Kathryn M. Munson

Omaha, Nebraska

Attended: Kaplan University—Omaha, Nebraska

Area of study: Paralegal program

Employer: Paralegal, Grossman Law Offices

If you take one thing away from this course, it should be this: Always be respectful of authority even when there is a difference in how you view the process, and follow the established rules.

Kaplan helped me reach my goals by providing me with the skills and education that I needed to reenter the work force. They were helpful by providing me with a wide range of subjects and classes that were vital for my success in the area of work I chose. They also helped me gain the confidence that I needed to step out into the work world and feel like I was capable of providing the services that my employer needed.

Chapter Summary

- Ethics is the study of right and wrong. All professions and societies have ethical guidelines, and a solid ethical foundation can guide you in difficult moments.

- The best decisions are made by weighing the advantages of a choice against its possible negative outcomes.

- If you're in doubt, follow the Golden Rule and treat others the way you would want to be treated.

- The best decision-makers have a system to assess the results of previous decisions.

- Confidentiality is important in order to gain the loyalty and trust of your colleagues.

To-Do List

☐ Define ethics.

☐ List examples of legal and ethical confidentiality.

☐ Write down three ethical questions that you can use as a guide for making good decisions.

☐ Make up a practice pro/con list for a major decision, such as buying or leasing a car, upgrading to a new laptop, or where to go on vacation next summer.

Important Terms

How well do you know these terms? Define them here or in your journal, or look them up in the glossary to help you remember them.

confidential

ethical behavior

ethics

Golden Rule

illegal behavior

risk-to-benefit ratio

unethical behavior

Online Resources

The Ethics Resource Center, an online resource devoted to studying and shaping ethics in the world

www.ethics.org

The Office of Government Ethics, with links to scenarios of common ethics issues

www.usoge.gov/common_ethics_issues/general_principles.aspx

Today's Workplace, a workplace fairness blog

www.todaysworkplace.org/category/workplace-ethics

Exercises

Write your answers in your journal or on a separate piece of paper.

1. Find a newspaper or magazine article that illustrates an ethical dilemma (not a legal issue). In your homework journal, analyze the ethical dilemma presented in the article. Try to really understand the nature of the dilemma and accurately present both sides of the issue.

2. Imagine you're working with someone who is gossiping about fellow employees based on her knowledge of those employees' insurance records. How would you react to her personally? How would you deal with this information in your workplace?

3. Practice assessing the outcome of your decisions. Choose a recent decision that you've made and write a paragraph or two discussing the outcome of your decision. Think about the concepts discussed in the chapter as you formulate your response. Were there any unexpected pros or cons that you didn't consider?

19 | Managing Finances

KEYS TO SUCCESS

- Creating a monthly budget to ensure that all of your expenses are paid on time
- Developing responsible habits for using credit and managing debt
- Adopting sensible safety practices to protect yourself from identity theft and related crimes
- Investing cautiously and wisely to build on your financial assets
- Taking full advantage of employee benefits such as medical insurance and retirement plans

Basic Money Management

Once you move from lower-level jobs into the professional world, you're likely to see a sizable hike in your paycheck. Not surprisingly, there are many more things you as a professional will have to spend money on—appropriate clothes, regular transportation, meals and coffee on the go, and perhaps child care or mortgage payments.

Many people think they can get by just by winging it: find a bill in the mail, and check if there's money to pay it; if not, wait; and repeat as necessary. It turns out that if you don't pay the cable bill, the company will helpfully tack it onto next month's bill. If the company cuts your service, then pay them off and let the phone bill slide, or put all your groceries on a credit card for a while. After years of letting things "work themselves out," you have experienced some lean times, paid some overdraft fees, and received some collection calls; but you've never gone to jail or anything, so everything's fine—right?

Wrong. You may be able to play the system in the short term. By doing so, however, you only create much bigger problems for yourself in the long term. If you don't develop a system for managing your money and expenses, you could end up paying thousands of dollars in unnecessary interest; you could lose your car or your home; and you definitely will damage your credit score, which can put any car, any home, and perhaps even certain jobs out of your reach.

Creating Your Budget

There is no way around it: you have to draw up a budget. Many software packages, such as Quicken, provide a ready-made template and do all the math for you. A spreadsheet program such as Microsoft Excel also does the trick cheaply and easily. But one way or another, you need to track and plan for your income and expenses.

A basic budget worksheet will keep track of how much money comes in and how much goes out, and when. Figure 19.1 shows a typical monthly budget worksheet. To keep track of your monthly expenses, document the following items:

- **Date:** When a bill is due and when it is paid.

- **Item:** The name of an expense (for example, "Gas bill").

- **Budgeted amount:** The amount you plan to spend for the item. Income is positive ($1100) and expenses are negative (–$420). You need to enter this information ahead of time.

- **Actual amount:** The amount you actually spent or received for an item budgeted earlier. Comparing the budgeted and actual amounts can help you identify places where your budgeting is off.

- **Balance:** The amount of money left in your bank account after you adjust for each item

Most bills come on a monthly basis, so plan to budget month by month.

Calculating Expenses

The key to successful budgeting is knowing as much as possible ahead of time. If your income is predictable, you don't have to spend much time thinking about that. Just make sure you budget for your *net* pay—the amount of your check—and not your *gross* pay, before taxes and other deductions are taken out. If you're paid on commission or if your work hours vary from week to week, make your best estimate.

Figure 19.1 (following page) from Judy Lawrence, *The Budget Kit*, 5th ed. (New York: Kaplan, 2008).

	Expenses	Amount	Date Due	Date Paid	Date Rcv.:				
Fixed Amounts	Mortgage/Rent								
	Car Payments								
	Other Loans								
	Internet Access								
	Day Care								
	Insurance								
	Clubs/Dues								
	Savings								
	Allowance/Mad Money								
Fixed Variable	Electricity								
	Oil/Gas								
	Water/Garbage								
	Telephone/Cell Phone								
	Cable TV/Satellite								
	Groceries								
	Meals Out								
	Auto Expense/Gas								
	Church/Charity								
Occasional	Household								
	Personal								
	Clothes								
	Medical								
	Child Expense								
	Recreation								
Installment	Credit Cards								
Total	Total Income								
	Total Expense								
	Total Excess								
	Total Short								

INCOME SOURCE: / Net Income Total Amount:

Figure 19.1 Monthly Budget Worksheet

Many expenses will also be fixed: your cable bill is probably the same every month, as is your cell phone bill, your rent or mortgage payment, your car insurance, and so on. You should try to make the same true for as many of your bills as possible. For instance, your power company may offer a "budget plan," where each month you make a fixed payment based on an estimated average of your heating bills for the whole year. That way, you pay a little extra during the summer, but you don't have huge bills in the winter.

> ### Practice Critical Thinking
>
> Step 1: Look at what you spend now.
>
> Step 2: Ask yourself what you really *need* to spend. What area of your spending could be better handled?

Expenses that can't be fixed must be controlled. Set out a specific amount each week for groceries. Save all grocery receipts for a month to see how much you spend on average. Do the same for everything else you spend money on: gas for your car, eating out, going to the movies, and so on. If you don't want to budget every single small expense, then consider budgeting a certain amount each week for petty cash. Each Sunday, take out your "allowance" from an ATM, and use that cash to pay for all the week's little expenses. Don't break out your debit card, and don't take out any more cash until next week.

Some expenses don't come up every month. For instance, you might pay $40 four times a year for an oil change, or you may take the dog to the vet for a checkup every six months. Any long-term expense that you know is coming should be planned for. Set aside a certain amount each month so that when it comes time to pay, you can do it without raiding your bank account.

Also, as contradictory as it may sound, plan for surprises: Open a savings account, and budget at least a small amount from each paycheck to deposit there; most banks will let you set up an automatic transfer. Even $20 a month will add up over time. Set a goal to build up an "emergency fund" that could cover three months' worth of living expenses. A savings account pays a small amount of interest on your deposits, but its real value lies in keeping a block of money separate from your regular spending.

Staying on Budget

Once you've accounted for all your expenses, it's time to take control of them. You may find that your monthly expenses total more than your monthly income. In that case, review your expenses and see what you can cut. Maybe you can scale back your cable TV to a more basic package or drop some of the extras from your cell phone plan. Maybe you need to put in some overtime at work, or consider an extra part-time job.

The next step is to plan your fiscal month. On your budget worksheet, list your bills in order by due date, and assign dates for other expenses (like taking out your cash each Sunday). If you get paid once a month, then your fiscal month starts on that date. For example, if your paycheck comes on the 15th of each month, it has to cover all your expenses from the 16th of this month to the 15th of next month. If you get paid twice a month or biweekly, then you have to split your bills in half; you may need to call certain companies and ask them to adjust your due dates to even things out. Try to get far enough ahead that you can afford to pay everything at the beginning of each month.

You should prepare your budget at least a month in advance. If you don't have all your bills for the next month yet, use your best estimate. Then, as you go through the month, fill in the "Actual Amount" column and add any unexpected expenses that come up. Save your receipts, review your bank statements, and check your account through your bank's website. You don't want to lose track of what you're spending and end up overdrawing your account.

Credit and Debt

For many people, part of the monthly budget is devoted to paying off debt: credit cards, mortgage, personal loans, car financing, student loans, and so forth. For the sake of your finances, not to mention your sanity, you should try to have as few outstanding debts as possible and keep current on all the payments.

Credit Cards

The most widespread type of consumer debt is credit card debt. If you charge only what you can afford and pay off your balance each month, a credit card can be a very convenient way of paying for things. And now that many cards offer incentives such as cash back on purchases, you can actually come out ahead.

The trouble begins when you don't pay off everything you charge each month. When you carry a balance, it's subject to the card's annual percentage rate (APR)—a charge that the company imposes on your account and that compounds (or grows) over time. APRs run from below 10 percent to 30 percent or more, depending on the company and your own credit rating. A 20 percent APR means that for each dollar you owe, you'll be charged 20 cents a year. In one month you'll be charged one-twelfth of that—about 1.66 cents. That may not seem like much, but it adds up. If you carry a balance of $500 for a year, it'll cost you an extra $100.

The average American credit card holder carries about $10,000 in credit card debt, racking up thousands of dollars in finance charges each year. You don't get anything at all for that money, except the privilege of carrying a big chunk of debt. The longer you delay

> **Financial Tip**
> Do you know what your credit card APR is?

payment, the bigger your balance grows. In the meantime, your minimum monthly payment keeps growing because it's linked to your balance.

If you're carrying balances on multiple credit cards, you may benefit from consolidating all of them into one account. Many companies offer special promotional rates for balance transfers from other accounts. For instance, they may charge you only 2 percent interest on your transferred balance. Just remember, though, that your regular APR still applies to the balance that is already on your card, and to any new purchases. The big advantage to consolidating is that you have to make only one monthly payment, instead of two or three or more.

Credit Reports

You've probably heard about your credit report and your credit score—mysterious numbers that control your financial life. A credit report is a list of all of the credit and utility accounts, loans, collections, and public records (such as court judgments or bankruptcies) in your recent history (generally going back about seven years). Each account's status is reported month by month—whether you paid on time, whether the account is in good standing, how much you owe, and for a closed account, whether it was closed at your request or the company's. The credit score is a number on the report that reflects the estimated level of risk a creditor takes on in lending to you, based on that full history.

When you apply for credit, the financial institution is likely to review your credit report. Based on what they see, they'll choose to approve or deny your request. The report will also be used to determine the mortgage interest rate and other terms. Prospective landlords or employers may also look at your credit report to assess your reliability.

Many companies advertise that they can give you access to your credit report, clean up a bad credit history, and beef up your credit score. There are a few important things to know about credit reports and scores:

- **You don't have just one.** In the United States there are three major credit bureaus—private agencies that compile data from your credit history. Their names are Equifax, Experian, and TransUnion. It's very common for different information to show up on each report. Some lenders will look only at one of the reports; others will check all three.

- **You have the right to see your data.** Many companies, including the credit bureaus themselves, offer a "free three-in-one credit report"—so long as you sign up for additional "credit protection" services that will cost you a monthly fee. However, federal law gives you the right to one free copy a year of each of your credit reports, no strings attached. Take advantage of this opportunity to review your credit reports for accuracy. To request copies, go to AnnualCreditReport.com, the site officially approved by the Federal Trade Commission.

- **You have the right to challenge them.** Inaccurate information gets into credit reports all the time, and sometimes it can seriously damage your credit. If you find a mistake, you can file a dispute with the bureau, including any supporting evidence or documentation. The bureau is required by law to follow up with the company in question. If the company can't prove its case, or if it doesn't respond, the item must be removed.

- **You can't fool them.** People try to beat the system by challenging every negative mark on their report, even if it's accurate, hoping that not all of the reporting companies will respond. This is, of course, dishonest and unethical. Beyond that, it doesn't work. Eventually, the company will report your debt again—causing a blow to your credit when you least expect it. Don't trust any company that promises to boost your credit score or scrub your report. The only way to improve your credit score is to make your payments on time and avoid getting in over your head.

Identity Theft

Identity theft is a crime in which somebody hijacks your name and credit for his or her own use, potentially leaving your financial affairs in ruins. Identity thieves operate by acquiring some important piece of personal information, such as a credit card number, Social Security number, or computer password, and then commit various frauds using the stolen identity. A thief may open a credit card account using the stolen identity, or use the victim's name to set up a bank account that is then used to write bad checks.

It's almost impossible to be completely safe from identity theft, but there are some simple things you can do to make yourself less of a target:

- **Guard your Social Security number.** Avoid giving it out if you can, and don't carry your Social Security card in your wallet or purse.

- **Guard your passwords and PINs.** Change computer passwords often, and don't use real words. Make it something you can remember, so that you don't have to write it down. Don't write down your ATM card PIN.

- **Guard your credit card.** Use your card only with merchants you trust. When shopping online, look for sites that offer secure transactions. Avoid giving your credit card number over the phone.

- **Report theft promptly.** If you lose your wallet or have it stolen, immediately call all of the companies to have your credit, debit, and ATM cards canceled and replaced with new ones (with new numbers).

Investing

The financial world offers many opportunities to put your money to work for you, be it through stocks, bonds, mutual funds, or other financial instruments. Investing is no longer just for Wall Street tycoons. Today more people are involved in some kind of investing than ever before. Just remember: every investment carries risk.

Where to Start

Investing can be very complicated. If you're interested, you should start out small and be cautious. Don't lay out more money than you can afford to lose, and expect to pay a price for learning the ropes.

A rule of thumb for all investors is to diversify—which means don't put all your eggs in one basket. If you own stock in only one company or industry, you'll lose everything if it tanks. Spread your bets around.

A good place to start may be with a mutual fund, in which you join a large group of investors in pooling your resources into a diversified portfolio that has been created by experts.

Some brokerage and investment companies offer entry-level accounts that don't require costly buy-ins. Using an online brokerage will be much less expensive than working with a personal stockbroker, although of course you'll have to make more decisions for yourself. If you have a good deal of money to invest and want to make sure you do it wisely, consider working with a professional financial planner. If you have friends or relatives who are experienced at investing, listen to their advice—but don't let them talk you into taking a bigger risk than you're ready for.

Getting the Most from Your Employee Benefits

In a job search, salary is obviously a top concern. It is also important, though, to be aware of the other kinds of compensation that different employers offer.

Medical Insurance

If your employer offers a health insurance plan, it's probably a better deal than you could get buying a policy on your own. Group plans have lower premiums, and your employer will usually pay part of yours. Whatever is left of the monthly premium is taken straight from your paycheck, so you don't have to think about it—and it's deducted *before* taxes are calculated, so you don't pay taxes on that money. Generally, a group plan also offers greater security than a private plan. A good employer-provided health insurance plan can add thousands of dollars a year to the value of your total compensation.

Retirement Security

Some employers—particularly those with unionized workforces—offer their employees pension plans that are designed to provide workers with a stable income after retirement. This is increasingly uncommon, however; most workers are expected to build their own reserves for retirement—and you'll want to start as early as possible, even if you're only

ON THE JOB

SCENARIO: You've been getting health insurance through your spouse's employer, but your spouse gets laid off. Both of you have pre-existing health conditions, making it difficult to buy affordable private insurance, and you've already declined your employer's health coverage.

QUICK FIX: There are laws in place to protect you. You can choose to continue your existing coverage through your spouse's employer for up to 18 months, although you'll have to pay the full premium. Or you could notify your employer of your spouse's job loss as a "life event," which will allow you to sign up for the employer health plan in the middle of the year, even though you previously declined it.

in your twenties. Many employers who don't offer pensions still offer some retirement benefits. The best known of these is the 401(k) investment plan. Basically, a 401(k) allows you to invest pre-tax dollars from your pay in a wide range of stocks, funds, and other instruments. Most plans offer the option of building your own portfolio or picking from a series of ready-made ones designed by experts. You don't have to pay taxes on the value of your 401(k) account until you start withdrawing funds from it, after you retire. That allows your money to grow tax-free for decades.

One of the most valuable things about 401(k) plans is that many employers offer "matching" contributions to your account, up to a certain limit. For instance, your employer might make a contribution of up to 3 percent of your total pay, provided you contribute at least that much yourself.

Another retirement plan is the 403(b). This option is available to employees of educational institutions and certain nonprofit organizations, such as some medical facilities, libraries, and schools. Taxes are paid on earnings from investments (annuities, mutual funds, etc.) after the money is taken out (usually at retirement).

Other Employee Services

While medical and retirement benefits are the big-ticket items, some employers offer many other services, including:

- Dental insurance

- Vision insurance

- Confidential counseling services

- Pre-tax Flexible Spending Accounts for health care or dependent care expenses

- Health club membership

- Travel agent services

- Transportation credits

- Discounts on company products

- Financial planning

- Legal advice

Depending on your particular lifestyle and needs, these benefits can add up to a lot.

Workplace Tip

Many 401(k) or similar plans offer ready-made investment choices based on how long you have to go until retirement. Plans for younger workers focus on higher-risk, higher-yield instruments such as stocks, as there's plenty of time for the young contributor to recover from losses. Older workers' plans are weighted towards safer, lower-yield choices such as government bonds, as they'll be needing to use their money sooner and won't have as much time to make up for any serious losses.

Lisarae Koch

North Huntingdon, Pennsylvania

Attended: Kaplan Career Institute—ICM Campus, Pittsburgh, Pennsylvania

Area of study: Associate in Specialized Business—Criminal Justice

Recent graduate; currently in interviews

If you take one thing away from this course, it should be this: Always remember you will be judged by your resume. Take pride when putting it together and keep it updated in a portfolio.

Kaplan made it possible for a single mother of two, in her 40s, to not only go to school, but to stay in school. The instructors and administration go above and beyond the call of duty. I also found career planning to be a valuable class in addition to my criminal justice classes.

Chapter Summary

- By calculating your monthly expenses against your income and by budgeting in advance, you can take control of your daily financial life.

- Wise use of credit can make your life more convenient, but taking on more than you can pay back will compound your money problems.

- Investing cautiously in a diverse portfolio can help build wealth, but you must be willing to live with risk.

- Employee benefits such as medical insurance and retirement plans can add thousands of dollars to the total value of your compensation at work.

To-Do List

- ☐ Practice cutting expenses by skipping an indulgence for a week: dinner out, afternoon snacks, expensive coffee, or something else you regularly spend money on but don't need. Calculate how much you saved in a week, and make an honest assessment about whether it was worth it.

- ☐ The next time you get a credit card offer in the mail, take the time to read all of the fine print, especially the standard APR. Get in the habit of doing this, to develop a sense of which companies really offer the best deals.

- ☐ Visit your bank's website and see if it offers a low-cost, entry-level investment account.

Important Terms

How well do you know these terms? Define them here or in your journal, or look them up in the glossary to help you remember them.

APR	credit score
benefits	diversify
budget	identity theft
credit report	retirement plan

Online Resources

About.com's Guide to Financial Planning
financialplan.about.com

Federal Trade Commission's Identity Theft Site, includes tips for avoiding ID theft
www.ftc.gov/bcp/edu/microsites/idtheft

Federal Trade Commission's Facts for Consumers, information on credit reports
www.ftc.gov/bcp/edu/pubs/consumer/credit/cre34.shtm

Exercises

Write your answers in your journal or on a separate piece of paper.

1. Create a personal budget for next month. Using the monthly budget worksheet on page 199, write down all of your expenses and paydays. Track your actual spending, and revise your budget as needed for the following month.

2. Go online and research opportunities for beginning investors. Start with a simple Internet search for "entry-level investing." In your journal write several paragraphs on the types of opportunities that are available and which ones you are most interested in.

3. Many banks offer the convenience of debit cards. Using your bank or the Internet for reference, describe the differences between debit and credit cards. When might you use one rather than the other? Which one is safer?

20 | Career Development Skills

KEYS TO SUCCESS

- Thinking critically about the larger organizational purposes behind your own routine tasks
- Understanding the concept of accountability and how it applies to your actions
- Remaining flexible in changing circumstances
- Preparing for performance appraisals by documenting your accomplishments throughout the year
- Developing a healthy attitude toward adversity and practicing techniques for staying positive
- Forming productive relationships with co-workers, collaborators, and peers
- Developing a career plan by deciding where you want to be in the future

Being Responsible

Classified ads will usually tell you what a position's job responsibilities are—anything from "count out cash from register at the end of each shift" to "forecast market conditions and opportunities." As you take the first steps into a professional career, you'll find that being responsible means more than simply performing your assigned tasks.

Being responsible to your job and your budding career means thinking ahead. You should think beyond merely performing assigned tasks and consider the following questions:

- What is the larger organizational purpose behind your current task? Are there other things you can do to help with achieving this larger goal?

- What are the next steps after your current task? Can you begin preparing now for the things you'll be asked to do later?

- What are your co-workers doing to work toward shared goals? How does it affect your tasks, and vice versa? Are there ways you can help out or team up?

This kind of thinking should not distract you from the importance of doing the basic assigned tasks, but combining solid fundamentals with big-picture thinking will make a huge difference in whether you're seen as just a hired hand or as a valuable asset with potential.

Being Dependable

Always show up on time—for work, for meetings, even for casual occasions like office birthday celebrations. Build a reputation as someone who is always there, always reliable in every situation.

Practice Critical Thinking

Think about some of the things you need to do this week, either in school or at work. How do those tasks fit into a larger purpose? How can you prepare now for tasks you'll be asked to do later on?

Accomplish all of your assigned tasks—early, if you can. Do them well: treat each responsibility, however trivial or low-level it may seem, as if it were crucially important. How you handle the little things is a big part of what forms your professional image. You want your boss to know that you'll do a good job on whatever you're asked to do and not cut corners because something seems unimportant.

Being Accountable

Being responsible at work means being accountable. Broadly speaking, accountability means that you assume responsibility for the consequences of your own actions. If you fail to complete a task or if you come in late, be prepared to explain why you fell short and how you'll ensure that it won't happen again. If you were hurt by circumstances beyond your control, say so—but say so simply. Don't make elaborate excuses for yourself, and don't blame others.

Always stay focused on the positive and on the future. Own up to what's already happened, and then move on to the things you can control, namely, what you do next.

Flexibility

The world is changing at a dizzying pace, and this kind of rapid change will affect your professional life. Over the course of your career you'll see many changes, including technological and organizational changes. Although you can't control the pace of technology or the global economy, you do have control over your reaction to change. The ability to be flexible in changing circumstances is one of the most valued qualities in the workforce. Employers value flexibility because having an adaptable staff makes the organization itself better able to adapt and remain competitive in a changing environment.

Attitude is often as important as expertise when you are facing change. The benefit of maintaining a positive attitude is twofold: First, it's easier to learn something new—whether it's a new procedure at work or an upgrade to a software program—when you go into it with an open mind and a positive attitude. Second, your employer will appreciate it. When unexpected things happen—and they do, frequently—employers value versatile employees who can take them in stride, all the while maintaining a positive attitude. If you are asked to take on a new responsibility or learn a new procedure, be flexible and look at it as a welcome opportunity to show your employer how adaptable you are.

Work Performance and Performance Appraisals

Being responsible, accountable, and flexible will help to prepare you for a more formal process: the performance appraisal. Every organization has its own system for evaluating employees' performance on the job. Some performance evaluations occur annually; some happen quarterly, or even more often. Some have a direct impact on pay, and others are geared more toward coaching and quality improvement. Whatever the specifics, you can expect to be regularly reviewed by your manager.

Performance reviews can be stressful, especially if employees are worried about their own performance. They can also be stressful for managers, who are trying to provide accurate, unbiased information, knowing that the performance review will end up in the employee's permanent record. The key to handling a performance review is to be prepared.

How to Prepare

Depending on your employer's performance appraisal system, you may be asked to participate a lot or a little in evaluating your own performance. In some companies, employees have almost as much input into appraisals as their managers. But even if all you're required to do is show up for the meeting, you should still prepare and be involved. Take advantage of the opportunity to talk one-on-one with your boss about your job.

> ### Workplace Tip
> When you're preparing for a performance appraisal, think about the accomplishments that meant the most, not just to you, but to your *organization*. It's important to link your achievements to the company's overall success.

Document your accomplishments on the job. Keep a regular log of the tasks you complete, the ideas you contribute, and the results you achieve. Think especially in terms of how what you've done has benefited your department or company. If you can link your accomplishments to the company's profit, be sure to record that. When review time comes, go over all that you've documented and identify the highlights to point out to your manager. Don't be modest; show how valuable you are.

Think about other things you want to bring up during your appraisal. Are there processes that you think could be improved? Areas of your work that you're interested in learning more about? Changes to your working arrangement that would help you to do a better job?

If you come to the meeting prepared and show that you're engaged with your work, you can turn even a fairly negative review into a positive opportunity.

What to Take Away

At a performance appraisal meeting, your supervisor will go over the duties listed in your job description and share his or her evaluation of how well you've performed each one. Your supervisor will identify what he or she sees as your biggest strengths and the areas of your work that need improvement. You may also be evaluated in terms of how you display certain workplace values that are important to the company, such as customer focus, teamwork, and passion for winning.

Listen carefully, and don't get emotional even if your manager says things that you think are unfair. It's one of the hardest things to do, but it makes a huge difference in whether you're seen as a responsible professional or a whiny and defensive clock-puncher. Ask questions to help understand what your boss wants from you. If the feedback is general, such as, "You don't work well in a team," ask for specifics. Ideally, ask what you could do to improve. You can and should defend yourself against unfair charges, but don't argue or get defensive. Make your appeal calmly and respectfully, with specific examples to back up your statements.

Of course, you hope for a great review, and maybe you'll get one. And even if your boss has nothing bad to say about you, make a point of asking about ways you could make yourself more valuable on the job.

Whatever your manager has to say about your work, try to keep your focus on your group, department, and company. Make it less about you, and more about what you can do for your organization.

Prepare for Next Time

At the end of the performance appraisal, you and your supervisor should go over what's expected of you between now and the next time you're evaluated. Try to develop a list of specific objectives, and be prepared to go back over them at your next appraisal. The point of this whole process is to get you and your boss on the same page.

Ultimately, performance reviews are designed to improve your work performance. Use the information and criticism as pointers. All employers like seeing employees take criticism seriously and work to become better at their jobs.

ON THE JOB

SCENARIO: Your employer has just reported a second straight quarter of disappointing profits. Word comes down that the main office is planning to close a branch, and yours looks like a top candidate. Morale plummets as people are worrying about losing their jobs—which of course causes productivity to drop at the worst possible time.

QUICK FIX: You talk with the co-workers you have good relationships with. You share concerns but quickly move the conversation into positive territory. You suggest putting together a group to brainstorm ways to improve performance and morale. Just by trying, you may feel better. You may actually perform better, and you could also get noticed and earn future consideration when changes come. What's more, you show yourself to be a strong leader.

Maintaining a Positive Attitude

Negative performance appraisals are only one kind of adversity you may encounter on the job. Work can be tough, and other parts of your life, such as your family or your health, can add to your stress. What's more, anytime your company, your industry, or your community goes through rough times, that tension gets passed down to you.

You'll find, however, that letting your stress affect you at work only adds to it in the long run. Taking out frustration on co-workers or displaying a bad attitude in the office puts a strain on your relationships, makes people less inclined to communicate with you, and tends to put others in a bad mood, too—and they may take it out on you. On a more basic level, it's just unprofessional.

If you find yourself feeling stressed out or frustrated at work, find positive ways of dealing with it. Break the mental cycle that keeps you thinking about negative things: change tasks for a while if you can. On your break, take a walk outside, or even around the inside of the building, to clear your head.

If everyone in the workplace is feeling stressed by the same things, then you can talk about it with your co-workers. Sharing with people going through the same experience can help everyone feel better. Just try to keep from complaining or turning on each other. Be honest about what you're feeling, but look for positives and focus on helping others through tough times.

Remember that nothing lasts forever. Think about things you can do to help make things easier on yourself and your co-workers, and look ahead to what you'd like to do in the future.

Building Relationships

It should be clear by this point that job performance and a successful career have a lot to do with how you interact with others. Relationships play a huge role in the workplace, whether they be with co-workers, customers, peers in your industry, or partners from other businesses. Every contact you have with another person is a potential opportunity somewhere down the road.

The Importance of Teamwork

Your most immediate and important professional relationships are the ones you have with colleagues at work. Already in this chapter you have seen how you can build an image as a reliable and considerate co-worker. That will be the basis for building good teamwork. (See Chapter 17, Teamwork and Leadership, for a detailed look at the components that make a successful team.)

Working well with others requires a clear understanding of roles. Every collaboration happens because one person's abilities, time, and perspective aren't enough to get the job done. When teaming up to handle a task, try to establish some ground rules from the beginning. If you're the team leader, then you'll be expected to define everyone's areas of responsibility, their objectives, and the timeline. If someone else takes the lead, make sure you know what's expected of you, and what will be handled by others; avoid stepping on toes. If you're working in a team without a specific leader, then everyone should work together to draw up a clear division of roles.

Suppose, for example, that your team has to make a presentation to a larger group. You might have to find a meeting place, make sure it has facilities for a PowerPoint presentation, order refreshments, produce handout materials, and so on. If no one is designated leader, then you can get things started by volunteering for one task, thereby encouraging others to step up. With some negotiation, team members will soon have assigned roles and a better chance of getting the job done.

If you're working on a task that requires you to go to someone outside of your group or department for help or information, take the opportunity to make a contact. If possible, walk over to where the person works and introduce yourself. Establishing a relationship means that beyond completing the task at hand, you've cultivated a resource for future collaboration.

Try to keep on everyone's good side. Avoid power struggles, pettiness, and personal grudges. If someone proves to be impossible to deal with, then be polite and try to minimize your interaction with that person. Maintaining goodwill is a top priority. You never know who might be asked for an opinion of you and your work, or who might think of you years later, long after leaving your company, when a good opportunity opens up.

Engaging with Your Peers

Don't limit your professional contacts to your own company. Build a network through trade and professional organizations. In Chapter 13 you saw the important role such connections can play when you're looking for a job. Even after you're working in your

Aundranique La Shay Fellows

Moreno Valley, California

Attended: Kaplan College, Riverside, California

Area of study: Pharmacy Technician

Employer: Pharmacy Assistant/Technician, Kaiser Permanente

If you take one thing away from this course, it should be this: My one word tip on professionalism would have to be "self-management." If you know yourself and the goals in life you would like to meet, nothing or no one can deter you from that.

Kaplan helped prepare me for the career that I wanted. Everything we did in class is necessary for what I'm doing in the field now, even down to the computer/typing training we received.

field, these contacts can continue to play a valuable role in your career. Not only will networking help you keep abreast of the latest developments in your field (usually via electronic newsletters), but many organizations also offer low-cost learning opportunities and career guidance as well as inside information on job opportunities.

Building a professional network is an ongoing process. Keep in touch with co-workers and classmates, even after they or you move on. They'll remember your success on a previous project or how easy it was to work with you. Attend conferences and seminars related to your field. Ask for business cards and share information about the industry. Don't wait until you need something to nurture these contacts. Networking is about good relationships, and it works best when you have a solid track record—and you give as much as you take.

Developing a Career Plan

You want to do something meaningful, fulfilling, or challenging with your life and career. And you want to earn at least a reasonable living. How do you reach those goals? You begin by having a plan.

Where Do You Want to Be?

Spend some time assessing your goals, as you learned in Chapter 1. Ask yourself where you'd like to be in five years, ten years, and fifteen years. Think not just about your job, but your whole life situation, because your family, location, and interests will have an impact on your career choices. There are many things you can't predict, so be flexible; but if you don't set your sights on a target, then you'll just wander aimlessly.

Maybe you don't yet know enough about your chosen field to know exactly what job you want to be doing fifteen years from now. That's fine; it just means that a major goal in the near future is to explore and learn as much as you can about the field and the people who work in it.

Professional Development

Even after you're working in the field of your choice, put some time into building up your knowledge and skills outside of work. It will show your employer that you're serious about your job, and it will make you a better qualified, more attractive candidate for future opportunities.

Continuing Education

There are many ways to pursue continuing education. Your employer may be willing to pay for you to attend professional or technical training courses, if they're relevant to your job. Your employer may also offer reimbursement of some or all of your tuition for academic courses at a community college, professional school, or university.

Learning on the Job

The regular workday also provides many opportunities to learn new skills and processes. Try to take advantage of them. Get out front when special projects come up. If a co-worker is out for an extended absence, volunteer to take on some of his or her duties temporarily. Be on the lookout for people with specialized duties who are looking to train a backup. If a task requires you to collaborate with someone from a different group, pay attention to his or her part of the work; take the opportunity to ask about what your co-workers do.

Remember that you're surrounded by people who have knowledge to share. Being a successful professional means picking up as much as you can, because you never know when it will come in handy.

Chapter Summary

- For a successful professional, being responsible means not just showing up and fulfilling your duties, but also thinking about the big picture: organizational goals, others' work, and the future.

- Being flexible and willing to adapt to change is essential in the workplace.

- Performance appraisals give you opportunities to understand what your manager expects regarding your performance and to demonstrate just how valuable you are as an employee.

- By learning to handle adversity with a positive attitude, you will decrease your stress and be seen as a reliable and level-headed co-worker.

- At the center of every successful career are relationships with co-workers, collaborators, and peers throughout your industry.

- A good career plan includes short- and long-term goals, continuing education, and involvement in your field.

To-Do List

☐ Practice being dependable. List five things that other people are counting on you to do this week and make sure you do them. Check them off your list when you do them.

☐ Write down a task you need to do that requires teamwork. Form a mini-team by asking someone to help you complete the task. Establish informal ground rules and objectives to ensure that you work as an effective team.

☐ Do an Internet search on your industry and see what professional conferences or seminars are available.

Important Terms

How well do you know these terms? Define them here or in your journal, or look them up in the glossary to help you remember them.

accountability   performance appraisal

career plan   positive attitude

organizational purpose   professional development

peers

Online Resources

Fifteen Essential Questions for Your Performance Review
www.asme.org/NewsPublicPolicy/Newsletters/METoday/15_Essential_Questions.cfm

International Association for Continuing Education & Training
www.iacet.org

National Career Development Association
www.ncda.org

Exercises

Write your answers in your journal or on a separate piece of paper.

1. Begin developing a long-term career plan by writing several paragraphs in your journal about where you'd like to be in five, ten, and fifteen years. Consider not just job titles but also family and personal goals.

2. As practice for a future evaluation by a supervisor, create a short performance appraisal for yourself. The appraisal can apply to your performance as a student, or it can apply to your current job if appropriate. Think about your work over the past

six to twelve months and list what you think are your five greatest strengths and weaknesses; three or four of your best achievements; three or four things you'd like to learn more about; and two or three objectives for your work over the next year.

3. How would you in your current role as student or employee build relationships with people at your level (student or worker) and different levels (instructors or supervisors)?

Portions of this chapter's content include material adapted from Brenda Greene, *Get the Interview Every Time*, revised and expanded edition (New York: Kaplan, 2008).

Appendix | Effective Research

KEYS TO SUCCESS

- Performing well-focused research that is targeted to your chosen topic
- Locating books and printed periodicals in a library's collection
- Accessing the wide range of sources available on the Internet
- Evaluating the credibility of your sources
- Documenting all sources to back up your conclusions and avoid committing plagiarism

What Is Research?

Research is defined by Merriam-Webster's dictionary as a "studious inquiry or examination," especially an "investigation of experimentation aimed at the discovery and interpretation of facts, revision of accepted theories or laws in light of new facts, or practical application of such new or revised theories or laws."[1] In a broad sense, the definition of research includes any gathering of data, information, and facts for the advancement of knowledge.

Why Is Research Important?

You already do research all the time, whether you think of it that way or not. When your car's check-engine light comes on, you go to the yellow pages to find a mechanic. Looking for a new job, you gather all kinds of information about where your skills are useful, who's hiring, what salary you can expect, and so on.

---

1. *Merriam-Webster's Collegiate Dictionary*, 11th ed. (Springfield, MA: Merriam-Webster, 2007).

Your studies and your job will sometimes require you to do very intense, specific research to explore an academic topic or solve a business problem. Your success will depend on how good you are at finding the best, most useful, and most accurate information and applying it to the task at hand. That's why understanding some basic research principles is essential.

The Purpose of Research

You will usually have a practical purpose for doing research. You want to write a paper, solve a problem at work, or make an important decision about your retirement account. You don't have the knowledge yourself to accomplish these things, so you need to go out and find it. The purpose of research is to:

- **Find answers.** Before you begin, develop a list of specific topics to investigate. If you can, put them in question form, like *How much will it cost to upgrade our desktop computers?* Break big topics down into smaller ones: *Which upgrades will make the biggest difference in performance? Which vendor can give us the lowest price on flat-panel monitors?* These questions will be the driving force of your research.

- **Think for yourself.** All that outside sources can do is *inform* you. They can't *decide* anything; that's your job. If you're writing a paper for class, your instructor will expect you to do more than just explain what other people think about your topic; he or she will want you to analyze, evaluate, and compare other people's ideas, and explain how you came to your own conclusion. If your boss puts you in charge of solving a problem or improving a process, he or she wants you to make recommendations. Always remember that the point of research is to help *you* to think and make decisions.

- **Back it up.** When you make your recommendation or state your conclusions, you want to be able to give some good, logical reasons for it. Gut instinct has its place, but the reason you're doing research is to be able to point to something solid to back up your decisions, something that will help to show why other people should agree with you. The difference between opinion and informed opinion is huge. Between two ideas, the one with facts on its side will always win.

Finding the Information You Need

There is much more information available to the average person than at any other time in history. It's an exciting time to be out there doing things, but wading into that sea of information can be overwhelming. To be effective, you'll have to be able to narrow your focus, and know how to find the sources you need.

Staying Focused

Remember as you research that you are in the planning stage of a writing project. You don't want to stray too far from your topic, but a little wandering can sometimes be fruitful. For example, if your subject is the financial difficulties of the American automobile industry in the twenty-first century, you can find magazine and newspaper articles on layoffs and plant closings, sales reports from the American and foreign car manufacturers, data on the resale value of different kinds of cars, explanations of how American cars lost their hold on the market in the late twentieth century, and commentaries on what might be done to remedy the situation. Reading and research take time. Set aside plenty of time to look for, read, and take notes on various sources.

Types of Sources

The type of information you find will depend on what kinds of sources you consult. Research sources fall into three basic categories:

- **Primary sources** include interviews with experts or witnesses, raw results of surveys, scientific experiments, and public documents such as birth and marriage certificates or census data. A primary source is *just information*; no one has interpreted it for you or expressed an opinion on it. It can sometimes be valuable to get a look at complete, unedited data, but only if you know enough about the subject to interpret it correctly.

- **Secondary sources** include books, newspaper and magazine articles, documentary films, and reports written by others. The authors of such sources are telling you *about* information that they or others have gathered; they're not giving you the raw, unedited data. For many topics, you'll need to rely mainly on secondary sources, because only an expert would understand the primary data. Just remember that you have to evaluate the author's credibility, because you're relying on the author to be your interpreter.

- **Tertiary (third-level) sources** include encyclopedias and any other collection of general-knowledge or topic-focused information that is compiled from secondary sources. These sources are usually not considered to be adequate or reliable for academic or professional research projects. They provide only a broad overview of a topic, and they get dated very quickly. Tertiary sources can be quite useful when you're dealing with an unfamiliar topic, because they serve as a starting point from which you can gain a basic understanding of the topic. They can also help lead you to good secondary sources.

Print and Human Sources

The Internet has made some research easier in recent years, but for most topics there's still much more information to be found in libraries and non-electronic ways than on the Internet. To be an effective researcher, you'll need to know the tried and true techniques.

Print Material

Libraries use two main systems to code their holdings: the Dewey Decimal System and the Library of Congress system. Some libraries use both systems at once, labeling some books with Dewey Decimal numbers and some with Library of Congress codes. In both systems, books and other types of materials are labeled with letter/number combinations called "call numbers," and the library organizes its shelves according to these labels.

Library shelves will typically be clearly marked to show the range of books they contain, and the books will be organized first by letter code (so that PS comes after PR) and then by number (so that PS 3537 comes after PS 1516).

You may have learned in elementary school how to find books using a library's card catalog—a bank of tiny drawers filled with alphabetized paper cards. Computerized filing systems are also available at most big libraries. These systems offer the basic functions served by the card catalog: you can search by author, title, or subject to find the call number and publication information for the books you want. Most computerized systems offer much more than the basics. Some of the common features you might find are:

- **Keyword searches.** This function helps you narrow your search by looking for combinations of subjects. For example, if you're researching a case study on the fast food business in Iowa, you might enter *fast food iowa*.

- **Search limitation.** Some systems let you limit the scope of your search by publication date, language, or other factors. Maybe you're researching a paper on Mexico's economy, and you're having to wade through all sorts of entries for books written in Spanish, which you don't read. You might be able to limit the search to English-language books and save yourself some time.

- **Book status information.** Computerized systems often let you know if the book you want has been checked out and when it's due back. And they will allow you to put a hold on the book if you can wait for the due date.

- **Remote access.** You might be able to access your library's filing system from home through its website and arrive at the library with a list of all the available books you want already printed out.

For many topics—particularly if they're related to business or industry—information is constantly changing. The books that are published often go out of date very quickly. In these cases, you'll probably find most of your information in periodicals—newspapers, trade magazines, and industry journals.

The best way to find information in periodicals is to search a big, comprehensive index by topic. Your library probably offers computerized versions of its periodical indexes, and you may be able to access the electronic index on the Internet. More and more frequently, the full text of the articles indexed is available for downloading and printing—so you might be able to do all of it from home.

> ### Research Tip
> Becoming familiar with the variety of trade magazines and industry journals while you are a student will serve you well when you are ready to begin looking for a job in your field. Journals and magazines that focus on your chosen field are excellent job-search resources.

Experts

A highly knowledgeable source can provide information that isn't available anywhere else, or offer advice on interpreting information you've picked up elsewhere. Examples of experts include government officials, specialists in different fields, and representatives of professional associations.

If the expert you want to talk to is nearby—for instance, your company's information technology director, or a professor at a local university—you might want to arrange to meet in person. Dress appropriately for the interview, and come prepared with specific questions. A phone interview will often be just as good, and much easier to arrange. Just be sure you do arrange it in advance; don't just call someone with a big list of questions.

If you don't think you'll need to ask a lot of follow-up questions or to interact directly, an email interview can be a great tool for research. You don't need to arrange an appointment, and you'll have a written record of everything. Remember to be professional, though: use a respectful tone, and proofread your messages very carefully. Make sure you ask directly for the exact information you need, because your source will probably get annoyed if you keep emailing back with more questions.

It goes without saying that you should make sure your source really is an expert. And remember that even experts may have biases that you should consider.

The Internet: Information at Your Fingertips

Through the Internet, you have access to a breadth and depth of information that is widening and deepening all the time. Just a few of the most useful things you can find on the Internet are:

- **Archives.** Many newspapers, magazines, and journals have digitized their content going back for decades. You can usually search these archives for free, and you can often read the articles at little or no cost. If you're doing research with any kind of historical angle to it, you may not have to spend hours taking notes at a library's microfilm viewer; you can search, download, and print in minutes.

- **Specialized information.** If you're looking for information on a narrow or unusual topic—high-level semiconductor engineering, rare diseases, regional sports leagues—the Web gives you access to journals with tiny subscriber lists, local newspapers from around the world, and other resources that aren't even available in print.

- **Primary sources.** Because the Internet has fewer size restrictions than printed publications, many authors, publishers, and organizations take advantage of the opportunity to post "bonus" material along with main articles. A newspaper might publish a short article in print about the president's address to Congress, and on its website post a complete transcript or even a video. Scientists might share the complete results of studies that are only summarized in print, supplemented with graphics, videos, and sound clips. If you want to dig deeper into a story or topic, you'll find a wealth of material online.

- **The whole world.** Online, you can call up an article from a Portuguese entertainment magazine just as easily as a menu from the restaurant up the street from your house. Of course, if you can't read Portuguese, that won't do you much good—but you get the idea.

How to Search the Web

The quickest, easiest way to find information online is to use a "browser" program such as Internet Explorer, Safari, or Firefox.

A good place to start your hunt for information is a search engine. A search engine is a website that lets you type in a few subject keywords—as you would in a computerized library catalog—and then searches the entire Web for pages that contain those words. Some of the most popular are:

- Google (www.google.com)
- Yahoo! (www.yahoo.com)
- Ask.com (www.ask.com)
- Bing (www.bing.com)

Search engines are very smart. They will make decisions about which of the thousands of search results are likely to be most useful to you. For instance, the pages that seem most relevant appear at the top of the search results. Still, there are some things you can do to get better results out of a search engine:

- **Be specific.** If your keywords are generic, you'll get the most general and popular information. The more specific you are, the closer you'll probably get to what you really want.
- **Use qualifiers.**
  - Enclose words in quotation marks ("energy policy") to search for an exact phrase.
  - Put a plus sign before a word (+wind) to return *only* results that contain that word.
  - Put a minus sign before a word (-politics) to *exclude* results that contain that word.
- **Limit your search.** Search engines such as Google will allow you to limit your search results in a number of ways—for instance, you can search for only news articles, images, videos, or maps.
- **Specialize your search.** The websites of most publications, companies, and organizations host their own search engines that work just like the general ones, but will search only their own site, or in some cases closely related sites. If you're looking for information about childhood vaccinations, try visiting the website of the American Academy of Pediatrics and searching the site for vaccinations. By using a medical site, you limit your results to medical information, leaving out news articles, opinion pieces, and millions of message-board posts by parents telling stories from the doctor's office.

The Catch

There is, unfortunately, a big catch to online research, and it's the same thing that makes the Internet so great: Anyone can post something there—experts, geniuses, students, crooks, and crazy people. If you're not careful, you could wind up basing your conclusions on a seventh-grader's class project.

Though it's certainly true that you need to use good judgment about which print sources you use, at least with print you know that editors and publishers have signed off on a book or article. Online, you'll want to seek out sources that carry a similar assurance, such as the websites of reliable print newspapers, magazines, and journals. Even with those sites, though, always be on the lookout for signs of bias, or for writers and organizations with a personal interest in influencing views on a subject. For instance, don't rely on air-quality data from a coal industry group.

Check out the statements that sources make: Do they say where their information comes from? If not, then for all you know it could be completely made up. If they do say, then take a quick look at the source's source. Does it seem reliable? Has it been fairly represented?

Some sources will have hyperlinks to the sources for the claims they make. If you want to be sure that the source is a good one, though, you'll have to click on that link to verify that the information is reliable. Sometimes it's just a link to another page on the same website or to another, very similar website advocating the same thing.

Your results may include entries from weblogs, or blogs—online diaries that tend to be casual in tone and focused heavily on opinion. Steer clear of blogs, unless you find the blog of a respected expert. Even then, be aware that blog entries carry much less credibility than thoroughly researched and edited articles.

Do not necessarily accept information on "user-edited" or "community-edited" sites such as Wikipedia as accurate. You should verify any fact you find on such a site with at least one other credible source. Also, these sites tend to be tertiary sources, which limits their usefulness even when they are credible. The best use of these sites is to help you find your way to some good secondary sources.

Practice Critical Thinking

Use a standard search engine to find the website of the U.S. Census Bureau. Now look for information about future job prospects in your chosen field. Is the site easy to navigate? How could it be made better? Do you think this site is a credible source?

Research Tip

When you use a source, you take personal responsibility for the information you get from it. If it turns out to be wrong, out of date, or biased, your reader will blame you for it.

ON THE JOB

SCENARIO: The office laser printer's performance is getting worse and worse. So you ask your manager to order a new one, and she says, "Sure thing—can you get me some recommendations and a price list by the end of the day?" You don't know a thing about laser printers, but you do want to impress your very busy boss.

QUICK FIX: You hit the Internet for some research. A computer retailer's website gives you a basic sense of the different types of printers and available features. Using several different online shopping sites, you narrow your search to a few models that have the features you need, and compare prices among the sites. You also look at the customer reviews and expected delivery dates. Finally, you take your top four choices to your manager. Based on your research, she can make a good, informed decision.

Working with Sources

Any time you bring other people's work into your own, you walk into a minefield of potential problems and missteps. The benefits of good research are worth it, but step carefully.

Plagiarism

Any time you use someone else's *information, ideas,* or *words* in your work, you have to say so. Partly, this is to give proper credit to authors and researchers who've done hard and useful work. It's also to let your reader know where your statements are coming from. Identifying your sources actually makes your arguments stronger, because you're backing them up.

When you fail to identify the source of a piece of information, an idea, or a quote, you commit plagiarism. That's one of the most serious academic offenses you can commit—it's seen as cheating—and can cause you to fail a class or be expelled from a school or program.

Employers are also very concerned about plagiarism. Content published in print or online is protected by *copyright,* a body of law that gives authors control over their work and guarantees their right to be paid for its use. If you sell or even release a plagiarized document to the public, your employer could be sued and publicly embarrassed.

Citing Sources

To properly credit a source, you need to do two things:

- **Cite it within the text**, where you use it. You can use footnotes if you really want to, but it's usually easiest to just work the citation into a sentence. (*King and Associates' 2008 survey of Midwestern agriculture found a steady rise in corn acreage after 2005.*)

- **Give full publication info**, either in a list at the end of your document or in a footnote at the bottom of the page where it's used.

There are a number of different formats for citations and reference lists, including popular formats from the American Psychological Association (APA) and the Modern Language Association (MLA). Here is the basic format for APA-style citations:

- **In text:**

  Identify the author and year of publication:

  > According to Maclay (2007), the initiative failed.

  If you're using an exact quotation, include the page number that it's on:

  > Giles (2003) felt that the mayor was "thoroughly corrupt" (p. 32).

- **Full info:**

  List all your sources alphabetically, by author. The specific format will vary depending on what type of source you're documenting. For example, a journal article would include the following information, in this order:

  - Author(s)—last name followed by initial(s)

  - Year of publication

  - Date of journal issue

  - Article title

  - Journal title, in italics

  - Journal volume number, with issue number in parentheses

  - Page numbers

- The information would appear in the reference list in the following format:

  > Rosenberg, W. L., & Summers, B. A. (1997). The growth of Wiccan groups in southern California. *North American Sociology Review, 15*(2), 215–227.

You can find much more detailed information on various style guides at websites devoted to research and writing, such as Purdue University's Online Writing Lab (http://owl.english.purdue.edu).

Appendix Summary

- The purpose of research is to find answers to questions, help you think for yourself, and back up your conclusions with facts.

- The three main types of research sources are (1) primary sources, which are unfiltered information; (2) secondary sources, in which an author interprets or summarizes information; and (3) tertiary sources, which compile information from secondary sources.

- Libraries' collections are organized according to a system of call numbers, and can usually be searched through a computerized catalog.

- The Internet allows you to access vast archives, useful primary sources, highly specialized information, and international resources; however, all sources' credibility must be carefully checked.

- To avoid committing plagiarism, you must document every source that you use, in an accepted format such as APA style.

To-Do List

☐ After deciding on a topic for your next research project or paper, write down as many possible search keywords as you can think of to get started on your research.

☐ Find out if your local library has a website, and explore it. Can you access the catalog from home?

☐ Try using one of the online search engines mentioned in this chapter the next time you're looking for a place to have dinner or go for an outing.

☐ Take a look at your local newspaper's opinion page. Are statements backed up with evidence and sources? How reliable do the sources seem?

Important Terms

How well do you know these terms? Define them here or in your journal, or look them up in the glossary to help you remember.

APA style

call number

citation

keywords

primary source

search engine

Online Resources

The Online Writing Lab (OWL) at Purdue University
http://owl.english.purdue.edu

Google search engine
www.google.com

Occupational Employment, Training, and Earnings
data.bls.gov/oep/servlet/oep.noeted.servlet.ActionServlet?Action=empeduc

How to Evaluate the Credibility of a Source
www.wikihow.com/Evaluate-the-Credibility-of-a-Source

Exercises

Write your answers in your journal or on a separate piece of paper.

1. Pick a topic you're interested in—baseball, strawberry preserves, anything—and search your local library's catalog for sources about it. Narrow your topic down to something that returns only a few results. Write down three sources' call numbers, and locate them on the library shelves. Make photocopies of their title pages and turn them in to your instructor to demonstrate your library research skills.

2. For the same topic you used in the previous exercise, perform some keyword searches on one or more online search engines. Keep refining your search until you get specific, useful information. Pick the three best online sources and print out the first page of each to demonstrate your online research skills.

3. Pick a specific fact stated by one of your online sources from the previous exercise and try to trace it back to its original source. Does the author of the page you found say where the fact came from? If so, try to find that source. If no source is identified, try using a search engine to find something that backs up the claim. In your journal, sketch the path you took back to the original source (or the earliest one you found).

4. For one of your online or print sources, write a complete reference entry in APA style. See the Purdue OWL website for additional format information.

Portions of this appendix content include material adapted from *Sharp Writing: Build Better Writing Skills* (New York: Kaplan, 2008) and Cynthia and Drew Johnson, *Caffeine Will Not Help You Pass That Test* (New York: Kaplan, 2005).

Glossary

accountability—being held responsible for your actions

active communication—deliberately conveying communication, as through speech, sign language, or gestures

APA style—the format used by the American Psychological Association for citing sources; one of the most commonly used formats in business

APR—annual percentage rate; the rate at which finance charges accumulate on a credit account

audience—a group to whom you deliver a presentation, or the intended readership for a written document

authority—the ability to command the attention of others and influence them based on your recognized expertise

behavioral interview—a type of job interview in which the interviewer asks questions about an applicant's behavior in past work situations, rather than questions about hypothetical situations; for example, a typical question might be, "Tell me about a time when you had to prioritize your responsibilities in order to meet a deadline."

benefits—services offered by an employer in addition to salary or wages

bias—a preference or inclination that prevents impartial judgment

blog—short for "weblog"; a personal website that combines the functionality of a daily diary with the ability to post photos and video online; usually offered in a fixed template

brand—a product line that is distinguished by careful tailoring and promotion of particular attributes; often identified by a slogan, logo, or identifying mark that is unique to the product

budget—a detailed plan for managing money

business etiquette—a set of standards for behavior at work that includes showing respect to superiors and co-workers and projecting a professional image

call number—a string of numbers and letters used to catalog and organize books in a library

career plan—a road map of where you're headed professionally, including where you'd like to be in five, ten, and fifteen years

chronic stress—the body's response to perceived threats that results in the body remaining in a continuous state of tension. Over time this state can lead to physical and psychological illnesses

chronological resume—a time history of an applicant's work experience, beginning with the most recent position; many recruiters prefer this format because it is easy to read

citation—the practice of identifying the source of a piece of information, an idea, or a quote within the text where it is used

confidential—privileged or secret

conflict resolution—the process of ending or minimizing disagreement among groups or individuals, with an emphasis on negotiating to create solutions that take into account the underlying interests and needs of all parties involved

corporate culture—the set of behaviors, values, and attitudes that distinguishes the way an organization pursues its objectives

cover letter—a letter sent with a resume or job application; often tailored to a particular job opening to provide information about specific skills and qualifications

credit report—a document compiled by a private agency listing all known information about an individual's payment history on credit accounts, loans, utilities, and other items

credit score—a number on an individual's credit report that estimates the level of risk involved in lending the individual money

culture—the particular set of rules, customs, values, and shared assumptions among a group

customer service—preventing conflict relating to the delivery of goods and services, and using negotiating skills to resolve conflict when it does arise

cyber bullying—harassing someone online, often through spreading malicious information or posting embarrassing content

difficult customer—a customer who is unhappy with the service or product received, has unrealistic expectations, or is otherwise abusive

diversify—to invest in a broad, balanced portfolio of stocks, bonds, or securities in order to protect against major losses

diversity—the quality of being different; in school or in the workplace, this term typically refers to the inclusion of people from different races, cultures, and backgrounds

divisional structure—a corporate organizational structure based on market, product line, or geographical location

draft—a written document that has not yet undergone revision

employment agency—a company that matches prospective job candidates with potential employers; the agency may be paid by employers or charge fees to job seekers for its services

ethical behavior—conduct that is in accordance with accepted social and professional standards

ethics—a system for determining moral behavior

external customer—an outside party doing business with a company or individual

format—the appearance and arrangement of a particular kind of writing

functional resume—a skills-oriented depiction of an applicant's work history; this format works particularly well for those who are changing careers, have limited paid experience, or have large gaps in employment history

functional structure—a corporate organizational structure based on the type of work that employees do

Golden Rule—a rule of conduct stating that you should treat others as you wish to be treated

gossip—rumor or sensational talk about others

group interview—an interview format in which the applicant is questioned by a group of people; alternatively, an interview style in which job candidates are interviewed in large groups

hard obligation—a task or commitment with a specific time frame or deadline

headhunter—a professional recruiter who helps people find jobs; headhunters are often paid by the companies in which they place people

hierarchy—the chain of command within an organization, running from the lowest-level employees to the CEO

identity theft—a crime in which an individual's name, personal information, or credit is stolen for criminal purposes; can cause damage to the victim's credit and financial standing

illegal behavior—conduct that is against the law

inflection—the intonation a speaker gives a sentence that affects the sentence's meaning; for example, an upward inflection at the end of a sentence typically indicates a question

informative presentation—a presentation intended to teach or inform the audience

intermediate goal—an important objective that is achieved over the course of one to three years; usually supports a long-term goal

internal customer—a person or department within an organization that receives support or services from another person or department within the organization

internship—a short-term employment opportunity, often unpaid or low-paying, available to entry-level job seekers to help them gain knowledge and experience in a particular field

job fair—a sponsored event designed to bring together employers and job candidates in a face-to-face setting

keywords—one or more words entered into a library catalog or online search engine to find sources on a certain subject

label—to identify a person in a way that reduces his or her personality to a single trait

leadership—the act or quality of providing vision and guidance to an organization or team

letter of recommendation—a letter written on behalf of a job applicant that evaluates the applicant's professional skills and qualifications

locus of control—a term that refers to an individual's perception of control over the events in his or her life. Individuals with an internal locus of control believe they control what happens in their lives. Individuals with an external locus of control believe that fate or chance determines outcomes.

long-term goal—a significant objective that is achieved over a long period of time

mission statement—a written statement detailing the main purpose and direction of a group (such as a company) or an individual

motivation—something that provides incentive to act

narrative—a story told by the documents in your portfolio that reinforces your image as a person who has accomplished things in the past and has goals and ambitions

networking—making connections with professionals who can help you in your career

nonverbal communication—communication that happens outside of language, such as through gestures, posture, and facial expressions

optimum stress—the level of stress that results in peak performance

organizational purpose—the larger goals of your department or employer that motivate the tasks you perform every day

passive communication—conveying information without directly intending or attempting to do so

peers—other people with the same or a similar job to yours; other professionals in your field

perception—how a person or entity is generally viewed; often an emotional response

performance appraisal—the formal process by which employees are evaluated by their supervisors

personal business—tasks from your personal life—such as paying bills, family business, and social and medical issues—that should be handled, to the extent possible, on your own time, not at work

personality—the set of behaviors, values, and attitudes that distinguish an individual or a group

persuasive presentation—a presentation intended to influence another person's values, beliefs, attitudes, or behaviors

plagiarism—the act of using someone else's information, ideas, or words without crediting them

policy—a fundamental rule of an individual or organization, either publicly stated or internally known

portfolio—a collection of documents, such as work samples, academic qualifications, and awards, that is designed to provide an overview of professional accomplishments

positive attitude—a mindset that emphasizes being flexible and looking for the good in any situation

practice interview—a mock interview staged before the actual job interview takes place, which allows an applicant to practice answering questions

prejudice—a preconceived opinion about a person or group of people

presentation goal—a one-sentence statement summarizing the goal of a presentation

primary source—original information presented without analysis; a secondary source offers analysis and a summary of information

priority—the level of importance assigned to a task; higher-priority tasks get taken care of before lower-priority ones

professional development—an activity, such as continuing education, job seminars, or learning on the job, that enhances job skills

reference—in a job search, a person who can provide information about an applicant's personal qualifications and character

reliability—in customer service, the practice of managing customer expectations and being accountable

resume—a brief written account of an applicant's qualifications, experience, and education, generally sent with or as a job application.

retirement plan—an employer-provided benefit that helps an individual build a reserve of income to draw on after retirement

revision—the act of improving an earlier version of a document. Revision includes not only correcting spelling and grammar, but also improving focus.

reward center—the part of the brain involved with producing the sensation of pleasure

risk-to-benefit ratio—a measure of the possible benefits versus the possible negative outcomes of any decision or action

search engine—a website that allows users to enter key words and search for pages throughout the World Wide Web containing those words

self-assessment—an evaluation of your own abilities, actions, and values

self-esteem—a person's feeling of his or her own worth

short-term goal—an objective that is achieved in a short period of time; usually supports long-term and intermediate goals

social networking sites—websites that allow people to link with friends, family, and colleagues through online networks

soft obligation—a task or commitment without a specific time frame or deadline

stereotype—a generalized assumption that is made about members of a particular group

stress—a chemical response of the body to a perceived threat or danger (stressor)

stressor—a perceived threat or danger that triggers the body's fight or flight response (stress)

task list—a list of all the tasks an individual needs to accomplish in the day

team—a group of individuals working together to accomplish a common objective

teamwork—the act of working within a team setting, with individual members working toward a shared objective

temporary agency—an agency that places people in short-term job positions

time management plan—a system for planning time that includes assessing available time, setting priorities, and scheduling tasks

trade journal—a professional magazine devoted to one business or industry; presents industry-specific news and events as well as classifieds

traditional interview—a type of job interview in which the questions are mainly focused on an applicant's experience and skills; for example, a typical question might be, "What are your biggest strengths and weaknesses?"

transcript—a record of academic achievement, usually including course titles and grades

transferable skills—skills learned in one situation that can be applied in another

unethical behavior—conduct that doesn't conform to accepted social or professional standards

values—a set of guiding principles for a group (such as a company) or an individual

verbal communication—communication that happens through language, such as speech, writing, email, or texting

visual aids—films, PowerPoint slides, models, or other material designed to supplement spoken information

"you-attitude"—the principle of business writing that uses a focus on the reader's reaction to a message as the basis for how to present that message.

Index

Date

_____

Name

Chapter 1 Goal Setting
Exercise

Write down one of your long-term goals, and brainstorm a list of actions you'll need to take to achieve the goal. Write down everything, even if it's something that sounds outrageous or silly. Once you have everything written down, review your list of actions and create a series of intermediate and short-term goals that will support your long-term goal.

_____

_____

_____

_____

_____

_____

_____

_____

_____

_____

_____

_____

_____

Date _____

Date

_____

Name

Chapter 2 Time Management Strategies
Exercise

Describe five things you can do that will help you stay motivated to keep your schedule.

_____

_____

_____

_____

_____

_____

_____

_____

_____

_____

_____

_____

_____

_____

_____

Date

_____

Name

Chapter 3 Managing Stress
Exercise

Write several paragraphs about a time you successfully handled a stressful situation at work or at school. First describe the situation and what made it stressful. Then reflect on your actions and identify three things you did that helped you overcome stress.

_____

_____

_____

_____

_____

_____

_____

_____

_____

_____

_____

_____

_____

_____

Date

_____

Name

Chapter 4 Your Professional Presentation Exercise

Write a description of what you think it means to be an effective professional in your chosen field. What characteristics are important for individuals working in this field? What characteristics might be a disadvantage?

_____

_____

_____

_____

_____

_____

_____

_____

_____

_____

_____

_____

_____

Date

Name

Chapter 5 Interpersonal Communication and Business Etiquette Exercise

Who is the most effective communicator you have known? A teacher? A coach? An employer? A friend? Write a three-paragraph description of what makes this person such a good communicator. Identify the person's specific communication strengths, both verbal and nonverbal.

_____

_____

_____

_____

_____

_____

_____

_____

_____

_____

_____

_____

Date _____

Name _____

Chapter 6 Writing Skills
Exercise

Imagine that you have just begun a new job in your field. Write a brief message (one to two paragraphs) to send in an email introducing yourself to your new co-workers. Pay careful attention to the style guidelines for business messages.

_____

_____

_____

_____

_____

_____

_____

_____

_____

_____

_____

_____

Date

Name

Chapter 8 Conflict and Negotiations in the Workplace Exercise

Make of list of ten guidelines you can follow to tactfully resolve conflicts.

_____

_____

_____

_____

_____

_____

_____

_____

_____

_____

_____

_____

_____

Date
_____

Name
_____

Chapter 9 Resumes and Applications
Exercise

What are your strongest skills? List the three skills you'd most like to emphasize on your resume and craft a description of your work history or academic background that highlights those strengths.

_____

_____

_____

_____

_____

_____

_____

_____

_____

_____

_____

_____

_____

_____

Date _____

Name _____

Chapter 10 Portfolios
Exercise

Write a paragraph or two about how you can use your portfolio during a job interview. What items in your portfolio do you most want to highlight during the interview? How will you work that into the interview?

_____

_____

_____

_____

_____

_____

_____

_____

_____

_____

_____

_____

_____

_____

Date
_____

Name
_____

Chapter 11 Personal Branding and Networking Exercise

Create some material to promote your personal brand:
- Develop a short statement (one to three sentences) that summarizes your brand. It should state who you are, what you do, and why you are distinct.
- Develop a one-minute pitch about yourself as a job candidate.

You can use these statements to introduce yourself and stand out when you are networking.

_____

_____

_____

_____

_____

_____

_____

_____

_____

_____

_____

_____

_____

_____

Date _____

Name _____

Chapter 12 Preparing for the Job Search
Exercise

Make a list of the top ten skills you need to get a job in your field. Next, look at your work history and educational background and write down examples of things you've done that demonstrate those skills. Be creative: skills that you developed working in unrelated fields often can apply to your new career goals.

_____

_____

_____

_____

_____

_____

_____

_____

_____

_____

_____

_____

Date _____

Name _____

Chapter 13 Job Search Resources
Exercise

Write several paragraphs describing why you want to work in your chosen career. Your statement should include what you like about the field and it should also describe strengths you have that make you a valuable asset in your profession.

_____

_____

_____

_____

_____

_____

_____

_____

_____

_____

_____

_____

_____

Date _____

Name _____

Chapter 14 Interviews
Exercise

Assemble research on a company you'd like to work for. Include all the relevant data you'd want to know before going to an interview with this company, including financial, personnel, and product information. Write down five questions that you could ask during an interview that would demonstrate your knowledge of the company. These should be specific questions related in some way to the company's business activities, methods, or recent successes.

_____

_____

_____

_____

_____

_____

_____

_____

_____

_____

_____

_____

Date _____

Name _____

Chapter 17 Teamwork and Leadership Exercise

Write a paragraph or two describing a team—either formal or informal—that you've participated on. Identify:

- The responsibilities of each member
- The goal that the team was working toward
- The decision-making method the team used

Now that you know more about creating successful teams, is there anything that you would do differently?

_____

_____

_____

_____

_____

_____

_____

_____

_____

_____

_____

_____

Date _____

Name _____

Chapter 18 Ethical Behavior and Confidentiality Exercise

Review the ethical issues examined in this chapter and make up your personal Golden Rule that reflects your individual values. Compare and contrast it to the traditional rule.

_____

_____

_____

_____

_____

_____

_____

_____

_____

_____

_____

_____

_____

_____

_____

_____

Date _____

Name _____

Chapter 20 Career Development Skills Exercise

List three characteristics of a reliable and considerate co-worker. For each one, write several sentences outlining actions you can take to display that quality in the workplace.

_____

_____

_____

_____

_____

_____

_____

_____

_____

_____

_____

_____

_____